OUR RED BROTHERS

LAWRIE TATUM

United States "Indian Agent."

Springdale, Cedar Co.
Iowa.

Our
Red Brothers

AND THE

Peace Policy of President Ulysses S. Grant

BY

LAWRIE TATUM

FOREWORD BY RICHARD N. ELLIS

UNIVERSITY OF NEBRASKA PRESS · LINCOLN

*The text of this edition is reproduced from the
1899 edition published by John C. Winston & Co.*

Manufactured in the United States of America

FOREWORD

In the spring of 1869 a balding and bearded farmer journeyed from the prairies of Iowa into the unknown. Lawrie Tatum, the portly Quaker, had been appointed agent for the Kiowa and Comanche tribes, and in May he joined his predecessor, Colonel W. B. Hazen, at Junction City, Kansas, and set out for the isolated agency at Fort Sill, Indian Territory. Tatum had little knowledge of Indians, nor did he have any special qualifications for this appointment other than the strength of his personality, his interest in education, and his fervent religious beliefs. He had not sought the position of Indian agent, and he had, in fact, been startled to read in the newspapers that he had been selected to fill this post. A desire to obey the wishes of God caused him to accept the appointment.

Lawrie Tatum was one of many religious men named as Indian agents during the early years of the first Grant administration, for changes were taking place in federal Indian policy and in the personnel of the Indian Bureau. Reform was long overdue in 1869, and criticism of the bureau and its policies was mounting.

The Indian problem had been the subject of debate from the beginning of English colonization in North America. Controversy continued after Independence as the new government grappled with the issue. In 1849 the Bureau of Indian Affairs was transferred from the War Department to the newly created Department of the Interior, but this was a change which failed to improve significantly the management of Indian Affairs. Criticism of government policies and of corruption within the bureau continued, therefore, throughout the 1850s and increased during the following decade despite the fact that the attention of the nation was centered on the Civil War.

During these years there were numerous proposals for reform by individuals both in and out of the Department of the Interior, but it was not until the outbreak of serious hostilities with the tribes of the Great Plains that the need for reform became crucial. Military officers observed many problems and quickly began to criticize federal policies and offer suggestions for improvement, and soon they were joined by others who were interested in the safety of the frontier settlements and the welfare of the American Indians. Special investigations were conducted, and in time a growing chorus of complaints led to the formation of new policies.

Among the leading critics of federal Indian policy was General John Pope, who directed operations against the Sioux following the Minnesota uprising of 1862. Pope bombarded his superiors with complaints and suggestions throughout the remainder of the decade without apparent success. He did, however, develop connections with Episcopalian Bishop Henry Whipple of Minnesota, who had devoted his energies to aiding Indians, and Pope, along with one of his field commanders, General Alfred Sully, also called upon American religious groups to open a new mission field among the western tribes.

Events in the West, meanwhile, attracted the attention of Congress as well as the American people. The brutal Sand Creek Massacre, a surprise attack by Colorado troops upon a Cheyenne village in 1864, led to a congressional investigation, and at approximately the same time a joint committee of Congress began a study on the conditions of the Indian tribes in the United States. Despite congressional interest, however, warfare continued. Soldiers stationed in the forts along the Bozeman Trail in the present state of Wyoming were under siege, and some were killed in the disastrous Fetterman Massacre of 1866. The continuing conflict stirred renewed interest in the Indian problem, leading to the appointment of the Peace Commission of 1867 to study the situation and negotiate treaties where possible with the hostile tribes. The report of this group, which included General William Tecumseh Sherman, Civil War hero and the leading military figure in the West, and Nathaniel G. Taylor, Commissioner of Indian Affairs, contained a suggestion that missionary groups devote more energy to work with the Indians.

Suggestions for increased religious activity among the Indians came from varied sources during the 1860s, but the concept itself was not new. The goal of Christianizing and civilizing the Indians was a major aspect of American Indian policy, and cooperation between the government and church groups had existed for some time. The Indian civilization fund to support this activity was tiny, however, and little had been accomplished. It was evident that greater efforts were needed, and these suggestions struck a responsive chord among officials in the Interior Department. Many of them believed that only Christian influence could save the Indians from extinction, and some had already suggested the appointment of missionary agents and Christian employees. Secretaries of the Interior such as James Harlan and Commissioners of Indian Affairs such as William Dole and Nathaniel G. Taylor reflected these beliefs.

Pressure for change increased as the decade of the 1860s progressed. Bishop Henry B. Whipple became a well-known figure in the Capitol lobbying for reform. Outraged at the low quality of the agents and the corruption in the Indian Service, Whipple proposed a commission of "men of high character" to reform the Indian system and soon received the support of William Welsh, an Episcopalian merchant from Philadelphia who was involved in the struggle for justice for the Indians throughout the remainder of his life. Whipple also attracted the attention of various Quaker groups, who began to cooperate with him, and by 1868 and the election of Ulysses S. Grant to the presidency a working alliance had developed between the Episcopalians and the Quakers. It was an alliance which provided needed pressure for reform.

Before the inauguration of President Grant, an issue arose in Congress which brought the matter of reform to a head. The introduction of a bill to transfer the Indian Bureau back to the War Department alarmed the Quakers, and both the Hicksite and Orthodox Friends immediately memoralized Grant opposing military supervision and suggesting that the government invite the assistance of philanthropic and Christian groups in working with the Indians. The result was a request that both organizations supply lists of individuals they would endorse as Indian agents.

It is ironic that the new president took steps to raise the standards of a government agency which was noted for an alarming level of malfeasance in office in an era characterized by corruption. The experiment which Grant inaugurated authorized the Quakers to nominate superintendents and agents, and its success, along with an act of Congress which prohibited army officers from also holding civil offices, caused the administration to bring other denominations into the program. Members of major religious groups were therefore nominated by their organizations and became the field officers of the Indian Bureau, thus removing this agency from the sphere of political patronage. At the same time a Board of Indian Commissioners staffed by ten unpaid philanthropists was created to watch over the Indian Bureau and make recommendations for policy changes.

These administrative changes were known as the Quaker Policy[1] because the program began with that group, and while it did not provide a final solution to the Indian problem, it was a marked improvement. On the whole the new agents were honest and capable men. Some like Lawrie Tatum were exceptional.

Like too many of the new agents, Tatum lacked experience in dealing with Indians. He was unfamiliar with the traditions and way of life of the wild tribes of the Southern Plains, but Indian agents were traditionally unprepared for this underpaid position. Tatum did possess, however, a strong personality and an ability to deal with others as human beings. These qualities, along with his honesty, a strong sense of justice, and a remarkable degree of patience, would stand him in good stead.

Born in New Jersey in 1822, Tatum moved with his family to Ohio, and in 1844 at the age of twenty-two, the devout young Quaker journeyed to sparsely settled Iowa. Locating near present Springdale, he was the first Quaker

---

[1] An excellent account of the changes in federal Indian policy can be found in Robert Utley, "The Celebrated Peace Policy of General Grant," *North Dakota History*, XX (July, 1953), 121–142. Utley distinguishes between the Quaker Policy, the administrative decision to use agents nominated by the various religious groups, and the Peace Policy, which was to move the Indian to reservations by persuasion or force. Many Americans of the period failed to make this distinction and used the term Quaker Policy for both of the above.

settler in Cedar County and one of the first in the entire Territory. He quickly became a leader among the Friends in the region, often joining with them in assisting runaway slaves in their flight to freedom. Tatum was also involved in community affairs and was a logical choice for a Quaker Indian agent in the eyes of the Quaker Executive Committee.

Like Tatum, the other agents appointed to the Central Superintendency were Iowa Quakers. Enoch Hoag was selected as Superintendent, while elderly but dedicated Brinton Darlington was sent to the important Cheyenne-Arapaho Agency. Other Quaker officials were Osage agent Isaac T. Gibson, Mahlon Stubbs of the Wichita Agency, and John D. Miles, who succeeded Darlington upon the latter's death in 1872. These men concurred in Tatum's belief that the Quaker Policy was a "holy experiment."

When Lawrie Tatum became Kiowa-Comanche agent in 1869, he needed faith that this holy experiment would succeed, for he stepped into an extremely difficult situation. The two tribes were under mounting white pressure, and although they had been defeated in Philip Sheridan's winter campaign in 1868, they were still determined to maintain their old way of life. Tatum found that newly constructed Fort Sill overlooked the agency itself, but despite the presence of the troopers, the Indians were not impressed with the power of the government in Washington.

Years later Tatum concluded that his Indians were probably the worst red men east of the Rocky Mountains and that the Kiowas were among the worst on the continent, and he was disappointed that he did not accomplish more. But Tatum should not be faulted for failure. The two tribes had always done as they pleased and habitually raided into Texas, where they literally ravaged the frontier region. Settlers were killed, captives were taken, and livestock was stolen. So serious were the raids that Tatum reported in 1870 that the Texas frontier had been driven back some 150 miles.

The destruction of life and property was extensive. In 1868, for example, one Comanche band made off with over 4,000 head of Texas cattle, and it is estimated that between 1860 and 1867 as many as 300,000 head may have been stolen. Equally serious was the loss of life. The massacre of Abel Lee's family is indicative of the suffering of the Texans. Lee, along with his wife and one child, were slain and three other children were taken captive. Nor were the soldiers or government property safe. Fort Sill, commanded by General Benjamin Grierson, a noted Civil War general, was manned by the Buffalo Soldiers of the Negro 10th Cavalry, but despite constant vigilance army livestock was stolen and people were killed in the vicinity of both the fort and the agency. Tatum's employees were in constant danger, and eventually most of the Quakers fled, leaving Tatum and a few brave employees to deal with the intractable Indians.

The Quakers believed that honesty, kindness, and generosity would provide a significant contribution toward the solution of the Indian problem. They also opposed the transfer of Indian affairs to the War Department and the use of force in dealing with the Indians, and although Lawrie Tatum approved of these principles, he began to question them soon after becoming agent. Many of his actions met with disapproval by the Quaker Executive Committee on Indian affairs.

In accordance with Quaker beliefs Tatum attempted to use peaceful methods to convince the tribes to terminate their raids and settle down on the reservation. He conferred with the tribal leaders and worked with various negotiators who visited his agency, but with little success. Tribal delegations were taken to Washington; Quaker officials counseled the Indians, and even the "civilized tribes" of Indian Territory were brought into the act, but the Kiowas and Comanches continued to do as they pleased. At one such meeting they told their agent that they would continue to raid into Texas as they had always done. If the president did not want them to raid there, they said, he should move Texas far away where the young men could not find it.[2] On another occasion, Lone Wolf, a leading chief, stated that they might consider peace if their reservation was enlarged until it

---

[2] See below, p. 126.

stretched from the Missouri River to the Rio Grande and all military posts were removed.[3]

Kiowa attitudes were further clarified by word and action. Satanta and other leaders often boasted of their success on the warpath and indicated that it was profitable to be bad because the government paid them to be good. They had only to point to the pitiable condition of the neighboring Wichitas, who were good Indians, as proof of this statement.

During one conference Tatum and General Grierson, who were trying to persuade the Indians to be good, were forced to listen to boasts and demands. Satanta, known as the "Orator of the Plains" because of his propensity for talk, announced that he preferred the breechloading rifle and other weapons to the more peaceful aspects of white culture. All the while the warriors were flexing their bows and sharpening their scalping knives while eyeing the bald head of their agent.[4]

This was the reaction to the peaceful methods of the Quakers, and it is little wonder that Tatum became discouraged at his lack of success and began to try new methods. He quickly realized that the warriors could not be trusted. They promised to be good, but did as they pleased, and Tatum began to warn his superiors that he

[3] *Annual Report of the Secretary of the Interior*, 1872, 42 Cong., 3 Sess., House Executive Document No. 1, pt. 5 (Serial 1560), p. 632.

[4] See below, pp. 40–43.

had no control over them. He also concluded that the warriors should not be rewarded for being bad and that they should be punished for their crimes. "I see no reason why they should not receive the same punishment as whites for similar offenses," he wrote to Enoch Hoag in 1871.[5] "To purchase a peace of the Indians by giving them an increased amount of rations and annuity goods upon their promise to cease raiding and war has a very injurious effect not only on the part who thus indirectly receives a bonus for their atrocities, but upon other Indians also," he explained. "We had as well attempt to hire the murderers and desperadoes in our large cities to cease their depredations as to pay the Indians to do the same." He urged that they be held responsible for their actions, for "the leniency of the government in letting guilty ones go unpunished is accepted on their part as cowardice or imbecility on the part of the whites."[6]

Convinced that he must have some control over his charges while still a practitioner of Quaker nonviolence, Tatum terminated the practice of paying ransoms to free captives. Experienced frontiersmen predicted failure, but Tatum was able to free twenty-six individuals by the strength of his character and his persuasive arguments. He also began to withhold rations and annuity

[5] Tatum to Hoag, May 25, 1871, Field Office Files, Kiowa-Comanche Agency, Records of the Bureau of Indian Affairs, National Archives, Washington, D.C., cited hereafter as Kiowa File.

[6] *Annual Report of the Secretary of the Interior*, 1872, pp. 631–632; Tatum to Hoag, Nov. 1, 1872, Kiowa File.

goods when Indians were involved in criminal activity
or were off the reservation. "My own view," he wrote to
Enoch Hoag in 1872, "is that they should receive nothing
more from the Government at present, unless they return
the stolen animals and then the leaders of the parties who
commit murders."[7] Once again Tatum startled old-
timers in the region, for some stolen livestock was returned when rations were withheld.

In 1871 Tatum went a step further, for an event occurred which was more than his remarkable patience
could bear. A large raiding party led by Satanta and
others struck a freight train after permitting General
William T. Sherman and a small escort to pass by safely.
Then they returned to the reservation and boasted to
their agent of their great success. Satanta, "Orator of
the Plains," obviously talked too much on this occasion,
for Tatum immediately authorized the army to arrest the
leaders of the war party. Satanta and others were seized
and sent for trial to Texas, where they were convicted
and held in prison as hostages for the good behavior of
the tribe. Tatum's account of these events and his actions
are described in the following pages.

Although Tatum achieved some control with these
methods, Kiowa and Comanche intransigence continued,
and despite his strong religious convictions the Quaker
agent began to look increasingly to the military for assistance. Differences of opinion existed between the agent

_____
[7] Tatum to Hoag, June 5, 1872, Kiowa File.

and army officers but did not prevent cooperation, and 10th Cavalry troopers watched over the agency and maintained order on ration day. In 1872 Tatum plaintively informed Enoch Hoag as he had so often done before: "The Kiowas and Quahadas [a Comanche band] are unmanageable by me."[8] In that same year he also concluded that "nothing less than military authority, with perhaps some punishment by troops, will bring them into such subjection as to again render the services of a civil agent of benefit to them."[9]

Tatum and his employees devoted their energies to convincing the Kiowas and Comanches to settle down and live in peace. Other Quaker and governmental officials worked for the same end, and the army attempted to prevent depredations, but little progress was made. Kindness and fair dealing had little effect, and gradually it became evident that Tatum and his superiors were drifting apart over the question of how to deal with these Indians. The use of military guards and the authorization to arrest Satanta and other guilty chiefs was looked upon with disfavor by members of the Quaker Indian committee and by individuals in the superintendent's office. Soon the agent was subjected to unwarranted criticism, although if he was aware of it, he did not complain. He did resent, however, the rejection of his recommendations and the implementation of policies which he

[8] Tatum to Hoag, June 5 and July 1, 1872, Kiowa File.
[9] *Annual Report of the Secretary of the Interior*, 1872, p. 521.

believed were ill founded. Unable to approve of the decisions of his superiors, the doughty Quaker resigned.

The imprisonment of Satanta and Big Tree had a salutary influence upon the Kiowas, and Tatum found them better behaved than ever before. Tatum intended to have the chiefs remain in prison, but the Quakers and other humanitarians thought otherwise. As a result, the Indian Bureau promised to release the prisoners. Tatum viewed this repudiation of his position as a disastrous move. He could not accept this decision, and in March 1873, Pot-ta-wat Pervo, Bald Head Agent, as the Comanches called him, was replaced by James M. Haworth, a new Quaker agent. It was evident that the Quakers desired a more amenable agent, for Haworth was carefully instructed to be more conciliatory.

Lawrie Tatum disagreed with these changes but bore no resentment. He wrote in his journal that Haworth's "heart was in his work." Time proved that this was not enough. The return to a policy of conciliation did not improve the situation on the Southern Plains, and slightly over a year after Haworth took office war broke out with the Kiowas, Comanches, and Southern Cheyennes. Some of the causes of this conflict are found on the following pages.

When Lawrie Tatum returned to Iowa in 1873, he departed with a sense of failure, but in retrospect it is evident that he had set his goals too high. He was, in fact, a good agent, and the Indians were sorry to see him go. Bald Head Agent had won the respect of Indians and frontiersmen alike.

Tatum was most effective in recovering captives and stolen property, but he instituted other changes as well. Efforts were made to change the Indians into an agricultural people; religious instruction was provided, and schools were established. Concrete results were few because these nomadic tribes had little interest in education, Quaker beliefs, or farming. The apparent lack of success was misleading, however, for subtle changes did begin during these years.

When Lawrie Tatum returned to Iowa, he once again became a leader in his community. He helped organize a bank, and as he had always been interested in education, he was involved in the establishment of Springdale Academy, which he believed was one of the best schools in the state. In later life he was appointed guardian for Herbert Hoover, future president of the United States.

Tatum's interest in Indians continued after his resignation from the Indian service in 1873, and he kept informed of conditions at the Quaker agencies in the Central Superintendency. In 1899 he published *Our Red Brothers*, an account of his own experiences and the work of his Quaker colleagues. Although written years after he retired from the Indian Service, *Our Red Brothers* is far more than a hazy memory of past events. Tatum kept a personal journal and apparently had access to copies of his correspondence while agent, for his com-

ments on specific events often closely follow his official
reports and letters. It is probable, also, that he drew on
the knowledge of his friends and former associates for his
account of the other agencies.

Our Red Brothers has been used repeatedly by his-
torians and has become a classic in the literature on the
Southern Plains. It is an invaluable source for the history of the Kiowas, Comanches, and other tribes, as well
as of an important period in the development of federal
Indian policy. The portion dealing with Tatum's tenure
as agent is, of course, a first-hand account of an exciting
era on the Southern Plains. It is useful, also, for the history of the other Quaker agencies and for illuminating
Quaker attitudes toward the Indians and federal Indian
policy.

RICHARD N. ELLIS
University of New Mexico

OUR RED BROTHERS

PREFACE.

THE prime motive for writing this volume has been to record some important items of history in connection with the Indians and the overruling providence of God, and to show that "The Peace Policy" in dealing with the Indians, which commenced in 1869, has proved a great blessing to them, to the government, and to people of the nation. If the volume proves to be the means of causing greater interest in the welfare of the Indians from a religious, literary and political standpoint, it will accomplish its purpose. May God bless it to that end.

THE AUTHOR.

Springdale, Iowa.

CONTENTS.

LIST OF ILLUSTRATIONS.

INTRODUCTORY REMARKS BY T. C. BATTEY, AUTHOR OF "A QUAKER AMONG THE INDIANS."

MORE than two hundred years have transpired since the organization of our Government by the adoption of the Constitution. During this period nearly one thousand treaties have been made with the various Indian tribes within our boundaries. Since by the definition of the word "treaty" only independent states or nations can constitute treaty-making powers, our Government has acknowledged the different Indian tribes as independent nations whenever it has ratified treaties with them.

According to Article VI. of the Constitution, treaties duly signed and ratified by the contracting parties become the supreme law of the land, and must be so regarded by all citizens and state officials, whatever the law of the state may be. Among civilized nations treaties are regarded of such binding force that each party is held to a strict accountability by the other for any infringement of their provisions; and in the present condition of international law a violation of a treaty is considered sufficient cause by the civilized world for an appeal to the force of arms.

(7)

Our treaties with Indians have been designated for various purposes, viz.: " The purchase of land," " peace and friendship," " to define boundaries " and thereby " remove cause for further dissension," and for " the protection of the person, property and life of Indians." In many of these treaties the United States has bound itself to provide for the education of the children of the tribe or nation treated with, and " thereby promote the civilization of the Indian."

A treaty made with the Cherokees in 1828 provides that their remaining lands " shall never in all future time be embarrassed by having around it the lines, or placed over it the jurisdiction, of a territory or state, nor be pressed upon by the extension in any way of the limits of our existing territory." Ten years after this solemn guarantee on the part of our Government, without any provocation but the request of the people of the state of Georgia, who desired possession of their lands, the Cherokees, numbering sixty thousand souls, were forcibly driven from their homes before the army into an unknown wilderness, suffering great loss of property. Fully one-fourth of their people perished.

Not only the Cherokees, but many other tribes have been forcibly removed several times within the century. Every removal has been attended with great suffering and sacrifice of life and property of the tribe thus removed. Several times have the Delawares been removed by our Government, despite the most solemn treaty guar-

anties to the contrary. In 1785 they were removed to
Ohio and Indiana. They then numbered, according to
their own account, over fifty thousand. In 1818 they
were removed to Missouri and Arkansas, and in 1828 to
Kansas. Chief " Journey Cake," who had been a minister in the Baptist Church for forty years, said, in a
speech made before the Indian Defence Association in
April, 1886: " We have been broken up and moved six
times; we have been despoiled of our property. We
thought when we moved across the Missouri River, and
had paid for our homes in Kansas, we were safe. But in
a few years the white man wanted our country. We had
made good farms, built comfortable houses and big
barns. We had schools for our children and churches,
where we listened to the same gospel the white man listens to. We had a great many cattle and horses. The
white man came into our country from Missouri, and
drove our cattle and horses away across the river. If
our people followed them they got killed. We try to
forget these things, but we would not forget that the
white man brought us the blessed gospel of Christ, the
Christian's hope. This more than pays us for all we
have suffered." Seven hundred and seventy Delawares,
the survivors of the former 50,000, were removed to Indian Territory, broken and disheartened, still robbed by
white horse thieves. (See Report of the Commissioner
of Indian Affairs, 1887.)

In 1876 the Ponca Indians were removed from their

homes, their harvests, and much of their property, and were driven before the bayonet a fifty-five days' march into a strange country and an unfavorable climate, to make another beginning in the way of civilization, losing nearly one-fourth of their number inside of a year from the date of their removal.

At the time of the annexation of Texas, according to a speech delivered in the U. S. Senate by Sam Houston (I think in 1855), southern planters rushed into the northern part of that state upon land which had been set apart for the Indians, and, regardless of treaty guaranties of the former republic, took possession of their improvements (for they had at that time commenced farming). This being resisted, on the return of the troops from the Mexican war they were sent against the Comanches, who were driven from their homes into the wilds of Indian Territory, where they relapsed into a lower state than they had ever before known. As might have been expected, with revenge ever rankling in their breasts, they for many, many years, continued a course of murderous depredations upon the people of that state.

The Brunot treaty with the Utes was ratified in 1874, which provided that they should receive rations and annuity goods. No part of the first annuity had been paid two years afterwards; only a half month's rations had been issued to them for a whole year. Arms and ammunition were withheld from them, though their sustenance in the absence of rations depended upon the chase. Though reduced to the verge of starvation, and squatters were crowding upon their best lands, yet in all this time not one deed of violence is shown to have been committed by them. At length, when human nature could bear no more, they fell upon the border robbers, and the Ute Indian war was begun.

Our Indian wars have nearly all originated in broken treaties and gross injustice on the part of our Government. Bishop Whipple, in a letter to the New York " Tribune," January 30th, 1877, says: " I have asked scores of brave officers who have grown gray in the service if they knew of a single instance where Indians were the first to break a treaty, and they always answered ' No.' " H. H. Jackson, after an examination of all the treaties made by our Government with Indian tribes, and the causes of our Indian wars, did not find that a single treaty had been first broken by Indians; that every one had been first violated by whites.

Forts Phil Karney, Smith, and Reno were built in the Sioux (Su) country in violation of explicit treaty stipulations. The Indians, knowing that the Government had no enemies in their country, and that soldiers sent there were either sent against them or to protect invading squatters, took up arms in resistance; war followed, costing the United States $4,000,000 per month. (See Speech of Rev. H. A. Stinson before the American Missionary Association, Chicago, October 29th, 1879.)

Immediately after the discovery of gold and silver in Colorado, notwithstanding articles in the treaties with the Cheyennes and Arapahoes solemnly covenanting to protect their lands from invasion of whites, they poured in upon them, not always respecting or even caring for the rights of the Indians. Misunderstandings arose, and some collisions took place. To correct these, instead of protecting the Indians in their homes, a new treaty was made, in which, in consideration of a reservation being set apart for them on both sides of the Arkansas River in Kansas, they ceded their lands in Colorado to the Government. Congress failed to ratify this treaty, but the squatters retained possession of their Colorado lands, and the Indians were left *without any home*. Their rations were also withheld in violation of the agreement. Still they kept peace until an Indian was charged by a white man with having stolen his horses. Without any investigation soldiers were sent to seize Indian ponies, and war was at once precipitated. The Cheyenne Chief Black Kettle applied to the Governor of Colorado for protection, which was refused. Still anxious to preserve peace, he sent a flag of truce to meet the approaching troops, and two of his brothers were killed beneath its folds. As might be expected some depredations were committed upon the settlements. The Cheyenne village of Cedar Bluffs was attacked, and several Indians were killed. Petty hostilities continued until fall, when application was made to Major Wyncoop, commander of Fort Lyon, to negotiate a treaty of peace. He ordered the Indians to assemble near Fort Lyon under assurance of protection. While here, in a defenceless condition, having surrendered arms, Colonel Chivington, at the head of a company of United States troops, surrounded and slaughtered without mercy the whole band, including women and children, consisting of five hundred persons! This inaugurated a war which withdrew 8,000 troops from those engaged in suppressing the rebellion, at a cost to the Government of $30,000,000. (See "Quaker Among Indians," pages 22 and 23.)

Less than three years after this "Sand Creek Massacre," in 1867, General Hancock, without any known provocation, according to the report of the Commissioner of Indian Affairs for that year, surrounded and burned a Cheyenne village consisting of three hundred lodges, destroying Indian property valued at $100,000. As a result of this unprovoked attack a three-years' war followed, at a cost of many lives and $40,000,000! In 1868 a village of peaceful Cheyennes, situated on land assigned them near Fort Cobb, was surrounded by General Custer and his troops, and not a man, woman or child was permitted to escape! (See Rev. H. A. Stinsons' speech, before referred to.)

The late difficulty with the Bannocks in Wyoming is but a continuation of wrong and outrage. In the last treaty made with that tribe, before Wyoming was organized as a territory, large game being abundant, the Indians were granted full privilege of hunting and killing game on any unoccupied land in the country, without reference to reservation lines, and as usual the United States entered into solemn stipulations to protect them in their rights. It is well known that Indians seldom, if ever, wantonly destroy game, or kill it in greater quantity than their needs for home use or trade require. On account of the abundance of large game, Wyoming became the grand resort of sportsmen from the East, and even from Europe, and much large game, as the elk and buffalo, was needlessly destroyed. This led the legislature, after the organization of the state of Wyoming, to pass stringent laws to protect the wanton destruction of game, and guards were appointed to see to their proper enforcement. Eastern sportsmen were permitted—under certain restrictions and accompanied by some of the guard—to exercise their cruel sport.

As by the Constitution of the United States treaty stipulations are the supreme law of the land, and state laws cannot supersede them, Indians were not bound by state laws regulating the killing of game, and, being under no restrictions, continued to kill such game as they needed wherever they found it. As this brought no money to the pockets of the state guards, they became irritated, and deliberately shot and killed a number of Indian hunters, who were quietly pursuing their legitimate business on land assigned them by the treaty with the Government. This led to retaliation, and troops were called into requisition to restore order. Explanations followed, and another Indian war was but narrowly averted.

Without one instance on record in which the Indians were the first to violate a treaty with our Government, our nation has sacrificed many thousands of lives and $500,000,000 in Indian wars. That the Indian has not been chargeable for this, the testimony of several Generals who have commanded in Indian wars, bear incontrovertible witness. General Harney, whose campaigns against various Indian tribes extended through a period of forty years of military service in the West, in his official report maintains that " In every war that has been waged between the United States and the Indians justice was on the side of the Indians. The Indians have in every case been simply defending their rights and their homes against the treachery and bad faith of the civil and the cunning brute-force of the military department of the Government.

Generals Crook, Terry and Miles have each in turn endorsed these statements of General Harney. General Crook, in an official paper, says: " It goes against my conscience to fight Indians when I know that the right is on their side and the wrong on ours." Similar sentiments to these may be found in the official statements of Generals Sherman, Augur and Pope. In view of existing facts as here stated, Professor Seely, of Amherst College, declares: " There has not been an Indian war for the past fifty years in which the whites have not been the aggressors."

It is well known that a belt of country lying between the frontier settlements of the whites and the lands usually occupied by the Indians has been for many years infested by bands of horse thieves and other desperate characters who have fled from civilized society to escape from that justice which their crimes merited. These desperadoes were continually prowling about in secret, committing depredations upon frontier towns and outlying settlements, selling whiskey, arms and ammunition to Indians, and stealing large numbers of Indian ponies, which, under the title of Indian traders,they would sell at public auction far from the scenes of their depredations.

Again, in the disguise of Indians, they have been known to commit depredations upon the frontiers, which, in numerous instances have been published in paragraphs furnished to newspapers as having been committed by Indians, who, from their ignorance of written language, were unable to repel the charges even were they to know of them. (See " Quaker Among Indians," pages 230-240, especially footnote on page 239.)

These newspaper items would be copied by the press throughout the land; but when cut out of any paper, and forwarded with an explicit answer to the editor by the writer of this article, who, under government employ, was residing in the camp of the wildest of the wild tribes for many months, and knowing whereof he wrote, while he could thus secure its publication in one paper, it would be, with very few exceptions, overlooked by those others who had extended the publicity of the original false paragraph—the vindication being read by the patrons of one paper only, while the calumny would be read by hundreds.

In consequence of these onesided representations the great mass of the people of the United States were so poorly informed of the true status of the case as to be very greatly, if not unjustifiably, prejudiced against the Indians. The excitement ran so high about the time of General U. S. Grant's election to the Presidency as to manifest itself in a very extensive clamor for a war of extermination against the whole race.

After the election of General Grant he was waited on by a committee of Friends, representing all of the Yearly Meetings of Orthodox Friends in the United States, who suggested to him to take into consideration the propriety of appointing religious men for Indian agents, who would secure religious employees so far as practicable, which they thought would have a better effect on the Indians than was sometimes seen in Indian agencies. After listening to them with great interest he replied, " Gentlemen, your advice is good. I accept it. Now give me the names of some Friends for Indian agents and I will appoint them. If you can make Quakers out of the Indians it will take the fight out of them. Let us have peace." The memorable words, "Let us have peace," will in time to come cast a halo of glory over his character. The President asking the committee to nominate Indian agents was totally unlooked for by them. He wished them to nominate a superintendent for the central superintendency, and agents to be under him to have the control of the Indian agencies in Kansas and the wild tribes in Indian Territory, and then a committee to have the moral and religious oversight of them, and to nominate successors should vacancies occur. In compliance with this request of President U. S. Grant the Yearly Meetings of Orthodox Friends appointed some well known and influential members to constitute an "Executive Committee," who acted in behalf of the Society in all their deliberations. This committee were to consider the qualifications, the business capabilities, and moral and religious adaptation, of all who were proposed for the position of superintendent and agents, and only such as had the approbation of this committee were recommended to the President for appointment.

Applications were also usually made to this committee for the position of teachers of the agency schools and other important employees. Thus great care was exercised that only suitable, judicious persons should be appointed to any important station under the care of that religious body.

Among the wilder tribes thus brought under the supervision of Friends were the Southern Cheyennes and Arapahoes, the warlike Kiowas and Comanches, a small band of Apaches, besides several remnants of tribes called the Affiliated Bands, such as Caddoes, Wichitas, Kuchies, Wacoes and several others, more or less civilized.

Of the labors of Friends among these and other tribes belonging to the Central Superintendency, the attending hardships and exposures they endured, and the results attained, it is the object of this book to briefly set forth, together with the result of the missionary labor of Friends with the Indians.

CHAPTER I.

In the early history of the colonies that subsequently constituted the United States there were two object lessons in the treatment of the Indians that were very telling on their character. One was in Pennsylvania and New Jersey, where they were treated honestly and candidly on the basis of "peace, good-will towards men." The other was in colonies with treatment towards the Indians based on the adage, "might makes right."

William Penn and the Friends of Pennsylvania and New Jersey regarded the Indians as brethren in tne Divine sight, with souls that needed to be "redeemed with the precious blood of Christ." "We are all one flesh and blood," said William Penn to them. With this feeling prominently in their minds it was not difficult to treat them kindly and justly. The Indians appreciated and reciprocated their kindness. "We will live," said they, "in love with William Penn and his children as long as the sun and moon shall endure." Harmoniously they lived together during the period that Friends controlled the Government of Pennsylvania, which was about seventy years. During that time there was not even a serious difficulty, much less a war. Their effort was to do their Indian brethren good, and direct their minds to the " Lamb of God which taketh away the sin of the world." The blessing of God was upon both parties.

Very different was the condition in the other colonies. There the Indians were not regarded as brethren. They were not uniformly treated from the standpoint of justice; hence the sad results stated in the introductory remarks by T. C. Battey.

From the day of William Penn to the present time, members of the Friends' Church, with but little if any exception, have taken a deep interest in the welfare of the Indians. In 1868 a number of the Yearly Meetings of the " Orthodox Friends " appointed committees to confer together, and see if there was anything more that they should do to befriend the Indians and advance them in civilization and the Christian religion, besides sustaining the schools that they already had among them. The committee met in Chicago in Twelfth month, 1868, and petitioned Congress not to transfer the care of the Indians to the Military Department, as proposed by a bill then pending in the House of Representatives. The petition further stated: " We earnestly appeal to you to extend to the Indians the fostering and protecting care of the Government; to search out and supply their immediate needs, and afford every facility and encouragement by legislation and approbation, to induce earnest, efficient and humane persons to labor among them as they have so successfully labored among the freedmen of the South."

The committee again met in the spring of 1869 in Baltimore, and after canvassing the subject, concluded to visit President Grant, with the result stated in the introductory remarks. The minutes of their third meeting, held in Indianapolis, Indiana, state: " The present condition of the Indian tribes, and the suggestion of the President in reference to the appointment of suitable Friends to labor among the Indians for their civilization and improvement, claimed the serious consideration of the meeting.

" In entering upon the consideration of this important subject, we are duly impressed with its responsibility. Rarely in the history of our Society has a work of greater importance been presented for its consideration, and we are fully sensible that, unless our reliance is upon that wisdom which cometh from above, we shall fail. Appreciating the generous offer of our President to receive nominations for Indian agents from Friends, we have greatly desired the opening might be embraced and suitable Friends appointed to take those positions. It is our united judgment that we should recommend none but such as are deeply imbued with the love of Christ, and who feel willing to accept the position from Christian and not from mere mercenary motives—men fearing God and hating covetousness.

"That in addition they should be men of sound judgment and ready tact in managing such business as will necessarily claim their attention. Possessing, first, a practical knowledge of agriculture and general farm management; second, a capacity for financiering. They should be capable of keeping correct accounts of the receipt and disbursements of all funds placed in their hands for the benefit of the Indians.

"They should also be such members of our Society as will faithfully represent us, possessing firmness combined with patience and mildness, so as to secure the esteem and confidence of both the Indians and those interested in their welfare."

After prayerful consideration they nominated Enoch Hoag, of Muscatine, Iowa, for superintendent, whose headquarters would be at Lawrence, Kansas, to have the oversight of the nine Indian agents, whose duty was to report to him quarterly, and he to report to the Commissioner of Indian Affairs at Washington. The agents nominated were Isaac T. Gibson, Dr. Reuben S. Roberts, Thomas Miller, Hiram Jones, John D. Miles, Brinton Darlington, Mahlon Stubbs, Joel H. Morris, and Lawrie Tatum, the author of this volume. I was living on a farm in Iowa, and knew nothing about being nominated for an Indian agent until I saw my name in a newspaper with others who had been appointed Indian agents, and confirmed by the Senate.

My appointment was for the Kiowas and Comanches,

who were wild, blanket Indians, and the Wichita and affiliated bands, who were partially civilized, some of them wearing citizen's clothes, all located in the southwestern part of Indian territory. The Cheyenne and Arapahoe Indians, on a reservation north of mine, and the Osages, in the northern part of the territory, were "blanket Indians,"—i.e., their principal clothing consisted of buffalo robes and blankets. The Indians in other agencies were civilized, and generally wore citizen's clothing. Those in the southwestern part of the territory were still addicted to raiding in Texas, stealing horses and mules, and sometimes committing other depredations, and especially was this the case with the Kiowas and Comanches. They were probably the worst Indians east of the Rocky Mountains. The whole number placed under the care of Friends was about 17,000.

Soon after assigning the central superintendency to Friends, the President requested other religious denominations to select and nominate some of their members for appointment as Indian agents, watch over their nominees and assist in the scholastic, industrial, moral and religious education of the Indians. Under President Grant's administration of two terms nearly all Indian agents were church members.

After my appointment I soon received official notice of it, with instruction to meet Colonel W. B. Hazen at Junction City, Kansas, May 20th, 1869, and he would convey me to my agency. I knew little of the duties and responsibilities devolving upon an Indian agent. But after considering the subject as best I could in the fear of God, and wishing to be obedient to Him, it seemed right to accept the appointment.

My friend, James G. Southwick, arranged to accompany me, and serve in some capacity at the agency. Israel and Ruth Negus also went with us to Kansas City on their way to the Cheyenne and Arapahoe agency, to assist Brinton Darlington, the agent of those Indians. We met Colonel Hazen at Junction City, then a small village, but the proprietors were very hopeful of its expansion. The colonel took us in his ambulance, drawn by four mules, nearly south about 350 miles, camping out at nights, with a good tent to sleep in. I believe there was not a house seen by us from Junction City to where Wichita now is. At that place there were several grass lodges made by the Wichita Indians during the rebellion, and two or three stockade houses. We saw no other buildings until we reached Fort Sill. Three or four miles from the Fort was the adobe house for agency use that was being constructed by order of Colonel Hazen, the military agent. He was afterwards placed at the head of the Weather Bureau at Washington.

He had several small tracts of land plowed for the Indians, and hired a man to show them how to plant and cultivate the crops. The women fenced the lots by planting stakes into the ground, and then with bark tying small poles to them. By keeping their ponies away from the fences they raised corn, melons and pumpkins. So craving was the appetite of the Indians for vegetables that many of the melons were eaten before they were half grown! They feasted bountifully on the corn as soon as it was old enough to use. A common mode of cooking it was to remove nearly all of the husks, and then cover it with hot ashes and coals of fire. They dried large quantities of corn and pumpkins. The " squaw fences " were too frail to last until the corn was gathered; hence the ponies would break through it if not carefully watched.

On July 1st, 1869, the care of the agency, with the Government property belonging to it, was transfered to me, except the commissary stores in charge of the Military Department, which were not transferred until a year later.

There had been an appropriation for agency buildings, but the adobe house was the only one contracted for. It was but a few rods from Cache Creek, which flowed from the Wichita Mountains, and sometimes rose very suddenly, so that it was too high to ford, and thus prevented our reaching the postoffice or commissary, and, being on low ground, I thought the location unhealthy. Therefore I selected high ground on the other side of the creek, and commenced building a schoolhouse, and houses for physician, carpenter and other employees, and in the autumn went to Chicago and bought a steam-engine and fixtures for a saw-mill, and a shingle machine and small mill-stones for grinding corn. The mill was well put up, and we could then have lumber for our buildings without paying one hundred dollars for a thousand feet, which had been the price.

About the middle of July, 1869, a sub-committee of the Executive Committee of Friends on Indian Affairs met at Lawrence, Kansas, to arrange for visiting the agencies under the care of Friends. John Butler and Achilles Pugh, of Ohio, were to visit the two agencies in southwestern part of Indian Territory, and Thomas Wistar, of Philadelphia, was to visit the agencies in Kansas. Superintendent Hoag went with T. Wistar, and to some of the tribes he paid their annuity funds. The newly-appointed Friend agents had not yet arrived at some of the agencies, and some of the tribes were expecting soon to remove to their new reservations in the Indian Territory. Affairs seemed unsettled, and some tribes were discouraged.

In the report of John Butler and Achilles Pugh they state that they visited, with their newly-appointed agent, Brinton Darlington, the Cheyenne and Arapahoe Indians near Camp Supply. In the Cheyenne camp there were two hundred and seventy lodges. Each lodge represented a family. " The tribe generally bore the appearance of great destitution, said to be occasioned by the removal of their traders and the long and exhaustive wars with the whites and with the other Indians, but they were scrupulously clean with what clothing they had.

. . . At the Wichita and Comanche agency we found
Lawrie Tatum at work on his location. He had about
seventy acres of land enclosed and cultivated in corn,
etc., a new agency building in process of erection, a
pretty good stone house, and things generally looking
thrifty and businesslike. On talking to him about his
prospects, both present and future, we were impressed
with the idea that we had the right man in the right
place. His ideas, like his duties, seem to be expansive
and generous. . . . We attended a council held with the
Indians by the President's Commission, in which we
were much instructed by the speeches of the Commissioners and the Indian chiefs. Several of the chiefs expressed much satisfaction with having the Commissioners
with them, and also a wish to endeavor to walk in the
white man's road.

" Satanta, a Kiowa chief, made two speeches, which
were said to be characteristic of the man, who is a daring
and restless man. He said that ' he took hold of that
part of the white man's road that was represented by the
breech-loading gun, but did not like the ration of corn;
it hurt his teeth.' He also said, ' The good Indian, he
that listens to the white man, got nothing. The independent Indian was the only one that was rewarded.'
They wanted arms and ammunition."

The Commissioners answered that the Indians would
get no arms nor ammunition, but they would be protected if they came onto the Reservation. "It was peace

on the Reservations; it was war off of them. If they left the Reservations without leave they would be punished. The buffalo came through the reservation twice a year; that was enough." ... "We desire to acknowledge the kind and generous hospitality of the Commander [Colonel Grierson] and other officers of Fort Sill."

During the spring and summer the Indians had been raiding in Texas, and they seemed very sanguine that they could not be restrained. A prominent chief told me that if Washington—i.e., the President—did not want his young men to raid in Texas, then Washington must move Texas far away, where his young men could not find it. One motive for raiding was to get an increase of annuity goods and rations. They told me that when they made their last treaty they got a large amount of annuity goods and a liberal supply of provisions. Since then they had not got so much. They told me a number of times that the only way that they could get a large supply of annuity goods was to go out onto the warpath, kill some people, steal a good many horses, get the soldiers to chase them awhile, without permitting them to do much harm, and then the Government would give them a large amount of blankets, calico, muslin, etc., to get them to quit!

The Indians came for rations every two weeks, and the chiefs generally ate one to three meals at the agency when they came. They frequently said that it made their hearts feel good to have such bountiful meals.

Colonel Grearson, the commanding officer at Fort Sill, a few miles from the agency, was very kind to them. The chiefs often ate at his table, and then he would sometimes give them an order on the bakery for bread to take to their families. He did all that was reasonable for such an officer to do to keep them satisfied and make them comfortable

As previously stated, I went to Chicago in the fall of 1869 to purchase machinery for a steam saw-mill. While in the state I procured several employees to assist at the agency. Among them was Eli and Mahala Jay, of Indiana. The latter was to serve as clerk. My wife and youngest child, seven years old, returned with me. There were ten men, four women and two children in the company. At Lawrence, Kansas, I purchased some wagons, spring seats, animals and harness; also a camping outfit, and started on our trip of about 400 miles, the most of the way with no house in sight. One day the monotony was broken by the sight of a small herd of buffalo, a new sight to a majority of the company. We halted, and I told the men that they might shoot buffalo, as several of them had guns, hoping that they might see game to shoot, and I would drive the leading team, and the women would drive the teams following. The men started ahead of the wagon train. I held in the mules, and they walked slowly. When the buffalo saw us moving, although a considerable distance from the road, they started to cross it ahead of the wagons, according to their custom. They were walking forty or fifty yards in front of the men when they shot, but there was no appearance of a buffalo being hit. The noise frightened the huge animals, and they soon ran out of sight. We had supper without buffalo meat—quite a disappointment. The next day I told the men that they might try their skill at hunting again. We were to cross a stream where there was jack oak timber, and I thought many wild turkeys were in it. They soon shot all the turkeys we could eat for several days—until we reached the agency. This force of mechanics and workmen was much needed in erecting the buildings. The winter is so mild that there was but little hindrance on account of inclement weather.

Through the summer I had more ground plowed, so as to have a small field for each band of Comanches who seemed willing to locate. In the fall I contracted with parties to have all of the Indian fields enclosed with a good post and three-rail fence, the rails to be mortised into the posts, and strong enough to bear the weight of a man after the fence was made. I then estimated for funds, but was informed that there were no funds applicable for fencing. I then made another contract, providing that the fences were to be paid for when funds were appropriated and forwarded for the purpose. Under it the land was inclosed, much to the satisfaction of the Indians, and it was paid for in the spring.

In the winter the Indians promised to furnish teams

in the spring to plow their fields. They seemed very hopeful of raising crops. In the latter part of the winter some of Pen-e-teth-ka band of Comanches went to Texas and stole some horses and mules. As soon as I learned of it I compelled them to return the stolen animals to their owner, who came after them. When I called on them for teams to plow, Asa-hany, one of the chiefs, said that I ought to have used the mules that he gave up to me. He urged the other chiefs to not let me have teams. Without his help I got their lots all plowed and planted.

As spring approached nearly all of the Indians became uneasy, and many of them manifested much dissatisfaction. Some of the Comanches signified that there would be trouble in the spring. My wife and other women made many dresses for the women and children, which they were glad to receive. The women seemed much more friendly than the men. They do not covet the "war path." In the latter part of May about twenty horses and mules were stolen from the agency and adjacent places by thirty or forty Indians, led, it was said, by Tob-a-nan-a-ca, a Comanche. They cut the tent occupied by the farmers to pieces, so as to render it almost worthless, stole the blankets and clothing in the tent, and left for the mountains. This raid was without any provocation whatever.

About the middle of June the Qua-ha-da band of Comanches stole seventy-three mules at night from the Quartermaster's corral. Captain Walsh, with a hundred men, were sent on the trail, but lost it among fresh buffalo tracks. A week or two later my wife and I were wakened one morning by the report of a gun. Five Indians had gone to where some men had camped for the night, about two hundred yards from the agency, and shot Levi Lucans, an employee of the Quartermaster. The ball went through the lower part of his body, apparently just inside of his back bone.   In a few minutes we heard another report of a gun. The same Indians killed a man at the beef corral. They stole some horses and rode towards the mill and houses that were being erected; but observing that they were being watched, and not knowing that Quakers did not shoot Indians, and no doubt feeling guilty, they turned their course towards the mountains. Another party killed and scalped a man about six miles from the agency the same morning.

Levi Lucans was carried to the agency building, and I supposed that he would die in a few minutes. The post physician reached there as soon as practicable and dressed the wound. I let him have a room in our house, and he was well cared for, and finally recovered, and again worked for the Quartermaster.

About the time of the foregoing depredations a herd of cattle that was being driven from Texas for Indian supplies was attacked by Indians, one man killed, some of the cattle killed, and many of them stampeded and lost. The Indians evidently wished to provoke an attack by Colonel Grierson, and then be hired to quit their depredations.

The latter part of June I called the Friends together who were working for the Government, and told them that, dangerous as it seemed to be there, I expected to remain, but wished them to use their own judgment as to remaining there or returning to the states. Eli and Mahala Jay, my clerks, and my wife, had expected to return early in July. All of the other Friend employees decided to leave except Josiah and Lizzie Butler, who were teachers. It was a great disappointment and injury to the work.

July 4. Two Kiowas came to see me and wished to know if the Comanches might come and draw rations. I told them that they might, provided they would bring in and return to Colonel Grierson and myself the animals that they had stolen. I consulted Colonel Grierson on the subject, and we both thought that it would not be right to let them go without some punishment after such atrocities committed without cause, except with a hope that their rations and annuities would be increased. My fervent desire was to be supplied with heavenly wisdom sufficient for the responsible business devolving upon me. My trust was in the Lord, who could restrain the evil intentions and passions of the Indians.

July 5, 1870. My wife and Friend employees started to their homes. Under the circumstances the parting was peculiarly trying. In the evening Israel and Ruth

Negus, from the Cheyenne and Arapahoe agency, seventy miles north, came to see us. There had been no trouble there. The Indians told their agent, Brinton Darlington, that he might sleep, and if hostile Indians came they would attend to them.

On the 1st of July the commissary stores, including 4,299 head of fat cattle, had been transferred to me from the Military Department. This greatly increased my responsibility and care. I was then responsible for the safe keeping of that large herd of wild Texas cattle until they were issued to the Indians. I divided the cattle into three herds, with a foreman over each herd, and under him one herder for every hundred head of cattle. William Broddus, who assisted in buying the cattle in Texas and driving them to the agency, I employed as foreman of one of the herds, and he also had oversight of the other herds. He superintended the whole herding business, including the delivery of cattle at the beef corral as they were needed for issue to the Indians. The large herds were kept about sixty or seventy miles east of the agency, in the Chickasaw nation, so as to have them out of reach of my Indians. William Broddus proved to be a very competent, energetic and efficient man for the position, and I was very fortunate in securing his services. He remained in my employ until I left, in 1873. He and one of the other foremen herders—Mr. Jorden—then went into the cattle business in Texas, and became wealthy.

When Mahala Jay, my clerk, left I was at a loss to know where to procure another. It was impossible for me to perform clerical and other duties devolving upon me. The Government is very particular to have the accounts clear, correct and self-explaining. Three copies of the reports showing the receipts and expenditures, and the amount of Government property on hand unexpended, had to be sent to Superintendent Hoag every quarter. He retained one copy and forwarded two to the Commissioner of Indian Affairs at Washington. I also retained a copy for my use.

I employed George H. Smith, a graduate of Girard College, to succeed Mahala Jay as clerk. He had been Commissary Clerk under the Military Department, and was acquainted with the mode of keeping Government accounts. He proved to be very efficient, and remained with me until I left the agency. Our business, interest and danger were so closely allied that there grew up a strong attachment between us. Soon after I left, he, with his family, went to Washington, and for many years he has been employed as clerk in the Treasury Department.

The Qua-ha-da band of Comanches, and some of the Kiowas, had remained on the plains away from the agency since the last treaty was made, and they committed many depredations. They had a bad influence on the Indians who would like to locate and be friendly.

July 10. Two runners came from the Kiowa camps with information that Little Heart, and one or two other chiefs, with their people, had gone to the Qua-ha-da camps, and did not intend to come to the agency. The other Kiowas wished to come in. I repeated my terms, that before they could have rations they must deliver the stolen stock. They said that Kickingbird was collecting it, and they would soon be at the agency. They assured me that there would be no more raiding here; that we might sleep now, and turn out our mules without fear of being molested. Black Eagle said after the medicine dance he went to the Rocky Mountains to fight the Ute Indians. On his return, finding that some of the Indians had committed depredations at the agency, he gave them a big talk for raiding on their white friends, where they received their rations. He thought they acted very badly. But now he wanted us all to live as friends, and let them have plenty of ammunition and provisions. Ten-Bear wanted the agent and General Grierson to have large hearts and overlook all that had been done. He hoped that the good road of the whites would be as an arch right over the blood of the white men that had been spilt, and that it would not be thought of or mentioned any more, and make no inquiry as to who had committed the murders in this vicinity.

I told him that the Great Spirit did not wish the Indians and white people to fight or injure each other, and the white people did not wish a war with the Indians, and we had given them no cause for one, but they had murdered the white people without cause, and stolen our horses and mules without provocation. On the return of the stolen animals they would get rations, but they need not talk about ammunition. They would not get that. I wished to know who committed the murders, but did not know what would be done with them.

Ten Bear then addressed the Kiowas, telling them how badly they had acted, and to bring in the stolen stock. They had plenty of mules, and they could not kill buffalo on them.

Little Raven, a prominent chief of the Arapahoes, who was there on a visit, said there had been no trouble at their agency on the North Fork; that he and his band had moved close to Agent Darlington and his friends, and had told them that if the Kiowas came there the Arapahoes would attend to them.

Buffalo Good, the Waco chief, told the Kiowas that he had long known them; that they were treacherous and bad Indians. Time after time had they made treaties and promised to behave, and then in a few days would murder some white people. He did not know when to believe them. He did not know whether they were sincere now in their promise or not. He had two hearts about it.

Asad-a-wa, the Wichita chief, said that the Great Father above, who was the Good Spirit, and our mother, the earth, were witnesses of what had passed to-day. The Great Spirit knew whether the Kiowas were sincere or not. He hoped they were, and that there would be no further depredations or trouble.

It was a trying and wearing day on me. The Kiowas had probably thought that if they committed some depredations they would be hired to be peaceable; also that they would obtain an increased amount of annuity, goods and rations, and be allowed to keep the stolen animals. But instead of that they were required to return the stolen stock and then only to obtain their usual amount of provisions, and no back rations.

About a week after the foregoing "talk," Ho-we-ah, one of the few reliable chiefs, reported that while Black Eagle was at the agency some of the Kiowas and Comanches were in Texas, and had killed two white men, and had taken a woman and six children captives! The way the Indians were acting was very discouraging.

August 7. The Kiowa chiefs, with two or three hundred of their young men, women and children, came to see me and obtain rations. They returned twenty-seven of the seventy-three mules stolen from the quartermaster, and one that they stole from Agent Richards, of the Wichita agency. I wished to have "a talk" with them, and invited Colonel Grierson to be present. He came with his orderly and post interpreter, H. P. Jones. My interpreter was Matthew Leeper, son of a former agent, who, in childhood, had lived much in the Comanche camps. He was very efficient and reliable. We had in one of the large commissary buildings an exciting coun-

cil. I reproved them for their raiding. Told them that
it was the people in Texas with the people in other states
who paid for the annuity, goods and rations that they
received without paying for. The only people in Texas
who had ever come onto the reservation to do them any
injury, so far as I knew, were a few whiskey peddlers,
who took foolish water (the Comanche name for whiskey) to their camps to trade to them. That class of people
did them an injury. Those foolish water people they
did not molest, but they went to Texas, to their friends,
who helped to feed and clothe them, and killed some of
them, carried off their women and children, and drove
off their horses, mules and cattle. The Texans were good
to them in helping to feed and clothe them, and in return
they were bad to the Texans. Washington (the President) had sent me there to issue annuity goods and
rations, to make fields for them, and show them how to
raise corn and melons, pumpkins and vegetables, for their
benefit. It was too bad for them to go to raiding on the
agency where they were fed and clothed and assisted and
instructed in what was best for them. They were the children of the Great Spirit, and the white people were the
children of the Great Spirit, and he wanted us to live
together like brothers. The white people want to live
that way, and it would be better for the Indians to live
that way.

Lone Wolf said that he had been looking and looking
to see what they had got mad about, but could find

nothing. The chiefs all claimed to have opposed the war and depredation movement, but were compelled to go with the current. There was so little dependence to be placed in their word that we did not know when they were telling the truth.

They said that White Horse led the party who stole the quartermaster's mules, and also led the recent raid into Texas and killed Mr. Koozer and took his wife and five children captives, one of them a young woman. They also got a boy named Martin B. Kilgore. It was distressing to think of those savages having white captives, and especially women. According to long-established usage, the Indians offered to sell their captives. A Mexican who was living with the Indians asked two mules and a carbine for the mother, who was in his possession, demanding the price in advance, and promising to bring her in next time he came. They all demanded pay, and that in advance. Their plan, no doubt, was to get their pay then, and again when they were brought. I told them that I should give them nothing at that time, and they need not come again for their rations until the captives were brought to me.

While we were in council the Indians had their guns, bows and arrows lying at their sides, which could be seized in an instant. As I was speaking, one of them took the cartridges out of his breech-loading gun and put them back again, to let me see how many loads he had in readiness! Another one strung his bow and was snapping an arrow on it! Another one, who was sitting about fifteen or twenty feet in front of me, drew out a butcher knife and whetstone and went to whetting his knife, turning it over from side to side, making all the noise he could with it. I thought they were doing it to intimidate the colonel and myself. After the council closed an Indian came to me and ran his hand under my vest over my heart to see if he could " feel any scare." But it was beating calmly as usual.

The next time that the Indians came to the agency I told them that they had been trying to scare me with their weapons, and in future when they came into my office or commissary building they should leave their guns, revolvers and bows outside. I carried no arms, and they did not need them when they came to see me, and they should not bring them into my quarters. It was with great reluctance that they yielded to that regulation. But as I would not have them in my office with their arms, they soon learned to leave them with their women outside.

August 18. The Kiowas came to the agency with their women and children and brought the captive Koozer family.

Some of the children were soon delivered to me, and then the bands that gave them up wanted their rations, but I refused to give any rations until all the captives were delivered. The chiefs then went to work in earnest with the Mexican, a contemptible fellow, who had the mother and one child, and soon procured them, the last of the family. A mother and five children! I felt thankful to my Heavenly Father that through His help and providence I was able to procure them, and they felt very thankful to get from under the clutches of those cruel Indians!

The Indians then wanted a council. They claimed to be entirely peaceable and friendly, and wanted a large amount of coffee and sugar, and their usual supply of flour and beef. As they had quit the war path, they wanted me to give them a liberal quantity of ammunition. They said that they had been very liberal in giving up those captives, and they wanted me to show a corresponding liberality in making presents in return for them.

I told them that they would get no ammunition, and no more than the usual supply of rations. The Government had been liberal to them a long time, in giving them rations and annuity goods, and asked nothing from them in return but good behavior. This they had not done, but had been off stealing horses and mules, murdering and taking captives. Their liberality was very small compared to ours. But I was willing to make them a present of one hundred dollars for each captive delivered to me. The Department approved of it, and paid the amount advanced by me.

I was afterwards told by H. P. Jones, the post interpreter, that he had no idea that I would get the captives without paying several hundred dollars for each one. He had been acquainted with the Indians for twelve or fourteen years, and during that period captives had never been returned without paying several times that amount; that two years before they were paid fifteen hundred dollars each for returning some captives. Sometimes they would agree to deliver captives if paid a certain amount in advance, and then when they were brought would have to be paid again.

September 1, 1870. The remaining captive was brought to the agency. Asa-havey told me that the boy would not be delivered unless I would pay more than one hundred dollars for him. I told him that the band would get no rations until the boy was delivered. While they were consulting in the tent, where they had the boy, as to how they could manage to get more for him than was paid for the other captives, they saw a company of cavalry coming to the agency. This caused them to deliver the boy, Martin B. Kilgore, to me, and I paid one hundred dollars for him.

I then called the chiefs into my office and told them that four weeks ago some of the Kiowas committed depredations at the beef pen, and two weeks ago, when they were there after rations, I told the Kiowa chiefs to go with their young men to the beef pen and see that they behaved, which they promised to do. The chiefs went with their young men, but instead of having them to behave they assisted in killing ten or a dozen beeves

and thirty or forty calves more than they were entitled
to, and robbed the herders of their provisions and cooking utensils, and now I was going to punish the Kiowas
by keeping back half of their coffee and sugar. Lone
Wolf told me to issue them as commonly and they would
behave. I told him that they promised to behave two
weeks ago and they had not done it, and now I expected
to punish them. He then shook hands with me and
stood back to make a big speech, as he termed it. Addressing me, he said: "It is very foolish for you to get
mad just as we have got entirely over our mad. We have
left all of our bad young men at home; brought nobody
but our women and children, and they are extremely
hungry for coffee and sugar. It is the most important
part of our rations. Now, if you cut that in two in the
middle and only give us half, it will only go half way
around to our families, and half of them will be mad.
If you wish to pay the herders you may keep some of
our beef, and some of our flour; we can do without it,
for we can get plenty of buffalo, but we can't do without
the coffee and sugar at all. If we can't have all of it, we
will do without any, rather than to have half of our
women and children mad, and you may keep all of our
coffee and sugar, and all of our other rations and pay the
herders good, and we will go home hungry." Other
chiefs made speeches to the same purport. Then I told
them that I did not want their beef or flour, but I wanted

half of their coffee and sugar, and half I should keep; but if they wished me to keep all of it, and their other rations, I should be satisfied with it if they were.

Lone Wolf then went to the door and called to the women in Kiowa, and they began to take down their little tents and pack up, and soon they were on their way to their camps without anything. We went to issuing to the other Indians, and before we were through Lone Wolf and the other Kiowas returned. They said that they had changed their minds, and would take what I would give them.

I now had all the captives that I knew to be in the possession of my Indians, except one or more that I believed to be with the Qua-ha-das, who did not come to the agency. They had sent word to me that they would not go to the agency and shake hands until the soldiers would go out there and whip them.

My plan of withholding rations from a tribe or band that had white captives until they were delivered was new and experimental. No one knew whether it would work well or not. But I thought it was right, and therefore the thing to do. In practice it worked grandly. I procured many captives of them afterwards without paying a dollar. That treatment made no inducement for them to obtain captives, while paying for them was an inducement.

To prevent the Indians from going into the commissary building and doing their own issuing, as they did at the beef pen, I had requested General Grierson to send a company of soldiers on that day to the commissary. When soldiers come under a civil officer for duty, it is to perform civil, and not military, duty, so that I had no more hesitation in using them than I would have in using a sheriff or police force. On the foregoing occasion I thought there would be danger in attempting to punish the Indians as I did, without the presence of some soldiers stationed in front of the "issue door," and that there would be no danger with their presence. As it was, "the issue" went off smoothly there and at the beef pen. Afterwards I had no further trouble of that kind with the Indians.

New difficulties, however, were frequently arising. One of them was with Satank, who was probably the worst Indian on the Reservation. He rode a mule to the agency which was claimed by a Texan. When there was a controversy between a white man and Indian, the Indian Agent was to sit as judge, hear the case and decide. The Texan proved that the mule had his brand, and the evidence was further shown that it was his. Satank said that some time ago he and one of his sons went to Texas to steal a few animals without intending to hurt anybody, but while they were trying to get the animals the Texans were so mad that they shot his son. He afterwards went to the same vicinity and stole the mule that he was riding, and now he loved it instead of his son. For that reason he thought that he ought to be allowed to keep it. Satank then proposed for me and him to go out on the prairie alone and have a fight, and the one who killed the other should have the mule. But I got the mule without the fight.

On another occasion he told me that some of the Indians had informed me that there was to be peace and quietness there now, but there would not be, unless he could get what rations and other things he wanted, which was far beyond what he was entitled to. Believing that it was not best to be swayed by the threats or complaints of any of the Indians, I gave him no more than usual. But he continued teasing and complaining. At length I told him to please suspend his teasing until we got through issuing, and then come into my office, where we would both have comfortable seats, and then tease and tease all he wanted to and I would listen. When he teased all that he wished to he could quit and go home, but he would get nothing more. " If that is the way it is to be, I will quit now," he said.

September 25. J. B. Maxcy, who lived about six miles south of Montague, Texas, went to the agency and reported that on the 5th inst. some Indians went to his house, killed his father, T. Maxcy, shot his wife through an arm, and killed a small child that she was holding. Then they took two of their children captives—a girl of about three and a boy six years old. There was living in the house with him a family by the name of Buls, who had two children killed, and Mrs. Buls slightly wounded. The men were away from home, except the one who was killed.

Another party of Indians, about the same time, went south of Montague and passed around east of it, stealing many horses. The Indians frequently asserted that they were going to continue raiding in Texas until the soldiers would go to their camps and fight them. They were well armed with revolvers, carbines and needle guns. They were very sanguine of being more than sufficient for all of the soldiers that the Government could send against them. They appeared to have very little comprehension of their dwindling condition or the benevolence and power of the Government.

It was reported that the Indians had a " trail " up the Canadian River, where they drove cattle, horses and mules stolen from Texas, to New Mexico, and traded them for guns, ammunition, blankets, etc. There were Mexicans among them, and many of the Indians could talk the Mexican language, so there was no difficulty in making the exchange, as the same language was largely spoken in New Mexico.

Mr. Maxcy remained at the agency until the Indians came for their rations, but I could hear nothing of the captive children. Their poor father went home disconsolate. He had but three children—one killed in the arms of its mother, the other two taken captive! I employed Pacer, a reliable Apache chief, to go to the Indian camps and see if he could learn anything about the children, or of Dorothy Field, a woman captured the previous winter. On his return he reported that he could hear nothing of any of them. He did not go to the Qua-ha-da camp, as they are mad, he said, at the people in Texas and here, and at the Indians who are friendly to the Government. Through the overruling providence of God, I procured Mr. Maxcy's son about three years afterwards, from the Qua-ha-da band of Comanches. The little girl was killed on account of her crying so much. I think that we never heard of Dorothy Field after she was carried off.

November 27th, 1870. Enoch Hoag, Superintendent; Edward Earl and Dr. William Nicholson, members of Friends' Indian Committee; also Agent Darlington and J. J. Hoag, from the Cheyenne and Arapahoe agency, came to see how I was succeeding in that remote agency, in charge of such refractory Indians. It was a great satisfaction to me, and some of my employees, to have them with us a few days. They seemed well satisfied with the way I managed business, and encouraged me to continue as I had been doing. The usual raiding season of the Indians had now passed, and we did not expect much, if any more, during the winter.

The superintendent instructed me to attend a meeting at Lawrence, Kansas, December 26th, 1870, of the Friend agents, and the committee of Friends who nominated and had the oversight of them. It was with much anxiety that I looked towards going, to be absent about two months, as I wished to go to my home in Iowa if I went to Lawrence. The annuity goods due, according to treaty stipulation, two months before, had not arrived. The Indians were needing their blankets and other goods that the Government was to furnish them. These supplies had been at Fort Hacker, in Kansas, several months, awaiting transportation by the Military Department, but it had its own stores to transport, which delayed the Indian supplies. The school was not yet started, but I hoped to have it in operation soon. The teachers, Josiah and Lizzie Butler, were ready to take charge of it. The latter has since become an evangelist in the Friends' church.

My " Friend " carpenter left in the spring, and for some time I was without one. Before he and others left the Government mill had been erected and some houses built. The stone schoolhouse was being built by contract. One day William Wykes went to my office and told me that he was a carpenter, working for the quartermaster, and he would like to work for me. I told him to return at a certain time and we would talk further about it. On his return I told him that I had made inquiry about him, and had learned that he was industrious and would work without being watched, and could do anything in wood from making a wagon to building a house, and that would suit me very well, but that I had also learned he was addicted to drinking and swearing, and that would not suit me at all, and I did not wish to employ him. "Mr. Tatum," he said, "I am guilty of both of these habits, and I can't quit them while in military employ. My reason for leaving there and working for you is that I may quit. I know that you don't allow your men to drink or swear, and if you will employ me I will give you my word that I will quit both of these vices." He seemed so candid and honest about it that I employed him. As a carpenter he was all that I could desire. His wife was highly pleased to have him under better influence. At the time that I was to leave for Lawrence he had been at work for the agency a few months and had, I thought, kept his promise. He was afterwards overcome twice with drink, but was so sorry for it that I did not discharge him. He and his wife were both converted while I was agent.

I left my clerk, George H. Smith, in charge during my absence at Lawrence. He was a sober, reliable man, and very good at office work. After traveling several days with my mule team, and camping at nights—one night the mercury four degrees below zero—we reached a " stage station " and had one day's ride in the stage to the railroad, and took the cars to Lawrence. Here the ten Friend agents and Superintendent Hoag were congregated, and met thirteen of the committee who nominated and had the oversight of them. The committee were from New England, New York, Pennsylvania, Ohio, Indiana, Iowa and Kansas—a very important committee, engaged in an interesting work. Our difficulties and trials, failures and successes were discussed. The agents were encouraged to use every effort to Christianize and civilize the Indians on the peaceable principles of the gospel, and to deal with them honestly, firmly and lovingly, and so far as practicable to procure religious employees, and look to God for a blessing on their labors. This, I believe, was the wish and intent of every agent.

CHAPTER II.

AFTER visiting my family in Iowa and making arrangements for carrying on my farm work there, I
returned to the agency in March, 1871, by railroad to
Baxter Springs, Kansas, then by wagon fifteen days' journey. Affairs had moved smoothly during my absence.
The bracing air of Iowa had invigorated my system,
which seemed like breaking down, in that southern clime,
with malaria and the mental strain of trying to properly
control those restless, raiding Indians.

When I took charge of the agency, in 1869, there were
under my charge about two thousand five hundred Comanches, nineteen hundred Kiowas, five hundred
Apaches, and twelve hundred of the "Wichita and
affiliated bands." The latter were partially civilized,
and were not addicted to raiding. They cultivated small
sections of ground near the timber, and planted corn,
beans, pumpkins, squashes, etc. General Hazen had
some ground plowed for them before I first reached the

(55)

agency, and I had more plowed and fenced, and they were ready to cultivate it. In additioin to their ponies, some of them had cattle and hogs.

The Wichitas numbered about three hundred. They had long claimed the country from the Red River to the Canadian, and were formerly much more numerous. The Wichita mountains were in their country and named for them. They were among the few tribes who never attacked the white people, and they assigned that as the reason why their country was taken from them and given to the Kiowas and Comanches, who did fight. They never received any compensation for their country, and had no land assigned to them. It seemed as if they had not been treated justly; but they bore it patiently—not, however, without making frequent complaints to me, and I reported their case to the Government, and there was eventually assigned to the Wichita and affiliated bands a tract of land about ten by twenty miles in extent.

Before they had a home assigned to them, the Kiowas and Comanches frequently brought my attention to the Wichitas as being poor and without a reservation because they would not fight the soldiers. They (the Kiowas and Comanches) fought and got a large tract, about sixty by one hundred miles in extent, assigned to them by treaty. They seemed confident that they not only had their reservation, but were treated better and commanded more respect, on account of their fighting the soldiers. A proof of it was the Wichitas!

The origin of the Caddoes—I was told by one of their number, named George Washington, their chief—was in Louisiana. He said that near Red River, below Shreveport, there is a hole out of which came ten men and ten women, from whom sprang the tribes of Osage, Wichita, Waco, Kuchi, Hieni, Tomac-o-ni, Caddo, and three other tribes that have become extinct. The Caddo man and woman were the last to come out, and the Great Spirit, who made them, gave them some corn, beans, watermelon, gourd and tobacco seed. The women were to cultivate these, do the cooking, dress the skins, etc.; the men were to do the hunting. He said that he did not know where the other Indians came from.

He told me that after living a long time near the place where they originated there was a strange object made its appearance in their village, which filled them with awe. They supposed that it had been sent down from the Father above. They did not know whether it was one or two beings. They all wanted to see it, but for some time were afraid to venture near it. It proved to be a Frenchman on horseback! They had never heard of a white man or horse. As he could talk the sign language that is common to all Western Indians, he told them that a long way to the East there were a great many white people who were coming West, and after a time they would be thick all around them. This they disbelieved, thinking that they were too far off to even reach the Caddoes.

The Wichita and affiliated bands were thirty miles north of the Kiowa and Comanche agency, the location of which was established by General Hazen. As those bands were so much further advanced in civilization than the Kiowas and Comanches, I urged the appointment of an agent for them, instead of a sub-agent that I was allowed to have. If they could have a separate agency, they would have their supplies there and not have to spend two or three days every two weeks in going after them. I thought, also, that it would be better for them to be kept away from the Kiowas and Comanches as much as practicable. The Department acceded to my request, and the Indian Committee nominated Jonathan Richards, of Philadelphia, a Friend of high character, formerly President of Haverford College, who was appointed, and he made an excellent agent. His work will be mentioned in future pages.

The Object of Taking Captives.

This was twofold. It was first to thus secure servants or slaves. The boys were obliged to herd ponies for their masters, and when they were old enough they tamed the vicious horses. The girls had to wait on the women, cut wood, and do the drudgery. When "Black Beaver," a good Delaware Indian, was asked why the Indians stole children, he replied: "Ingen, him whip squaw; and squaw, him want white child to whip." Captives were sometimes sold to other Indians. Another motive was to procure ransom money. From a few hundred to more than a thousand dollars had been paid for them. If the boys remained with the Indians until grown, and then should go on a raid and steal some horses or mules, they could then get married and be recognized as Indians. Among the Kiowas and Comanches there were many Mexicans of that class. They could generally be distinguished by their waving hair, while the hair of the Indians was straight.

POLYGAMY.

This was not uncommon with the Kiowas and Comanches, as well as with some other tribes in the southwestern part of the Indian Territory. So many of the men were killed in their raids and wars that the women were much more numerous. An Indian with two or three wives claimed that one could cut the wood for fire, another do the cooking, and another could care for the ponies, and none of them would have to work hard. And if one of his wives died he would not be so badly broken up, nor feel so lonely if he had one or two left. They frequently had a separate lodge for each wife.

Marriage with the Indians was frequently a one-sided affair. A mother would sell her daughter for one, two or more ponies, and pay little or no regard to the wish of her daughter. Whether she loved or hated the man to whom she was sold, she generally had to live with him, and submit to the powers that be. It was the " Indian road " and must be followed. Sometimes, however, that custom was varied. A Mexican woman who was captured by the Comanches when she was an infant, and knew nothing but Indian life, told my wife and myself about her marriage. When she was of adult age her Indian mother (as she called the woman who claimed her) told her that she was old enough now to go home with a certain Indian whom we will call " Blueleggings " to be his wife. " No," said the girl, " I won't go home with him; I won't be his wife. He is the most homely and meanest Indian in the tribe, and I won't live with him. Her mother replied: " You will have to live with him. He has been waiting a long time for you to get old enough to be his wife, and you must go home with him." " No I won't," the girl replied. " He may just kill me here in the lodge if he wants to. I would rather be killed than to live with him." " Who do you want to live with?" the mother asked. " I would like to live with Mr. Chandler," the daughter answered. " Well, I will send for both of them" said the mother, " and they may come and fix it up." " All right," the daughter said, " but I won't live with ' Blueleggings.' "

Both of the Indians went there, and the mother said to the girl: " Here now is ' Blueleggings ' come to take you home for his wife, and you must go home with him." " I won't go home with him. I won't be his wife," the girl answered. " You will go home with me," said " Blueleggings "; " I am going to have you for my wife. I have been waiting a long time for you, and I am going to take you home with me, and you will have to be my wife." " No! you won't take me home with you alive," the girl replied, defiantly. " You may just kill me right here if you want to. I won't live with you." " Who do you want to live with?" said the Indian mother. "I would like to live with Mr. Chandler," said the girl. " You see," said the old woman, " what the girl thinks of you, and you must fix it up between you." Mr. Chandler then asked "Blueleggings" what he would take for his interest in the girl. " You see," said he, " how mean she is, and how ugly she acts, and if you will give me three dollars and a crowing chicken you may have her." The offer was accepted and she went with Mr. Chandler a happy bride and was a good wife, and he was a good husband to her. He was half American and could talk English; was a truthful and upright man. He improved a farm, built a good log house, had outbuildings and yards for his cattle, made a good living, and had a family of attractive, well-behaved children. She also was truthful and industrious.

DEATH AMONG INDIANS.

The death of the head of a family, whether man or woman, was the occasion generally of burning the lodge in which the death occurred, with all that it contained. If a woman died the cooking utensils were destroyed. I have seen good brass kettles with holes cut through the bottoms with an axe. They account it as giving to the deceased. Sometimes, in order to save the lodge, they would remove the sick person into a small tent to die. I was informed when "Kicking Bird's" wife died he burned the lodge, and almost all they had, except some poor clothing that he and his little girl wore, and he killed one or two ponies for her. He loved his wife, and his grief was real. He had but one wife and one child. After her death he did not come to the agency for several weeks. I sent some blankets, calico and other things to him with the request to "wash the cry off his face" and come and see me; that I pitied him and his little girl. When he came he expressed much gratitude for my kindness and remembrance of him in time of need.

The burial of the dead was generally done by old women, who took the corpse to a secluded place, wrapped in its best blankets, where they would dig a grave and cover it too deep for the wolves to dig it out. The family did not wish to know the place of interment, or even see the grave.

Mourning for the dead commenced about sunset and continued at intervals during the evening. It was a dismal wailing by the family and others—sometimes real grief; occasionally for mercenary purposes. I once heard an Indian tell about hearing of the death of one of the tribe, and he remembered his nice saddle that he wanted. He immediately repaired to the lodge of the deceased and cried lustily for some time, and then asked for his friend's saddle, which was given him. The mourning continued for several evenings, and if for the death of a prominent person it might continue each evening, if it commenced in the spring or summer, until the leaves began to drop in autumn; or if the death occurred in the fall or winter, the mourning would continue until the leaves put out in the spring.

KILLING BUFFALOES.

This used to be the great harvest time for the Indians, and occurred in the spring and autumn. In the autumn the buffaloes went South; in the spring they returned to the North. Their movements were usually slow, deliberately grazing. Not in compact herds, but thinly scattered over the plains as far as the eye could reach. This was sometimes the scene in passing from Kansas to the agencies in southwestern Indian Territory until about 1880. Different tribes of Indians had somewhat different modes of killing them. The Kiowas and Comanches' mode was for some of the Indians to surround a portion of them and keep them herded together, while the hunters would go inside of the line and kill them, but were not to follow one outside of the line. Each man would select a buffalo, ride up by the side of it, horse and buffalo on the run, and shoot at the heart. They preferred the bow and arrow, as they made no noise. If the shot appeared to be fatal, they would turn from it and pursue another. It was dangerous to continue riding at the side of one after it was seriously hurt, as it was liable to throw its hind parts around enough to turn and gore the horse, dismount the rider and horn him to death.

After the men had killed all that were inclosed the work of the women commenced. They had to skin the buffaloes and take care of the hides and meat. All of the lean portions were dried. It was prepared by cutting into thin slices around and around a piece of lean meat until it was a yard long, more or less, and then hang them on poles. If the sun was shining the meat would dry in a day or two. But if it was damp or cloudy, it had to be dried with fire, which added much to their labor. If dried without getting tainted it was very palatable and nutritious. After it was perfectly dry, they packed it in tanned skins, and it would keep for six months, or until the buffaloes returned.

The skins were taken to camp, stretched tightly on the ground by cutting holes near the edge through which small stakes were driven into the ground. Then, with an instrument like a little hoe, they were to be fleshed, i. e., all the flesh scraped off the skin. This had to be done before the women retired to rest. The hides could then be dried and tanned at a future time. Killing buffaloes was great sport for the men, but curing the meat and skins was very laborious for the women.

" Buffalo Robes " were made of the skins of the animals that were killed in the fall and winter. The brain of an animal, whether buffalo, deer, bear or panther, was considered sufficient to tan its skin. This was also the work of the women. It took a great deal of hard rubbing and other work to make a soft, pliable buffalo robe. In the spring the buffaloes shed their hair, which came off in patches, and they presented a very ragged and homely appearance. At that season of the year the skins were dressed after the hair was taken off, and were used for lodges and other purposes. It took from ten to fifteen skins to make a covering for a lodge. They were sewed together with sinews so tightly that they would shed water, and they would last several years. The frame of the lodge was made of poles fifteen or twenty feet long; cedar was preferred. It was set up in a circle, and tied together at the top. The skin covering was put around the poles and fastened together, where they were joined, with wooden pins. The opening into the lodge was always in the east, about four feet high, with a skin fastened on one side that could be thrown over the opening to close it.

THE INDIAN CAMPS.

These were always near wood and water. Sometimes one chief and his people, and sometimes several chiefs and their people, would be camped near together. The families belonging to a chief varied from five to thirty or forty. Each family had a lodge. When the boys were nearly grown they generally had a small tent, near to the parents' lodge, to sleep in. In counting the lodges that a chief had the small tents were omitted. An objection to having a large number of Indians camped near together was on account of pasturage for their ponies. Some Indians had a large number of them. I knew one who had three hundred. Some of them were fine large horses. Their wealth was estimated to a large extent by the number of their ponies. Their large herds would soon consume the grass in the vicinity of the camp, and they would have to move to some other location. It was an interesting sight to see them take down their lodges, pack up their effects and move. The large end of some of the lodge poles were fastened to each side of a pony or mule, and the small end resting on the ground. On the poles back of the pony was sometimes tied some of their baggage. Occasionally some blankets and bedding were arranged on them, and upon it laid a sick person. There was sufficient elasticity in the poles to make the transportation comparatively comfortable for an invalid.

Small children were tied on gentle ponies, and then these ponies were turned loose to follow those that the mothers were riding. Frequently the mother would have a small child on the pony in front of her, and anther riding behind her, holding to her clothing. The chief would lead the caravan to the new camping ground. The women would erect lodges, dig a small hole in the centre for the fire, place some short poles around the fireplace, about four feet from it, except in front of the doorway. Behind the poles they placed some fine brush and grass, then spread blankets on it for seats or bed. Behind the beds, and against the lodge, was room for packages of meat, flour, sugar, saddles and other goods. In

"LODGE" MADE OF BUFFALO SKINS

an incredibly short time the tents, or " lodges," were erected, their effects stowed away, and the women would be engaged in cutting wood for cooking their meals, with no appearance of a recent moving.

INDIAN MEDICINE.

This included many articles and devices. With apparently good results they used some roots and herbs. For the bite of a poisonous snake or reptile they chewed the root of a weed that grew in that country, and rubbed the spittle on the bite and around it. They claimed that it never swelled where the saliva was applied. If applied soon it appeared to be a specific. A sweat bath was administered by placing the patient in a small tent with red hot stones near, upon which water was sprinkled. From the sweat bath he would plunge into a stream of water and then wrap in dry blankets.

Their medicine was generally witchcraft, sorcery and enchantment. Occasionally they would dig a hole in front of the lodge, and on the fresh dirt place a buffalo head facing the opening into the lodge where the sick was lying, expecting healing virtues to pass from the buffalo's head to the sick person! At one time, " a medicine woman " went with a party to Texas on a raid. When they crossed Red River, on their return, the woman made " bog medicine " in the river, so that if soldiers or others attempted to follow them their horses would mire down and they could not cross the river. Having entire confidence in the medicine, they camped before going far, killed a buffalo, and were roasting some of its choice parts when a squad of soldiers came upon them and killed some of the men. They afterwards killed the medicine woman for not making stronger " bog medicine "!

On the return of some Indians from Washington, one of them said that the strongest medicine that he came in contact with in his travels was in connection with his trunk that was given to him in Washington. He put his clothes and other presents in it and took it with him to the depot, thinking of the good time he would have when showing them to his people after reaching home. But at the depot a couple of strong men jerked the trunk away from him, gave him a little brass money with a hole in it, and away the men went with the trunk out of sight, and he was hurried into the car. He could not help thinking how mean some of the white people were to steal his trunk just as he was starting home, and had no chance to recover it. They traveled on and on and on. A short time before arriving at Kansas City, a man came through the car trading for brass money. The interpreter told him to let him have his, and when he gave it to him the fellow gave him a little paper! Worse and worse, he thought—one party steal his trunk and give him a brass money, another steal it and give him some soiled paper. The interpreter told him to take care of it. At Kansas City they were taken to a very large house, and in a few minutes the very trunk that was stolen from him in Washington was taken to the same house, and nothing had been stolen from it. What kind of medicine caused his trunk to be taken to the very house where he was he knew nothing about!

KIOWA MEDICINE DANCE.

This annual gathering and ceremony occurred at the time of the falling of the cotton from the cottonwood trees. In 1873, T. C. Batty, the teacher in the Kiowa camp, attended the ceremony by invitation. It was seldom that a white person was permitted to attend those festivals, as they regarded them sacred. It was expected that the whole Kiowa tribe should attend—men, women and children. If any member of the tribe was not present they expected that person to die before the next one occurred. On that occasion nearly all of the Apaches belonging in that agency were there. Also about five hundred Comanches, many Cheyennes and Arapahoes and other Indians, numbering in all about three thousand souls.

The work of constructing the " Medicine Lodge " was commenced by the women cutting down small cottonwood trees, to which ropes were tied, and they were dragged by several hands to each rope, accompanied by music and dancing, to the place of the lodge, in a beautiful broad valley. To larger trees ponies were attached by tying the ropes to the saddles, a young brave and a young woman riding each pony, several of which were tied to a log and pulled abreast. Some of the men beat

Indian drums, and all sang, having a merry time. It was the duty of the young women to hitch and unhitch the horses. The lodge was circular, about sixty feet in diameter, covered with cottonwood brush with the leaves on. Horizontal poles were tied on the outside of the posts, and against these were leaned small cottonwood poles, with limbs and leaves on, which made a shade several feet thick for spectators. On top of the highest post was fastened a freshly killed buffalo head. The lodge was soon completed, and then, within the enclosure, commenced, under the direction of the "medicine chief," the drumming, singing, dancing, tumultuous shrieking and smoking.

The medicine was an image lying on the ground, but so concealed from view by cedar and cottonwood boughs that its form was indistinguishable to T. C. Batty. Above this was another image, concealed with eagle and other feathers. On each side of this were decorated shields, buffalo robes, and various articles of clothing, to be medicated so as to preserve the wearers from sickness or harm during the year. The medicine dance continued six days. A minute and interesting account of it is given by T. C. Battey in his "Quaker Among the Indians."

INDIAN RATIONS.

These included beef, bacon, flour, coffee, sugar, soap, tobacco and soda, which were "issued" every two weeks to the chiefs, who divided them by having a woman of

each family sit on the ground in a circle around him
with her sacks, and he would divide it among them, except the beef, which was issued alive, one or more head
of cattle to a chief or his representative, who had " beef
paper," according to the number of families in his band.
The last four weeks' issue that I made, in March,
1873, was to three thousand seven hundred and sixty Indians. To these were issued beef, gross two hundred
and ninety-three thousand six hundred pounds; bacon,
five thousand and forty pounds; flour, fifty-one thousand
eight hundred pounds; coffee, four thousand one hundred and forty-six pounds; sugar, eight thousand two
hundred and ninety pounds; soda, one hundred and
thirty pounds; soap, one thousand and twenty-one
pounds; tobacco, five hundred and eight pounds. The
beef was sometimes killed near the beef pen, a few miles
from the agency, and carried on their ponies to the
camps, and sometimes they were driven there to be butch-
ered. If the supplies of a family were exhausted, they
would go to the other lodges to eat, until the supplies of
the whole band were exhausted. Then, if they could not
fast until ration day, they would probably kill a mule
or pony for food. Some time subsequent to 1873, by
order of the Department at Washington, the rations,
including the beef, were issued to each family separately.

Annuity Goods.

According to treaty stipulation of 1868, the Kiowa
and Comanche Indians were to receive to the value of

thirty thousand dollars (I think this was the amount), annually, for thirty years. The goods consisted of "blankets, brown muslin, satinet, calico, hosiery, needles, thread, a few suits of men's clothes, beads, tincups, butcher knives, iron kettles, frying pans, hoes and small axes."

Mow-a-way and the Iron Horse.

The following is a verbal account of Chief Mow-a-way's journey with his people:

Before I went to the agency, probably in 1867, Mow-a-way, a Comanche chief, with a few young men, went to New Mexico on " a raid," and were arrested by soldiers and taken across the plains to Fort Leavenworth, Kansas. He told about the trip substantially as follows:

" I supposed when we started that the soldiers were going to take us away off and then kill us. But we traveled on and on, day after day, in the wagons and were kindly treated. When one of the Indians was taken sick, I supposed that the white men would be glad for him to die. But instead of that they doctored him, and seemed to do all that they could to cure him. But he died, and then they did not throw him onto the grass for the wolves to eat, as I expected they would, but the commanding officer sent some of his men to dig a grave for him. They made a box and put him into it with all of his clothing, his bow and arrows; everything he owned they gave him. The hole that they dug was the nicest one that I ever saw. They made a little mound over him, smooth and nice. I could not understand why such mean people, as I thought the white people were, should be so kind to an Indian in sickness and after death.

" When we had traveled many days we came to where there was a new kind of road that I had never heard of. There was a very large iron horse hitched to several houses on wheels. We were taken into one of them, which was the nicest house that I ever saw. There were seats on each side of it. As soon as we were seated the iron horse made a snort, and away it went, pulling the houses! Our ponies could not run half so fast. It only run a little while and then made a big snort and stopped at another white man's village. The iron horse kept running and snorting and stopping at the white men's villages, and the villages kept getting larger and larger. I had no idea that the white people had so many villages, and that there were so many white people. At length we reached Leavenworth, which was the largest of any of the villages. There the people were so numerous and the land so scarce they built one house on top of another, two or three houses (stories) high. These houses were divided into little houses (rooms) inside. The houses were built close together on both sides of the road. They were full of people, and the roads between the houses were full of people. I know not where they all came from, but I saw them with my own eyes. I had no idea that there were so many people in existence.

" After we were taken over one of the houses built on

top of another, we were taken into a house down in the ground right under the other one. There was nobody living in it, but there were barrels of foolish water (whiskey) in it. There was some of it offered me to drink, but I saw that it made white men foolish who drank it, and I was afraid to take any, for fear I would get as foolish as they did.

" We were taken into a house that was built on the water (Missouri River), and it could swim anywhere. It made no difference how deep the water was, it could swim. There is where the sugar comes from. I saw men rolling great big barrels of sugar out of the house on the water, and so many of them! Nobody need talk to me about sugar being scarce after seeing the large amount come out of that house that was swimming on the water."

After being kept at Fort Leavenworth for some time, Mow-a-way and his little party reported themselves to Colonel Grierson, at Fort Sill, as his prisoners, stating that they " had been sent from Fort Leavenworth in the custody of a white man who took some foolish water to the Wichita camp, and had been drinking there for several days and had lost his senses," and they had come on without him. " Well," said the Colonel, " if that is the case, I won't treat you as prisoners. Orderly, take these Indians to the agency, and turn them over to Agent Tatum." They were soon at my office and I released them, telling them to go to their people and behave. After that Mow-a-way was one of my best and most reliable of the Comanches.

BLACK BEAVER.

This chief was a Delaware Indian. In early life he had been a successful trapper of beavers, otters and other fur animals. He had traveled up the rivers to the Rocky Mountains, in and across the mountains from Washington to California, New Mexico and other States. He was a truthful, reliable Indian, and could talk English so as to be understood. His knowledge of the Western country and of Indians was so extensive that he was employed as guide for explorers and naturalists. When employed by Captain Marcy in his explorations, many years ago, the party met with some wild Indians, whom the Captain wished to impress with the great superiority of the white people. He told them about railroads, and with what rapidity people could travel on them. Black Beaver interpreted it with some hesitation. The Captain then told about the telegraph. He said that he might be ready to take a seat at his dinner table and send word to his friend twenty days' journey away what he had for his dinner, and before he would have time to eat it his friend would receive the message and send word back what he had for his own dinner. He then waited for Black Beaver to interpret, but he said nothing. "Black Beaver," said the Captain, "why don't you interpret that to the Indians?" He replied: "General, me civilized Injun; but me don't believe that meself, and me can't make these wild Injuns believe it." He was a truthful Indian, and he was not willing to interpret what he regarded as an untruth. After becoming better acquainted with the white people, he could laugh at his own ignorance.

FARMING AT THE AGENCY.

General Hazen had two hundred acres plowed in the Washata valley for the thirty Delaware Indians in the agency. I contracted with a party to inclose it with a good post and three-rail fence. After the contractor had been at work a short time, I went thirty miles to see how he was progressing. I got out of the ambulance and stepped onto the middle of the lower rails to test the work. All that would break or spring out of the mortise with my weight were displaced. The new fence looked terribly demoralized. I told his cook where I would camp, and wished to see the contractor in the evening. When he drove up with two or three loads of little rails and saw the fence torn to pieces, he censured the Indians, supposing they had removed the worthless rails. When told that the agent wished to see him, he anticipated the difficulty. I told him that the contract provided that the rails should be strong enough to bear the weight of a man standing on the middle after the fence was put up, and I expected him to put one up that would bear the test. He then made a good, substantial fence.

Black Beaver was the only Delaware Indian who located near the two-hundred-acre field. The others pre-

ferred their small fields near the timber. He wished to
cultivate all of it, but I thought it too much for him,
and I reserved forty acres, and had a white man cultivate it on shares for the Government. I told the Indian
that we would see who raised the most weeds and who
raised the most corn. In the fall I looked over the large
field with Black Beaver, and we decided that my white
renter had raised about as many weeds on his forty acres
as Black Beaver had on one hundred and sixty acres,
and the corn was much better on Black Beaver's part.
I told the Indian that he was ahead of me in farming,
and he might have the whole field after that, which
pleased him very much. He was a successful farmer,
respected by all the Indians who knew him, and his
influence with them was always good. He was a Christian, and tried to do what was right in the sight of God
and towards his fellow-men.

THE INDIAN STYLE OF SMOKING.

The Indians very generally smoked, and a few of
them chewed tobacco. Their mode of smoking, however, was very different from that of the white people.
I have no recollection of ever seeing an Indian fill his
pipe and smoke it all himself. If he wanted a little
smoke alone, he would roll some tobacco in a leaf, or
small piece of paper, and smoke it. They smoked, with
rare exceptions, in companies. Unpleasant as tobacco
smoke was to me, when in usual health, I let them smoke
in my office. A half dozen or less would leave their

seats and sit in a circle on the floor, and then the one who was to light the pipe would prepare his medicine by taking off a moccasin, or putting a smooth stone, which he carried with him, in the palm of his hand, and resting the bowl of the pipe on it to fill and light, or do something else of like importance. Then gravely he would fill and light the pipe. The first full puff of smoke he would blow up for the Good Spirit, the Father, who gave them the tobacco seed and caused it to grow. The next puff he would blow to the floor for the mother, the earth, from whom the tobacco came. He then appropriated a puff or two for himself, and passed the pipe to the next one on the left. He would take a puff or two and pass it on. The pipe would go around the circle until exhausted, and then it was put away. I do not remember ever seeing it immediately relighted and smoked by the same company. It was not unusual for them to draw the smoke into their lungs and expel it through their nostrils. In that way they seemed to get the full benefit of it, without wasting so much as the white people do.

They frequently mixed kinnikinic with their tobacco for smoking, which consisted of the leaves of sumac, which had turned red in the autumn. It gave quite a different odor to the smoke, and was more injurious to the lungs than pure tobacco. When they decided to go on the " war path," they would smoke " the war pipe."

On another occasion they would smoke " the peace pipe," both being solemn occasions.

"FOOLISH WATER."

This was the name by which the Kiowas and Comanches designated all intoxicants. I heard of a few of them who would not drink liquor, but they were generally fond of it. I was informed that when the Comanches had procured it, before they commenced drinking they would select two of their number to keep order. These were not to drink any, and if the others got drunk, it was with the understanding that the two were to preserve order and be obeyed. I think it was seldom, if ever, that they had serious difficulty at their drunken sprees.

SIGN LANGUAGE.

There was a sign language common, I believe, to all of the uncivilized Indians east of the Rocky Mountains, and it may have extended to the Pacific coast. Indians of different tribes, who could not understand each other's spoken language would converse by the hour with signs, which were very natural and significant. In making speeches they were apt to use the sign language as gestures in connection with their speaking.

JESTING.

The Indians appeared to be social and to enjoy company. They would sometimes pass a jest, but they generally wilted under one. They did not like to be laughed at, especially by white people. The teachers of the school soon learned that it would not do to even smile at a child for mispronouncing a word. If they did, it might be some time before they could persuade it to speak again.

I once met with a Chickasaw woman who had been sent "to the States" to be educated, and on her return she spoke English fluently for years, as occasion required, but on being laughed at for a mispronunciation, she would not afterwards speak a word of English.

A delegation of Indians from the three agencies in southwestern Indian Territory was taken to Washington. Before starting, I urged the officer in charge of them to take them to a penitentiary and let them see what was done with white people who stole horses and mules and killed people. I thought it would do them more good to go there than to the Treasury Department, as it was very provoking to them to see so much money, and the men in charge of it so stingy that they would not give each of them a handful! They were taken to a penitentiary, but they did not want to be taken to another house like that. They pitied the poor fellows who were penned up there for offences of which they were guilty.

While in Washington an Indian who could speak a little English, imitating some of the white men, went to the bar in the hotel and said, "brandy and ice." The barkeeper gave him and each of the other Indians who were with him a glass. It tasted so good that the Indian said "brandy and ice" again, and each was given a second drink. He then handed a ten-dollar bill to the clerk, who gave him back the change. Jim counted it, and thought the clerk had kept too much, and told him so in Wichita. As the clerk did not understand him, Jim jumped over the counter to teach the white man a lesson on honesty. Just then the intepreter stepped in and " halted " the Indian, and wished to know what was the matter. After hearing the case and counting the change that the Indian had, he told him that he had paid no more than white people did for drinks, and if he partook of brandy and ice he must pay for it and behave.

After their return from Washington, Agent Richards and I had a council with the Indians of the agencies. When we were through, the Indian referred to said that he wanted to talk. We told him that he might. He then addressed me, saying that when he was in Washington he was shown a large amount of money, and was told that it was for him and his people. He had now been at home a long time, and had heard nothing about his money, saying, " Now I want you to tell me the truth about it. Have the people in Washington stolen it, or has it been sent to my agent, and he has stolen it? I want you to tell me the truth. Tell me who has stolen that money ? "

I thought that he wanted to get into a wrangle with his agent, which seemed wholly unnecessary. So I replied, " Sometimes when Indians go to Washington they drink so much brandy and ice that their heads get to whirling around, and they don't know what is said to them." The other Indians had heard of the incident. They laughed. He wilted, and said no more about his stolen money.

SCALP LOCK.

This was a small tuft of hair at the crown of the head that was plaited or braided, and worn by all of the uncivilized men. It generally hung down behind their heads, and was in some instances two feet or more long. When they had their pictures taken some of them would draw it over one shoulder, and have it hang in front. This was not to be cut on any occasion unless they concluded to adopt the habits of white men, and have all of their hair cut short and wear " citizen's clothes." As the scalp lock grew, it was sometimes unplaited and braided up again. The men plaited the remaining portion of their hair in two braids, frequently with different colored flannel or with fur, one on each side, which hung in front of their shoulders. These braids were sometimes cut off about even with their ears in token of mourning. For a near relative both were cut off and buried with the deceased or burned. One braid was severed for a distant relative.

ORNAMENTS.

The Indians appeared to be as fond of ornaments as white people are. Men and women wore ornaments in their ears. We frequently saw brass rings an inch in diameter in their ears, to which were attached hair-pipe beads or brass chains, terminating with a small piece of German silver, tastefully cut. Hair-pipe was said to be made of sea shells. They were from one to six inches in length, near the size of a lead pencil, with a hole through the centre. They cost the Indians twenty-five cents per inch. The men wore a breast ornament of hair-pipe beads in four rows. The center beads were six inches and those outside four inches long. The number in a row varied from ten to twenty or more. They were attached to strong leather which went around the neck. Kicking-Bird used to wear one that probobly cost him twenty-five buffalo robes, or one hundred dollars. The women wore brass rings around their wrists and lower part of their arms. They were made of coarse wire, cut so as to meet around the wrist or arm. Some of them wore fifteen or twenty of them.

Then men and women parted their hair in the middle, and the place of parting was frequently painted red. The men generally painted their faces when they wanted to " fix up " to visit the agent or some other important person. Each one painted according to his fancy.

HOSPITALITY.

This seemed to be universal with the Indians. They had to be very destitute indeed if they could not furnish a stranger with a meal and lodging. Go to their camp at any time of day and they would want to prepare " chuck-a-way," the Comanche word for something to eat. After eating they were ready to hear from the visitor. He might be a person that the Indian would be willing to kill if found alone on the prairie, but if he could get to the camp and go to the lodge of the chief, he thereby would show his confidence in the Indian, and in placing himself at his mercy, his life and property would then be sacredly protected. If on friendly terms it was a real satisfaction to entertain a white man, and especially their agent. I have eaten many meals with them and slept in their lodges. On one occasion, after riding all day on horseback, my interpreter and I reached a camp, tired and hungry. We went to the lodge of the chief, who sent one of his wives to take care of our horses; another wife prepared some fuel for the fire in the tent, and a third wife prepared our supper. After getting materials ready she fried some meat, made light biscuits, and coffee, etc., cooking our supper while sitting down on her heels. She did not get nervous by having us siting on the bed about four inches high on the opposite side of the fire watching her. When she had it cooked, she placed a board on the laps of her husband and visitors, spread her cleanest blanket on it, and placed the provision before us, and we had a sumptuous meal. Just as we got through eating an invitation came from another chief to eat with him. I told the interpreter that I had not anticipated that and had eaten heartily. He said we must go and show our respect. So we accepted the kind invitation, supped a little more coffee, and partook of enough food to show that we were not above eating with him also.

As the Indians were very hospitable to others they expected hospitality extended to them. When they went to the agency my Irish cook roasted a large piece of beef, and prepared to feed a number of them. After the family was through eating the Indians went to the table and ate. If they could not consume it all they remembered their squaws and pappooses who would like to have the remainder. I have known Indians to eat a hearty meal at my table, and then go immediately to my clerk's, a few rods distant, and eat another.

The Wild Animals.

These in the Kiowa and Comanche agency were buffaloes, deers, antelopes, elk, black bears, timber wolves and prairie wolves (or coyotes), panthers, wild cats, jack rabbits, and prairie dogs. Wild turkeys were numerous in the oak timber districts. The elks, bears and panthers were largely confined to the Wichita Mountains, a detached range about ten by sixty miles in extent, with the highest peaks about twelve hundred feet above the surrounding country.

The prairie dogs, which belong to the "marmot" family, seemed much more like squirrels than dogs. They were about a foot long, of a yellowish-brown color. They lived on grass and weeds. The prairie dog " towns " were sometimes many miles in extent, where they burrowed in the ground, and the dirt which was thrown out was always piled up several inches high around their holes. On top of the mounds they would stand and chirp as we passed along the road, but their position was always between us and their holes. If they were shot they would fall into one of these holes, and could not be obtained without digging for them. Sometimes there would be scores of them chirping around us, when one would give an unusual sound,—a note of alarm, apparently,—and every one would dart into its hole and their noise cease, and all were instantly out of sight. In a short time they would cautiously peep out, and if they saw no danger would resume their running around and their noise, which to me sounded more like the chirp of a bird than the bark of a dog.

MULTIPLIED OFFICES OF THE INDIAN AGENT.

First, the agent is governor.

It was his duty to see that the laws and regulations of the United States Government applicable to Indian reservations were executed. At the time I was agent it included the merchants, or "Indian traders." The application for trader had to be renewed every year. It commenced with the agent, and was then approved by the superintendent and Commissioner of Indian Affairs, and the appointment was, I think, by the Secretary of the Interior. The agent was not allowed to have any pecuniary interest in the trading business. I had one trader dismissed for not complying with the law in trading with Indians.

Second, the agent constitutes the legislature.

An order published by an Indian agent became a law for that agency unless it was countermanded by a superior officer. Soon after taking charge of the agency I published an order that traders should not sell " buffalo spears " to Indians. These were steel spears about a foot long, to which the Indians attached handles, and the only purpose that I could hear of their being used for was to kill people, and were never used to kill buffalo. My order stopped their sale.

On another occasion, after a party had made a contract with Colonel Grierson to raise corn on the Military Reservation, and furnish it for the cost of seventy-five cents a bushel, I published an order requiring that persons who raised grain on the Kiowa and Comanche Reservation should run all risk of depredations by Indians, and any depredation claim brought against the Government on account of Indian depredations on grain raised on said reservation would be opposed by the Indian agent. Colonel Grierson soon came to see me on the subject as he felt grieved that I had frustrated his contract, which he believed would save the Military Department some thousands of dollars, as the corn for the post had been costing twice that amount. I told him that it would no doubt cost the Interior Department much more to pay depredation claims than it would save the Military Department. The contracter also came to see me about the order. He felt chagrined. I told him to raise the corn, and run his own risk. He replied, " Why I would not raise it for twice that amount if I had to run my own risk." The contract was annuled.

Third, the Indian agent is judge.

Controversies between white men and Indians were heard and decided upon by the Indian agent. The decision was generally final. In cases of claims against the Government on account of depredations by Indians they were first heard by the Indian agent. If the Indians in council said that they committed the depredations with which they were charged the agent so reported, and the claimant would probably have it allowed and paid when he took it before superior officers. I examined and decided on many claims that I believed to be just and some which I believed to be fraudulent.

A fourth office of an Indian agent was that of sheriff.

Whiskey smugglers or other violators of the law were to be arrested by order of the Indian agent. If it was thought that proof sufficient could be furnished to convict him they were to be sent to Fort Smith, Arkansas, and tried in the United States Court. A great difficulty and obstruction to such suits was to procure witnesses, as the witness fee paid by the Government was not sufficient to meet the necessary expenses.

According to United States law any person, excepting

an authorized physician, who took spirituous liquor into the Indian Territory was liable to arrest, and if proven guilty, he should be fined, not to exceed $1,000, or he should be sent to the penitentiary, and all the property he had with him should be confiscated. The law also provides a heavy penalty for selling intoxicating liquor to Indians anywhere in the United States. I had a number of whiskey smugglers arrested. They sometimes went to the Indian camps and traded bad whiskey for good horses and mules. I tried to get the Indians to arrest them and take them to the agency, but they were too fond of whiskey for that.

The law was good and wholesome in its application to Indians. Why it would not be equally good and wholesome for all other inhabitants in the United States is difficult to see. The New York " Journal " states that in New York city, during 1895, there were six hundred and eighty deaths directly caused by drink. Three thousand, eight hundred and eighty-six persons died of sickness whom physicians believed might have lived if they had not used liquor; twenty-three thousand, four hundred and ninety-three men and eight thousand, four hundred and fourteen women were arrested for drunkenness. To procure these awful results there was paid for drink $105,410,208—a vast sum worse than wasted. Had it been used for procuring the necessaries and comforts of life it would have been a great blessing to families, procuring happiness instead of misery. If the Government would protect all of its citizens as well as the Indians, it would avert a vast amount of misery, destitution and premature deaths.

The fifth office of an Indian agent was that of accounting officer.

All moneys to pay employees, also for buildings and other improvements, also for provisions for the Indians, annuity goods, medicine, iron, lumber, and for other property belonging to the Government was to be accounted for on cash and property rolls, and every three months the agent reported to the Government at Washington what had been expended, for what purpose, and the balance on hand.

CHAPTER III.

UNDER President Grant's administration the agents
were expected to select and employ physicians, clerks,
teachers, and all other employees of the agency. Under
the ruling of the Indian Committee of Friends they
wished to select the important employees. I had long
urged the committee to send me a physician. I wanted
one who would not only attend to the medical department, but would do the preaching at the schoolhouse on
the Sabbath and take part in the Bible School. If a
Friend could not be found, I would accept one of another
church, but he must be a religious man and exhorter.
After looking for more than a year Dr. A. D. Tomlinson, of Bloomingdale, Indiana, was found—a minister in
Friends' Church. He came with his wife and daughter
to the agency in the spring of 1871. He was a skillful
physician, a good minister and valuable assistant to me.
I had put up a stone dwelling-house for himself and
family, and they had comfortable quarters.

AN INDIAN SCHOOL.

A school-building was erected, 30x60 feet, and Josiah
and Elizbeth Butler, of Ohio, now of Kansas, had been

appointed to take charge of the school. They were very useful at other work until the school opened in February, 1871, with a few scholars. No Kiowa or Apache Indian could be induced to attend school, and but few Comanches. I had permission of the department to fill up the school from outside of the agency. Caddoes were the principal students. One boy of about seven summers asked his grandfather, as he was taking him to school, if he thought the agent would give him a revolver and butcher knife to carry in his belt when he got to school. " No," said his grandfather, " I think he will not. What makes you think that he will ? " " Why I am going to school to learn to be a white man, and white men carry revolvers and butcher knives in their belts," was the reply.

The teacher could not understand the Indian language and the pupils could not understand English. He used No. 1 Wilson's illustrated charts. The first word was " Cap," with an illustration. The lesson was one of three letters. One word, and what it meant, and so going on from day to day for some time, they became familiar with quite a number of words. This was sometimes varied by taking an object, as an ax. They would repeat " ax, ax, ax." Then show them a box, and they would repeat the name. Then connections, " ax on box," " ax in box," etc.

A few days after the school opened I procured a Mexican woman for interpreter, who had from infancy been brought up by the Comanches and could talk English. With her assistance the students were soon able to speak in English. The teacher was kind, patient, and had good ability for governing the school. Every day for a period of about two weeks one or more of the older members of the family came from the homes of the students, twenty-five to forty miles distant, to see how their children were treated. Then the chief spent a whole day in the school, and was so well pleased with it that he brought twenty-seven more students, which filled the school. It was a boarding school, with "Aunt Jane," a colored woman, for cook.

GEORGE WASHINGTON'S TEST.

The teacher reported that George Washington, the Caddo chief, came one day, and never left the schoolroom when I was in from daylight until bed-time. He had an idea that I had what they called " medicine " that enabled me to have them do what I would. Hence, after I had gone he locked the doors, called the children up, and he took the pointer to test them (the children had to show him how to use it), and knowing some English, he could tell if they repeated right. The scholars spelled the words and pronounced them, and told him in Caddo what they meant. Then he tried the arithmetic tables in like manner, and so kept on until near midnight, when he was satisfied that they really had learned something, and it was not simply " white man's medicine."

I seldom was hasty in correcting an Indian, but gave serious thought before adopting my plan of rebuke. To illustrate: On Saturdays I furnished the boys with hooks and lines, and let them go fishing, having them return the fishing tackle in the evening. On one Monday morning a boy was missing. I asked, "Boys, where is Soloce?" "Gone a-fishing," was the reply. "Where did he get a hook and line?" "He no give it up Saturday," was the answer. So we went on with the school. At noon he returned. Several boys came to inform me, saying, "Soloce come! Soloce come." To which I replied, "All right." He ate with the rest, and all noontime they were watching to see what I would do, and different ones were saying, "Next time I go fishing; next time I keep back hook and line." When school called, I said, "Soloce has concluded to not learn any more in books, but is going to be a fisherman. I hope he will be a good one and keep us in fish. Soloce, now go and do your best." I was obliged to speak to him several times, and almost force him out. The other boys annoyed him with it for a long time. It became a severe punishment. I permitted him to return, and no one ever kept his hook and line after that.

The children made good progress in their studies, especially in reading, writing, geography and singing, and a few of them became acquainted with the first principles of arithmetic.

Tobacco was a part of the "ration," and the school children were entitled to their portion. As the boys had been accustomed to using it at their homes, the teacher and I thought it best not to refuse it in school, and by moral persuasion we might induce them to quit. The teacher therefore gave them a short lecture generally, if not always, when he furnished them with tobacco. One day he told me that some of them (perhaps three) had concluded to quit using it. As I had never smoked a cigar or chewed tobacco, I was ahead, compared with many people, on tobacco funds, and could now use some anti-tobacco funds. So I gave each one who had quit a pocket knife and a silver dollar. A week later he reported that eight more had quit. Each of them received a pocket knife and half a dollar In a short time only a few of the boys persisted in its use, each abstainer receiving a pocket knife and half a dollar. It was a great satisfaction to the teacher and agent to witness the tobacco reform. Sixteen months after school commenced I requested some of the scholars to write to me on the subject of tobacco. The following is an abstract from one of the essays:

"All the boys quit chewing tobacco. Tobacco no good, heap cost money. Buy good horse and wagon. No use tobacco in school. I like to go to school. All the girls good sew. I love God. I want to go to school eight years.

Your friend,

" JOE WASHINGTON."

The boy—Joe Washington—was able to speak English and use the pen in sixteen months.

June 20th, 1872, in writing to the committee, I stated: " The school was opened February 20th, 1871, with a few of the present students. There are now thirty-one. They are kind, tractable, studious and confiding. There are eleven classes. Besides the primary charts they have reading, writing, arithmetic and geography. The entire school forms a class for study of outline maps in the evenings. Three-fourths of them can name and locate the states, territories, capitals, mountains, and many of the rivers of the United States, and the political divisions, oceans, bays, gulfs, etc., of the Western Hemisphere. I think that every lover of the truth would be pleased to hear their Bible lessons, given every Sabbath by their teacher, whose ardent wish is that they may learn the way of salvation and experience Jesus to be their Saviour."

In the early part of 1873 Mr. Moncrief, a Chickasaw Indian, went to the agency to be treated for paralysis. Dr. Tomlinson did what he could for him. He soon realized that it was doubtful about his recovery, and felt anxious about his salvation. He could talk English, and enjoyed hearing the Scriptures read and expounded. Many were the prayers offered on his behalf as well as by himself. He was quartered near the schoolhouse, and the teachers gave much attention to him. Several days before his death he told me that he believed that his sins were all forgiven, and he felt prepared and ready to go, but was anxious about his children, and requested me to buy each of them a Bible, and write their names and a Scripture motto in them, which I think was done. Three of his children were in the school at the time.

The carpenter shop and blacksmith shop were not far from the schoolhouse, and as some of the boys seemed to take an interest in what was being done there, arrangements were made for three of the boys to work with the carpenter, William Wykes, and two with the blacksmith, William Hall. They were to work on Saturdays, also mornings and evenings, and during a part or all of vacation. They made very good progress in learning their trades. When they had been at work about two years the Caddo chief took a buggy to the carpenter shop to be repaired. The carpenter told me that it was not worth repairing; the wood was so broken and decayed. I asked him if the iron was good. He said it was. I told him to repair it with new wood, and have the Indian boys to do all of it that they could. The carpenter was very skillful in teaching the boys and set them at it. Wheels could not then be bought ready for use. The spokes had to be made by hand. With but little assistance the boys made nearly all the woodwork, and then painted and varnished it. The chief went after his old buggy, and when he was shown the nice new one that his boys had made he was not stoic enough to keep back the tears.

I reported to the department the progress that the boys had made in learning trades while attending school, and reported an estimate for a set of tools for each of them without saying anything to them about it, wishing to not foster a hope in their minds that might result in disappointment. The Commissioner of Indian Affairs wrote me that my estimate of tools had been honored, and would be forwarded. Soon after receiving that word the carpenter boys told me that they had decided to quit work, as they could not buy tools to work with, and their trade would do them no good. I told them that tools had been bought for them and for the blacksmiths, which was a great joy to all of them.

As only one family of the Comanches and none of the Kiowas would send their children to school, I felt very anxious to have a missionary teacher go to their camps, move with them in their wanderings, and teach them as best they could, and try to influence them to quit raiding, cease their nomadic habits and be converted to God.

I frequently wrote to the "Friends' Committee" on the subject, urging its importance. My preference was to have such person go under the auspices of the church, and to be paid by it. But if one went I wanted him called of God for the place, and qualified by Him to fill it. The committee never seemed to be enthused on that subject, but were very hopeful in carrying on the school at the agency. I have no recollection of ever asking our kind and generous Philadelphia Friends for any help for that school but that they gladly responded.

Here was a proposed school to be in the camps of a tribe of roving, raiding, rapacious, murderous Indians! I knew that it would seem dangerous to go among them, but as stated in a previous chápter, if they take a man in as a friend and he proves to their satisfaction that he is one, they will stand by him, and listen to his counsel, although some of them may not take it. Two or three times there seemed to be a prospect of obtaining a missionary teacher in the person of

Thomas Chester Battey,

a Friend, with whom I was acquainted in Iowa. He had been teaching school at the Wichita agency for eight or nine months, and had met with some of the Kiowas and Comanches. He knew their character and their needs. On the morning of March 30th, 1872, he distinctly heard the question audibly addressed to him by the Lord, " What if thou should have to go and sojourn in the Kiowa camps ? " I think that he was not aware that I had for more than a year been looking for a man for that place. The subject was on his mind almost constantly during the day. In the evening Kicking Bird, a Kiowa chief, and his wife went to see him, taking an interpreter with them. They told him that they wanted him to go to their camp, and be a father to their little girl, as he was to the Caddoes. They had lost five children, and they could not leave their little daughter with him at the agency school, as she was all they had. " You come and live with me," he said, " and I will be your friend. Nobody shall harm you. We will be brothers." The anxiety that I had for a Kiowa teacher, the voice of God to T. C. Battey, and the pleading of Kicking Bird, taken together, seemed very remarkable, and all converging to the same point, emanating, apparently, from God.

T. C. Battey informed me of his " call of God," and I rejoiced at the prospect of obtaining a man well qualified for a teacher in the Kiowa camps. I immediately wrote to the Commissioner for authority to employ him and for funds to pay him. A reply was returned, stating that there was a school at the agency, and there the Kiowa children could attend, and not to employ T. C. Battey. I wrote again, urging the importance of having such a teacher. Again the Commissioner refused to sustain me in the enterprise. I told T. C. Battey that I wished him to continue the Kiowa school, and if the Government would not pay him I would divide my salary with him. While I remained agent I wanted him with the Kiowas. The third time I wrote to the Commissioner. Superintendent Hoag, by that time, was interested in the matter, and urged the Commissioner to try it for a while at least. It might be the means of reducing the number of raids and depredations of the

CON-NE-ON-CO (KICKING BIRD), KIOWA CHIEF

Kiowa Indians. The Commissioner then authorized the employment of him, and put funds to my credit to pay him.

December 1st, 1872, T. C. Battey, riding a mule, accompanied Kicking Bird and Dangerous Eagle to their camps, some fifty miles northwest of the agency. I afterwards furnished him with a long tent, wagon and small cook stove. The tent was divided into two apartments, one of these for his school room, and the other for cooking and lodging apartment. There were so many hungry young men to feed that he quit cooking for himself, and lived with Kicking Bird. If he cooked for himself and did not feed the young men they would be angry at him, which would mar, if not wholly, destroy his usefulness. He had taught school in Iowa and at the Wichita agency, but this was an entirely new mode of teaching. He had charts and other appliances for teaching, but his chief usefulness was his general influence with the band. It was his custom to come to the agency every two weeks, when the Indians went to draw rations. So I kept informed as to his success and failures. As to the school, as is genearlly understood by the term, it did not seem to amount to much. But the school as an influence was very encouraging and useful. We will now leave him for a time with Kicking Bird, who belonged to the worst tribe of Indians in Indian Territory. He was an exception to that tribe, and was far in advance of any other chief of the tribe in wishing to quit raiding and to comply with the wish of the Government.   T. C. Battey was probably the first teacher ever employed by the Indian Department to live in an Indian camp and roam over the country with them.   To quote the words of William Penn, it seemed like " a holy experiment."

CHAPTER IV.

THE raiding Indians were usually quiet during the autumn and winter, which was the case with the Kiowas and Comanches in the winter of 1870 and 1871. As soon as their horses were recuperated on fresh grass, which, in their reservation, was mostly good in March, they were ready for raiding. March 11th, 1871, I wrote the committee: " I think the Kiowa Indians are determined to provoke a war. They have killed several persons lately in Texas, and have stolen many horses." They had the idea that if the soldiers went in pursuit of them they could scatter and keep out of the way, and then in the autumn they make peace and get a large amount of annuity goods.

At times there had been a large number of Arizona and New Mexico Apaches west of the reservation in Texas, who were reported to have made frequent raids in Texas, and occasionally committing murder and carrying off captives. I wrote Superintendent Hoag August 25th, 1870, that an Apache chief from New Mexico had recently visited the agency to ascertain if he and all of the Apaches of New Mexico and Arizona could come to this reservation to reside. He and several Kiowa chiefs with him claimed that there were about as many Apaches as the whole number of Kiowas, and that it included all of the Apaches that were not already belonging to this agency. Before arrangements had been made for them to remove to the Indian Territory they decided to remain at their old homes, and I learned that the Comanche Indians had traded for some of the captive children that these Apaches had stolen in Texas, and that these stolen children were now with the Comanches.

In the spring of 1871 the " civilized " Indians, at their council at Okmulgee, passed a resolution that they were willing to meet the Indians of the plains and " have a talk." Superintendent Hoag therefore appointed a council for them and the Indians of the southwestern agencies, to meet at the Wichita agency April 24th, 1871. That day was rainy, and no Indians made their appearance. After that they slowly collected until the 29th, when they met and decided who was to interpret, and made some other arrangements. As the next day was Sabbath they adjourned until Monday, one week after the council was to have been convened. The Indians selected the place of meeting in the shade of trees. Logs were placed in a circle of about fifty feet in diam-

eter.   Blankets were spread upon the ground in the center, upon which a principal chief of each tribe was seated.
The thirteen different tribes represented were Cherokee,
Muskokee (or Creek), Seminole, Chickasaw, Shawnee,
Delaware, Caddo, Wichita, Comanche, Kiowa, Apache,
Cheyenne and Arapahoe.   Each tribe spoke a different
language.   The Comanche was more generally known
than any other.   After the chiefs were seated on the
blankets and the other Indians, agents and visitors on the
logs in the circle, James Van, the second chief of the
Cherokee Nation, said: " I am glad to see my red brethren and smoke the pipe of peace with them.   We will
smoke the Cherokee pipe and tobacco."   He then gave a
few puffs from a large stone pipe which had a stem about
two feet long.   The pipe was held by a Cherokee, who
passed the stem to the mouth of each chief in the centre,
all of whom gave a few puffs except Kicking Bird, who
seldom smoked.   He took hold of the stem in sanction
of the custom.   Some of them gave a puff up to the
Great Spirit, and another to the earth.   It was again
filled and passed around the circle to those who were
seated on the logs.   The writer and some others followed
the example of Kicking Bird.   Thus we all smoked the
pipe of peace.

SMOKED THE PIPE OF PEACE.

At 12.30 the smoking was completed.   Then the
Cherokee chief, who appeared to be the chairman, said:
" The proceedings of to-day make me feel glad at my

heart because we are friends. It has been a long time since the red men met in such a council. When our forefathers met in this way they kindled sacred fire at their councils, to which all the red men of the various tribes flocked to have a smoke, and peacefully transact their business. In shaking hands they extend the whole arm to each other. The Cherokee is the oldest brother of the Indian tribes. To them is entrusted the white path and the key of peace. My young brothers, the head men of the various tribes are now sitting before me. It is our duty to assist each other in promoting peace and welfare. All nations should go hand in hand, and always have a good talk."

Micco Hutkee,

who was the Creek chief, then arose and said: " Brethren, we have heard the talk of our elder brother, and now I have something to say. I wish to talk of the pipe, tobacco and smoke. They are emblems of peace, and they speak that language. It was the tradition of our forefathers that when the pipe of peace was smoked that the smoke would ascend on high, and the surrounding nations would see it arise,—that is, when the people returned they would tell over the talk, and all would understand that the pipe had been smoked and the smoke arose. The talk of our forefathers was that we should have but one fire, one kettle, one plate, one spoon, and then with our five fingers we should all take the victuals from the same plate. This was a figurative expression, and meant that we should be friendly; all should be at liberty to pass from one nation to another without danger of having blood spilt on the white path. Keep in unity and love that we may all eat with one spoon from one plate the provisions cooked in one kettle over one fire.

" Our forefathers told us that there was something white coming up beneath the rising sun that would distress us. This represented the white man, who has distressed and impoverished us, and moved us from towards the rising sun in the direction of the setting sun. Although we are apparently of three races, the red, the white and the black, we were all created by the same Great Spirit, and should live in love and peace together. If the white man should not oppress us now we should not molest him, but live in harmony with him, for the Lord made us all."

The speaker then held up a bunch of white beads as an emblem of the white path, and all who wished to shook hands with it by taking hold of it with one or both hands, and the beads were drawn through as an emblem of being on the white path. He then gave to Kicking Bird, on behalf of the Kiowas, a small piece of tobacco with a string of white beads wrapped around it. In like manner a representative of each tribe was treated with some tobacco and beads, and the council then adjourned until next morning.

May 22d, William Ross, who to all appearance was a white man, addressed the council nearly as follows: " I come before you looking like a white man, and dressed as one. But I was born a Cherokee, and all my life has been spent with them. It is the heart, and not the color, that makes the man. I speak to you as an Indian. I feel as an Indian. You heard yesterday the speech of my chief, also the speech of my younger brother, the Creek. When we all came forward and shook hands with the white beads, my heart was as much gratified as any of yours. The different tribes might be compared with the different members of a man; what affects the hand or arm affects the whole system. Whatever affects the Kiowas, Comanches, Cheyennes, Cherokees, or other tribes affects all the Indians.

" There were thirteen different tribes represented at the last annual council at Okmulgee, each of whom had their own country. The tribes represented there would number about 60,000 Indians. We would like you to send some of your leading men to our next council. Our people are all living quietly and peacefully at our own home, and increasing in numbers, and not fading away like the snow in the warm sun. I hope that peace and prosperity will shine upon you, and upon all men as brightly as the sun shines upon us to-day."

Several other speakers were heard, among whom was Assadawa, the Wichita chief. In his long and complaining speech he said: " For many years Washington has been sending plenty of annuity goods for our people, but before they get here and afterwards they are missing, so that we get but little. For many years Washington has been sending a good deal of money to improve our condition, but it is not used for that purpose. The rations we get are not nearly enough. We have one swallow, and then it is all gone." (The rations that they were receiving of their agent, Jonathan Richards, an honest, upright, Christian "Friend," was: Bacon, ½ pound, two or three times per month for each Indian; beef, 1½ pounds per ration, except the days when they had bacon; flour, ½ pound per ration; coffee, 4 pounds; sugar, 8 pounds; soap, 1 pound; salt, 1 pound; tobacco, ½ pound, to each 100 rations, a ration being one day's supply. The rations were issued once a week. A large " swallow.")

Assadawa further said: " I feel badly about the prospect of having a railroad built through our country. I think it will be detrimental to the Indians. When you Cherokees return I want you to send my speech to Washington, as I see one of you taking it down."

William P. Ross, the person alluded to, then arose and said: " I hold in my hand a paper printed by the Cherokees, partly in English and partly in Cherokee. Assadawa's speech and the proceedings of the council will be printed in this paper."

Toshama, one of the oldest and best of the Comanche chiefs, said: " I was the first of the Comanches to make peace with the whites, which I have not broken. As a bright fire on the summit of a mountain is to a traveler in the night, so have I been to the Indians of the plains, drawing them into the reservations and causing them to cease their raiding. Now I see no reason why I should leave the road spoken of yesterday, represented by the white beads around my neck, long ago given to me on a similar occasion to this by my brother, Tuck-a-ba Che-me-co."

Kicking Bird, a Kiowa chief, said: " I like the talk of yesterday pretty well, but cannot promise to accept it all at this time, but may in future. You have often heard that the Kiowas were a bad and foolish people, which is true. The reason is our land has been taken from us, and we are not permitted to purchase ammunition. If you wish us to become a good people you must get Washington to do something for us, especially in furnishing us with guns and ammunition. Then, perhaps, we will." (All of the Indians in that section of country received rations and annuity goods if they went to their agents for them.)

Joseph James, a Chickasaw, and Joseph Ellis, a Shawnee, made short speeches. Then the Cherokees had as many as were willing to form in line, with the Cherokee chief at the head. There were probably fifty or sixty, including the agents and a few other white people. When all were ready the chief turned to the one next him, and they took each other by the right hand, and each with the left hand took hold of the other's right arm at the shoulder. Thus taking "the whole arm." In like manner the chief passed down the line, shaking hands with each one, and bidding "good-bye." As soon as the chief bid "good-bye" to the one next to him, then he turned and did the same, following the chief, and the next one following him, and so on. When the chief got to the end of the line there were two rows shaking hands and bidding "good-bye." Each one when he got to the end of the line passed away. As they passed down the line each one shook hands with all the others. It was a unique but warm-hearted conclusion of an interesting Indian council.

In making the speeches the speaker would utter a sentence, or part of one, and then wait for it to be interpreted into different languages, only one interpreter speaking at a time. A slow process of speech-making, but it gave you ample opportunity to report them.

About the time that we were "in council" at the Wichita agency some Indians committed a terrible tragedy in Texas. On the 22d of May, 1871, I wrote the committee: "I think the Indians do not intend to commit depredations here this summer, but from their actions and sayings they intend to continue their atrocities in Texas. I believe affairs will continue to get worse until there is a different course pursued with the Indians. I know of no reason why they should not be treated the same as white people for the same offence.

It is not right to be feeding and clothing them, and let them raid with impunity in Texas. Will the committee sustain me in having Indians arrested for murder, and turned over to the proper authorities of Texas for trial?"

May 23d General Sherman, the head officer of the United States Army, called at my office to see if I knew of any Indians having gone to Texas lately. He said a party of Indians, supposed to number about one hundred, had attacked a train of ten wagons belonging to the United States Government about seventeen miles from Fort Richardson; killed the train master and six teamsters. Five others escaped. He was at the Fort all the time, and gave orders for the available troops to follow them, with thirty day's rations, and report at Fort Sill. I told the General I thought that I could find out in a few days what Indians they were. Four days later the Indians came for their rations.

Before issuing their rations I asked the chiefs to come into my office, and told them of the tragedy in Texas, and wished to know if they could tell by what Indians it was committed? Satanta said: "Yes, I led in that raid. I have repeatedly asked for arms and ammunition, which have not been furnished. I have made many other requests which have not been granted. You do not listen to my talk. The white people are preparing to build a railroad through our country, which will not be permitted. Some years ago they took us by the hair and pulled us here close to Texas where we have to fight them. More recently I was arrested by the soldiers and kept in confinement several days. But that is played out now. There is never to be any more Kiowa Indians arrested. I want you to remember that. On account of these grievances, a short time ago I took about a hundred of my warriors to Texas, whom I wished to teach how to fight. I also took the chief Satank, Eagle Heart, Big Bow, Big Tree, and Fast Bear. We found a mule train, which we captured, and killed seven of the men. Three of our men got killed, but we are willing to call it even. It is all over now, and it is not necessary to say much more about it. We don't expect to do any raiding around here this summer; but we expect to raid in Texas. If any other Indian claims the honor of leading that party he will be lying to you. I led it myself." Satank, Eagle Heart and Big Tree were present, and assented the correctness of the statement made by Satanta.

That they were guilty of murder in the first degree I had not the shadow of a doubt, and thought that forbearance in the case would not be a virtue but a crime. There was no provocation whatever for the atrocity. I told the men to go to issuing, and I would go to the Fort. I went to Colonel Grierson's quarters, and requested him to arrest Satanta, Eagle Heart, Big Tree, Big Bow, and Fast Bear for the charge of murder. Scarcely had the order been given, when to our surprise Satanta brought the post interpreter into Colonel Grierson's quarters. He had heard that there was a big Washington officer there, and he probably wished to measure up with him, and see how they compared. When I was about to leave he said that he would go with me, but some soldiers stepped in front of him with their revolvers, and ordered him back; and he tamely obeyed. The Colonel sent for Satanta and Eagle Heart to come to his quarters. Satanta obeyed and was arrested. Eagle Heart was nearly there when he saw Big Tree being arrested, and he turned and fled. Kicking Bird pleaded eloquently for the release of the prisoners, although he entirely disapproved of their raiding.

A day or two after the arrest Colonel McKenzie, in command of the troops from Fort Richardson, arrived at Fort Sill, and reported that the heavy and continued rains so obliterated the tracks of the raiding Indians that they could not be followed. In a few days the Colonel with his troops took charge of the prisoners to convey them to Texas for trial. Satank was so refractory that he was put into a wagon with two soldiers to guard him, and Satanta and Big Tree were placed in another wagon. George Washington, a Caddo Indian, rode by the side of the wagons as they left the Fort. While on the journey Satank said to him: " I wish to send a little message by you to my people. Tell my people that I am dead. I died the first day out from Fort Sill. My bones will be lying on the side of the road. I wish my people to gather them up and take them home."

WHITE BEAR (SE-TI-TAH)—SATANTA, KIOWA CHIEF

Satanta also sent the following message: "Tell my people to take the forty-one mules that we stole from Texas to the agent, as he and Colonel Grierson requires. Don't commit any depredations around Fort Sill or in Texas."

When about a mile from the post Satank sang his death song. Then, with his back to the guard, drew the shackles off of his hands by taking some of the skin with them. With a butcher knife in hand, which he had secreted, although twice searched by soldiers, he then started for the guard in the front of the wagon. They both jumped out, leaving their guns. Satank picked one up and commenced loading it, wanting to kill one more man, when he received several fatal shots, and in twenty minutes died in much savage agony. There was cause to believe that he had killed many white people, also Indians, in addition to the last seven for which he was arrested. He was buried by the soldiers at Fort Sill. The Indians were told that they might take him up and bury him at their own camp, which they declined to do.

The Kiowas and Arizona Apaches had determined to do an extensive business at raiding in Texas, but the arrest of those three chiefs put a check on them.

M. Leeper, my interpreter (who was, in 1896, a practicing physician in Chicago), and H. P. Jones, the post interpreter, attended the trial of the two chiefs at Jacksonborough, Texas. The jury brought in a verdict of murder in the first degree, and they were sentenced to be hanged on the first of September, 1871. I had requested that the Indians be not executed, and independent of my principles against capital punishment, had given reasons for thinking that it would have a better effect on the Indians of the agency to imprison them for life. After the trial the Judge wrote me that he would request the Governor to commute the sentence, which was done. They were sent to the penitentiary for life. It seemed remarkable to me that General Sherman, Colonel Grierson, and the Judge on the bench should all so heartily co-operate with my views and judgment in connection with the disposal of those Indians. General Sherman assured me that so far as his influence and authority extended he would have my requests carried out.

I wrote to the " Friends' Committee " that " Colonel Grierson and Interpreter Jones, and many others who have been long known to Kiowas, say that they were never so effectually subdued before. I see much in the Kiowas and all of the other Indians to confirm me that it was right to have them arrested, and I see nothing to make me feel doubtful about it. It has probably saved the lives of many Texas citizens. He whom I endeavor to serve has, I believe, enlightened my understanding in times of need."

The Kiowa Indians delivered to me in August forty good mules and one horse. Part of them were stolen at the Satanta raid. I wrote to the owner, Henry Warren,

SATANK, KIOWA CHIEF

to come to the agency and get them. Near that time there were delivered to me forty-two ponies and two mules which had been stolen from the Kiowas in the spring by the Sioux Indians, which had been recaptured and brought here by the United States troops. They were returned to the Kiowas, greatly to their surprise.

About the time of the arrest of Satanta, White Horse and six other Kiowa men and one woman were in Texas, and murdered Mr. and Mrs. Lee and one of their daughters, and took three of their children, Susan, aged sixteen years; Milley F., aged nine, and John A. Lee, aged six captives to their camps, six days' journey.

The civilized Indians, at their Okmulgee Council, had appointed a delegation to meet the Kiowas, and try to induce them to cease their raiding. It was proposed to hold the council at old Fort Cobb, July 22d, 1872. I opposed having it at that time, as the Indians seemed nearly ready to bring in their captives and receive rations, and the council would probably delay the delivery of them. They had been doing without rations a long time, and the women and children were becoming clamorous for coffee and sugar. Cyrus Bedee, the superintendent's clerk, was there on behalf of the superintendent, and urged to have the council; hence we yielded, and went to it, about forty-five miles distant. After remaining there a week waiting for the Kiowas, I was sent for to return to the agency on account of my wife's sickness. A few days later the Kiowas went to the council.

White Horse said that he and the young men did not want peace, but would raid when and where they please. Lone Wolf said that they would return the captives and make peace when Satanta and Big Tree were released from the penitentiary, when all the military posts had been removed from the Indian Territory, and their reservation lines extended from the Rio Grande to the Missouri River.

The civilized Indians told the Kiowas that if they did not " take in " the captives and behave that the Government would surely inflict upon them severe retribution. After the council had adjourned Kicking Bird requested the interpreter to tell me that he did not like the talk of Lone Wolf, and that he should make a strong effort to have the captives delivered to his agent. Cyrus Bedee urged him to take them to his agent at once.

About a month later the girls were delivered to Agent Jonathan Richards. The Indians told him that they were afraid to go to their own agency on account of its being near to Fort Sill. Agent Richards gave them a liberal supply of rations, and hired Caddo George to take them to me. The next morning he put them in his wagon, and the Indians who took them to the Wichita agency rode their ponies with him, and they were delivered to me. The Indians told me that the boy was sick and not able to ride. His sisters said that he was well and cried to go with them. They had no idea when they left the Indian camps where they were going. But when they came in sight of houses it seemed like approaching civilization again.

The Indians told me that they had " a big talk " at their camps, and had agreed to " take in " the captives and cease raiding if the white people did not get foolish and do something to them. They only wished to be let alone. They pleaded with all the eloquence of which they were capable to obtain remuneration for delivering the girls. I told them that paying for them was an encouragement to steal more, and that they should not have a dollar, and that they could have no more rations until the boy was brought. These girls were the first captives ever recovered from the Kiowas without paying from $100 to $1,500 for each one. As their parents had been killed the children were placed in the agency school. I wrote to their relatives in Texas of their recovery, and an elder brother came to the agency for them. He was at the schoolhouse when their brother John was delivered, September 30th. They were all rejoiced to meet again. Two days later they started to their desolate home, about four months after they had been captured by the Indians.

About six weeks after the council of the Okmulgee delegates and C. Bedee with the Kiowa and Comanche Indians, there was another very important one held by Captain H. E. Alvord. Professor Edward Parish, of Philadelphia, and Captain Alvord had been appointed a commission to look into the condition of the three agen-

cies, Cheyenne and Arapahoe, Wichita and Affiliated
Bands, and the Kiowa and Comanche tribes, and to take
a delegation from each of the tribes to Washington, and
report their judgment " as to the best and most effectual
method of dealing with and controlling the disaffected
portions of said tribes." Soon after they arrived at the
Kiowa and Comanche agency Professor Parish was taken
sick with typhoid fever. He was treated by the agency
physician, and nursed and cared for as well as he could
be there, but died September 9th, 1872. He gave evidence that his end was peace and joy. His heart was
thoroughly enlisted in the work, and Captain Alvord felt
a great loss in not having his counsel and help.

The Cheyennes were out hunting and were not present. From some cause word had not reached them of
the Council. The commissioners were authorized to
promise the release of Satanta and Big Tree, but before
Professor Parish was taken sick the commissioners had
given the subject much attention, and decided that their
release " would be highly detrimental to the interest of
the Government," and it was not mentioned to the Indians. It was difficult to get suitable representatives of
the Kiowas to agree to go to Washington. They were at
length obtained with the promise that if they would go
they should see Satanta and Big Tree, and these prisoners
were brought from the penitentiary in Texas to Saint
Louis to meet the Indian delegation. Captain Alvord
reported this meeting as " proving to be a most impres-

sive and affecting occasion." He, Superintendent Hoag, and others present believed that it would result in good. After being with the delegation a few days the prisoners were returned to the prison in Texas, and the delegation went to Washington, where " the Kiowas were promised the release of their chiefs, by the permission of the Governor of Texas, at the end of six months, upon good behavior meanwhile of the whole tribe with other fixed conditions." Captain Alvord made an interesting and elaborate report, including many pertinent suggestions which were embraced in the report of the Commissioner of Indian Affairs for 1872.

WILLIE SMITH MISSING.

An exciting scene took place one day at the agency in early spring. The clerk's five-year-old boy, Willie Smith, was missing. His parents searched about the buildings and places where he was accustomed to playing, but he could not be found. He had been seen to pass through the office and the yard gate into the open prairie, and no one observed which way he then went. An Indian had given him a little bow and some arrows, and his mother was fearful that he had been enticed behind a hill near the agency by Indians, and that they had carried him off. Having recovered several children from the Indians, and talked with parents who had lost them, we knew something of the distress and anguish of mind experienced by parents whose children had been carried off by them. Some of these bereaved parents had told me that they would rather see their children killed than carried off in that way, and endure so much suspense and uncertainty of ever seeing them again. The day before Willie disappeared, as the agency families were returning from church service at the schoolhouse, one and a half miles distant, the little boy saw some wild flowers near the road and wanted to get some of them, but his parents thought it not best to stop the ambulance in which they were riding. The next morning he went after the flowers, and when he got them he thought that he would go to the schoolhouse, having no thought of the distress that he was giving his parents. The suspense was broken in about two hours by a schoolboy conducting him home, to the great joy of his parents and others.

CHAPTER V.

SATANTA, in the penitentiary in Texas, was claiming to be the principal chief of not only the Kiowas, but of all the nations in the three agencies in the southwestern part of Indian Territory, and if he were released he constantly declared he would keep all of them from raiding. It was understood that the Govenor of Texas favorably considered his release. The authorities at Washington also thought it might be best. The " Friends' Indian Committee " felt very hopeful that it would be right to release those chiefs, and thereby put an end to the raiding in Texas. The committee wrote me on the subject. But I took a very different view of it. Satanta was not the principal chief of the Indians in those agencies. The various tribes had their chiefs, but they had no leading one over all of them. I did not believe him sincere in his promises. He had made a similar one some years before when under arrest, and had been released. In-

(131)

stead of keeping others from raiding as he had promised he seemed afterward to be the leading raider.

My candid opinion of him was that he could not keep the other Indians from raiding if he wished to; and that he would not do it if he could. My judgment was to send some more of the leading raiders to the penitentiary, and in that way stop their unprovoked hostility.

The Kiowas, in 1872, had endeavored to get the Cheyennes, Sioux and Comanches to join them in a general fight against the white people, and compel the release of their chiefs. Failing to get those tribes to join them, they were committing more depredations than usual. The Comanches informed me that about one-fourth of the Kiowas had left the reservation and joined the Quahadas. In the spring of 1872 they stole one hundred and twenty mules from the troops north of Camp Supply; killed several men in Texas, and stole several hundred horses and mules, in some instances taking all the stock of frontier settlers.

Under date of August 14th, 1872, in answer to the committee relative to the release of Satanta and Big Tree, I wrote: " The action of the Kiowas has been such that I think it would be very wrong to release them at this time." My superior officers and the committee saw the subject so very different from what I saw it, and from what Captain Alvord and Professor Parish saw it after being on the field, that their release was finally promised. I felt that it would lead to bad results, and that it was hardly probable that I could have much further control over the Indians. It seemed clear to me that it would be right to resign my position, and if some other person could control the Indians with that kind of management he ought to have the opportunity. I therefore forwarded my resignation, to take effect March 31st, 1873.

The Indians are largely what the white people have made them. In all the years of intercourse with the whites, the Kiowas or Comanches never had a missionary or special religious influence in their camps until T. C. Battey went among them. They had learned and practiced many of the vices, and few, if any, of the virtues, of civilized nations. Hence to give them cause to believe that their raiding had compelled the white people to release their chiefs would only be a stimulus to them to continue hostilities, and keep the white people so afraid of them that they would yield to their demands. It seemed to me that from their standpoint it showed a weakness in the Government and a strength in them.

THE QUA-HA-DA BAND OF COMANCHES.

This band, it was reported, had never been to an Indian agency. Their haunt was the western part of Texas. They formed a rendezvous for disaffected or raiding Indians of any tribe. At Captain Alvord's council, in 1872, Tab-a-nan-a-ka, the leading chief of the Quahada band, said: " I see but three tribes whose young men, at least, have not been present and equally guilty with our people and the Kiowas in more or less of the forays of the last two years, and they are the Arapahoes, the Caddoes, and the Delawares. The Cheyennes and the Osages have also acted with us, and as to your promises—you could not control your young braves if you would, and you do not attempt it."

Raiding parties could go from the Quahada camps, and then charge it to them. They had repeatedly sent word to me that they "would never go to the agency and shake hands until the soldiers would go there and fight with them. If whipped they would then go to the agency and shake hands."

ILLICIT TRADERS.

Vicious men from New Mexico supplied the Indians with ammunition and breech-loading guns, taking in exchange horses and cattle which had been stolen from Texas. They ridiculed the reservation Indians for remaining there instead of doing as they did, roam over the plains unmolested, and raid in Texas when they wished without ever being called to account.

In the fall of 1872 Colonel McKenzie followed a raiding party from Texas to their camp and surprised them. Instead of fighting, as they said they wished to do, as many as could, including men, women and children, jumped upon ponies and fled. A few of the men were killed by the soldiers. Among them was a white man about forty years old, who fought desperately.

Another of the killed was an Indian who had declared that he would never go to an agency or submit to the requirements of the white people.

More than a hundred women and children who could not escape tried to secrete themselves in a thicket. After the soldiers chased the Indians, who scattered like a flock of frightened quails, they returned to the thicket and were preparing to shoot into it when a woman went out with a white flag. The Colonel, through his interpreter, asked what she wanted. She replied that they did not want to be shot. He told her to leave their arms in the thicket, come out and surrender to him, and they should not be hurt. Thereupon they surrendered to the soldiers, who, after burning many of their lodges (probably one hundred), marched them to Texas. Among the prisoners there were members of nearly or quite every band of Comanches on the reservation. That confirmed my previous opinion that every band of Comanches, as well as the Kiowas, participated in the forays of the Quahadas.

As a large number of their lodges were now destroyed, and with them much of their dried buffalo and other property, the near approach of winter and the hope of having their women and children restored to them, all combined to make it desirable to go to the agency, get rations, annuity goods, and if possible obtain their Texan prisoners. Lone Wolf and several other delegates who recently returned from Washington went to the agency with them. When the chiefs went into the office I was

engaged in the annuity room. For some time Lone
Wolf was instructing the Quahada chiefs, who had never
seen me, about their "bad lying agent." "He pretended," he said, "to have a copy of the talk that the
commissioner gave us in Washington. But the talk that
the commissioner gave us was entirely different." He
told them wherein it widely differed. "The agent," he
said, "was just lying to the Indians about that talk."
The interpreter came to me and told me how Lone Wolf
was talking. Then Lone Wolf came and told me to
hurry into the office. He wanted to talk to me. As I
walked to the office I prayed the Lord to direct me. I
did not know what to say to those chiefs whom I was
about to meet for the first time, and expecting that Lone
Wolf had a lying, vindicative harangue in readiness for
me.

After shaking hands with them, I told them that I was
glad to see them, and that I had been wanting to see
them for three years, and now hoped that we should all
be friends. Some of the Indians had recently been to
Washington and shaken hands with the officers there,
and "a talk" had been given to them, and the same talk
had been sent to me for all the Indians of the agency,
and I would read it to them. The interpreter who was
with them in Washington was present and interpreted
it to the Quahadas. The letter from the Commissioner
of Indian Affairs stated that the Indians must cease their
raiding and remain on their reservation. and deliver to

the agent the horses and mules stolen that year. That the Government could not longer permit raiding as it had been practiced. The letter was of some length, and was carefully interpreted. Then I asked one of the delegates if that was the same that was said to them in Washington. He said that it was. Several others said that it was just the same talk they heard in Washington.

I told them that the white people and Indians were similar in many particulars. Some white people would lie and some Indians would lie. When they found an Indian addicted to lying they should turn their backs to him, and have nothing to do with them. If they listened to his talk they were liable to be brought into difficulty by him. They should throw him away. When I got through talking I told the Quahadas that I should like to hear from them if they wished to talk, but they did not wish to say anything just then, and I told Lone Wolf that he might talk, but he had nothing to say. When I entered the office his eyes were shining like a black snake's, apparently thinking of how he was going to abuse me before those new Indians. But when I got through talking he looked like a kill-sheep dog. The Lord, I beileve, answered my prayer, and directed my mind in talking. To Him be the praise.

Lone Wolf soon withdrew, and then the Quahadas said that they had "a fight with the soldiers," and had been whipped. Now they were ready to be friends, and do as their agent advised them. They would remain on the reservation, send their children to school, and do the best they could at farming. But before they could do either their agent must restore to them their women and children who were prisoners in Texas. I told them that they had some of my children that I had been trying for three years to obtain. Before I would talk to them about their women and children they must deliver to me all the white children they had. In a few days they brought to the agency two boys, whom they said were all the white children in their camps. The name of the oldest captive was Clinton Smith. He was about thirteen years of age. He and a younger brother were herding stock in the vicinity of San Antonio, Texas, where some Arizona Apaches captured them. Clinton was sold to a Quahada Comanche. His father had been to the agency to see if he could hear about his boys, but previous to this time nothing had been heard of them.

The other boy that the Indians took to the agency was about nine years old, and said his name was Topish, and the Indians retained the name. He had been with them several years. As they were not permitted to talk English he had forgotten every word of his mother tongue. He remembered that his father had been shot in the yard when he was captured. His mother and an infant in her arms were both shot, and he thought killed. He and a younger sister were carried off. His sister for some cause was killed the first night. I advertised in the Texas and Kansas papers for his relatives or friends.

The boys had their hair cut, dressed in citizen clothes, and placed in the agency school. Topish's name proved to be John Valentine Moxie. It was his grandfather who was killed. His father was away from home at the time. His mother recovered from her wound in her arm, but the babe was killed. His father came to the agency and obtained the boy. As stated in a previous chapter, he had been there before, but at that time could learn nothing about him.

These returned captives informed me of two other white children in the Quahada camps. I told the Indians that I was not yet ready to talk about their women and children in Texas. They must deliver to me all the white children they had, and then I would talk about their captives. In a few days " Horseback," who delivered the first two boys, brought two more to the agency. He was one of the most peaceful and docile of the Comanche chiefs. In being active in taking in the captives, he wished to show his friendship to his agent, and he was anxious to have the Indian women and children returned from Texas. Several from his band were among the prisoners. The name of the oldest captive returned was Adolph Kohn, a German boy. He was captured about three years before, near San Antonio, and he said he was eleven years old; had a father, mother and nine brothers and sisters. The Arizona Apaches who captured him traded him to a Quahada Comanche. He was delighted with the idea of being restored to his parents, brothers and sisters.

TEMPLE FRIEND,

another captive, was brought to the agency with Adolph Kohn. He had forgotten his name, and could only speak the Comanche language. He thought that his father's name was John, but whether it was the first or last name he could not tell. He recollected that his mother and aunt were killed. The hair of the boys had not been cut since they were captured. It was shaved off, and they were bathed, dressed in citizen clothes, and placed in the agency school, where they soon learned to speak English. I had notices of Temple Friend put in the Texas and Kansas papers, and wrote to L. S. Friend, a Methodist minister, thinking that the boy might be his grandchild that he had for some years been looking for. He spent several weeks at the agency the previous summer to see if he could procure him. On reading my letter he was satisfied that he was his grandchild, and he started from El Dorado, Kansas, the next morning to the agency with his horse and buggy. When he arrived there my wife and I went with him to the schoolhouse. It was the custom for all the children to speak to us when we went there, and young Friend came in with the others. When he spoke to my wife she told him to speak to this old gentleman. He put his arm around him fondly and recognized his long-lost boy. As soon as he could control his feelings he said, " Temple Friend."

The boy looked at him with suprise. His forgotten name seemed to be remembered, and he said, " Yesh." His sister's name, " Florence Friend," was then spoken. With amazement he again replied, " Yesh."

The grandfather stated that the boy had been stolen in Texas five years before, and his mother was shot with an arrow, which went through both arms and her breast, knocking her down, and she pretended to be dead. The arrow looked as if it passed through the vital organs, and she was left for dead after taking off a small scalp which she endured without moving a muscle. When the Indians went into the house she knocked one of them with a flatiron, which showed her bravery, and for that reason they took a small scalp. After the Indians left she went to a neighbor's dwelling and had the arrow extracted, and she recovered from the injury. Brother Friend told me that he had traveled about fifteen thousand miles in the vain endeavor to recover the boy, having been to the Apache reservations in Arizona and New Mexico, hoping to find him, as those Indians raided so much in Texas. Several times he had been to the Kiowa and Comanche agency. He had a standing reward of a thousand dollars for his recovery, but at length obtained him free of cost, for which he felt very thankful.

These were all the captives that I heard of, and hence I could now talk about the Texas captives. " Horseback " was the principal spokesman, but there were some of the Quahadas present. They claimed to have surrendered all of the white children, and now wanted all of their women and children. I told them that they might have come to the agency at any time before their women and children were captured, and they might have been friends, but now I had no control over them. They belonged to the soldiers in Texas. They then wanted me to write to Colonel McKenzie and tell him how good they had been in delivering all the white children they had, and how good they intended to be in future, and now they wished to have their women and children returned to them. I wrote what they desired, and then on my own account wrote the Colonel that they had surrendered four white children, and so far as appeared that was all they had, and I would like him to please return a few of the women. I did not think it best to return all of them at that time.

After the Moxie and Friend boys commenced speaking English, I asked them why they ran away from the soldiers, instead of running to them, as they would have been so glad to have taken care of them and to send them to their homes. One of them replied it was because they were foolish little boys, and the other assented to it. Often have I since thought that there are many little boys and girls and grown up people who act very much like those white boys in the Comanche camps. They were far from their Great Father's home and in the enemy's camp. And when they had the opportunity to go to the soldiers, who would direct them to their

Father's house, they went flying off in the opposite direction. We have all been away from our Heavenly Father's house, and in the camp of our enemy. As those captive boys rode Indian ponies, probably racing and having jolly times in their camps, so do many go to riding hobby ponies in Christian lands, and having their jolly times while away from their Heavenly Father's house. Some will ride a whiskey-pony, but don't intend to ever let it get the advantage of them. Its course is always down and down, and never up. Some will ride a lying hobby horse, some a thieving one, some a swearing one, some a skeptical one. Many seem to be riding a blind hobby horse, drifting they know not where. While they are riding their hobby horses, seeking to have good times on them, here are the soldiers of the cross, under the direction of the " Captain of the hosts of the Lord " —ministers of the gospel, Bible School teachers, Christian Endeavorers, and many other soldiers, striving to induce them to abandon their hobby horses in the enemy's camp and ride the King's horse in " the highway of holiness." Many listen to them and make the exchange, and if faithful to the orders of their captain they uniformly realize a better and more satisfactory time than they had in the enemy's camp; and they have the assurance that when through riding on the highway of holiness, they will be promoted to a mansion prepared by the Captain and wear " a crown of righteousness," " a crown of glory," " a crown of life." The exchange is on condition of repentance towards God and faith in the Lord Jesus Christ. When a person will not make the exchange, does he not seem like the " foolish little boys " with the Comanche Indians?

Colonel McKenzie honored my request and sent back five Comanche women, one of whom was taken sick and died on the way. When the four reached the agency, I asked them how they had been treated by the officers and soldiers. They replied that they had uniformly been treated kindly and with respect, and had not been abused in any way. I asked them how it compared with the treatment of the Indians towards white women when they took them prisoners. They said that Indians never treated white women with the kindness that they had received, but always abused them.

I was impressed that the Quahadas had some Mexican captives who would like to leave them and return to their homes, and I said to the Indians that if they had any such captives they must bring them to the agency, to which they agreed, providing I knew of any Mexicans who wished to leave them, and if I would tell them who they were they would bring them to the agency. They knew of none, they said. I tried as best I could to get trace of one or more, but failed to find any. Then I procured a half-breed and his wife (the latter lived in that band) to see if they could find any, and they failed. After exhausting my ingenuity and skill, I asked the Lord in some way to make it manifest if there were any

Mexicans with the Indians who wished to leave them. A few days after I asked the Lord to do what I could not do. He answered my prayer, I believe, by putting the thought into the heart of Martha Day, a Mexican captive, to leave the Indians and come to the agency. This she decided to do while on the journey to the agency for rations. " Black Beard," who claimed her, asked " if she had any thought of running away to the agency?" She derided the idea. He told her that if she went to the agency or to the Fort she would probably be killed, as the white people did not want Mexicans; or, if she was not killed, she would be returned to him and he would kill her. She replied that she did not want to be killed and he need not be uneasy about it. In the evening she told the Indians that she was so afraid of the white people and of the soldiers that she could not sleep, and if they could sleep they might and she would watch them through the night and " herd " the ponies. They gladly accepted her proposition and she went to " herding " the horses and mules in the dark and rain. Before morning she left them to " herd " themselves. She reached the agency and met with soldiers who were patroling the buildings. Some time previous to that, on two occasions, the commissary building had been broken into at night and some stores taken, I supposed by white men. To prevent a repetition of it, I had asked Colonel Grierson for a guard to protect the Government property from thieves. As it took some time to pass around the buildings she had no difficulty in going through the yard gate and onto our portico, where she quietly waited, fearing to arouse us lest it might make us mad. When she heard a noise in the dwelling she made herself known.

She reported that she had been captured in the vicinity of San Antonio about two years before, while on her way to school, and she wanted to go home. I told her that I was glad to see her, and would send her there. My wife and her sister, Edith Painter, who was there on a visit, and my clerk's wife, had a busy day preparing clothing for her to take the place of the Comanche costume. My quarters were closely guarded that day by the Indians, who apparently intended to shoot her if they got sight of her. In the evening, when nicely dressed, she was a handsome young woman, about eighteen years old, and happy with the thought of returning to her home and people—a great contrast from the dirty, slovenly looking squaw that she seemed like in the morning.

The father of Clinton Smith was at the agency, having come there for his son, and he wished to start home that evening. The stage came to the agency and the whole household accompanied him and Martha Day to it, and the nicest dressed woman in the company entered the stage and off they went. It was the most opportune night for her to leave the Comanche camp that there was during the four years that I was agent. Mr. Smith and she lived in the same neighborhood and he could accompany her home. It seemed as if it was the ordering of the Lord.

The following morning a number of chiefs and other Indians came into the office to have " a talk." They told me that they had lost a squaw. and wished to know if I could give them any information about a stray one. I told them that I could tell them all about one. " She came to my house two nights ago and told me that she had been stolen in Texas by the Indians and wished to go home. Last evening I put her in the stage and started her home. She is now a long ways from here and you will never see her any more." That was a complete surprise to them. They had no idea of her being sent away so promptly. For a time they were as quiet as the old-fashioned proverbial " Quaker meeting." Then one of them said: " They did not care much; she was not worth a great deal, but we want you to pay for her." I told them that " I was not buying squaws, but was glad to get that Mexican girl without buying. You told me that you had no Mexicans who wished to leave, but she was so anxious to get away from you that to do it she jeopardized her life." She had informed me of three boys in the camp who wished to leave. I told the Indians their names and the names of the Indians who claimed them. They said the boys were there, " but the girl was just lying to you." They were sure that they did not wish to leave them. I replied that it made no difference how much the girl lied, that those boys have to come into my office and tell me with their own tongue which they would prefer, either to go to their homes or live with the Indians. "If they tell me that they prefer to live with the Indians they may be Comanches. If they say that they wish to go to their own people they shall go there."

They were brought to the office and my Irish cook prepared a good meal for them, which they greatly enjoyed. It was "the Indian road to not talk to a hungry man." After inquiring of them about their home people, I told them that if they wished to go to their parents and kindred I would send them there, and if they wished to throw away their parents, brothers and sisters, they could be Comanches. They said that they wanted to go home. So I took charge of them and had them bathed, their hair cut, and they were dressed in citizen's clothes and sent to the school house. They told of two more Mexican captives, and I demanded them of the Comanches; but when they came after their rations in two weeks they brought but one—Presleanno, a little fellow about eight years old. He was a smart, active boy, and was evidently "a pet" in "Parry-o-coom's" lodge, who apparently thought that if taken alone he would not remain with strangers whose language he could not understand. Parry-o-coom claimed that he did not belong to me, as he had stolen him in Old Mexico, and "Washington" had no jurisdiction in that country. I told him that the United States and Mexico were brothers, and if he wished to go to his own people I would send him to them if they could be found. The little fellow ate a hearty supper, and while eating he had no use for knife or fork. When the test question was put to him, he said that he would like to go to his own people. The tears immediately started in the eyes of Parry-o-coom, one of the prominent chiefs of the Quahadas. I told the inter-preter to take the boy into the kitchen. I did not wish him to see the tears. As the school was not in session, he was kept at the agency, where he became attached to all who belonged there and was merry and happy as a bird.

By the time that Presleanno was recovered, I heard of another captive who wished to leave and demanded the two. I told the little boy that when they came he might talk to them and try to induce them to leave the Indians. My first talk to captives was in the presence of the In-dians. After he talked to them in the office he went out, and told me that one of them expected to leave the In-dians and the other intended to return with them. I told him to take them into the bedroom after they had eaten dinner and talk to them again. A clerk at J. S. Evans' store, who understood Mexican, went into the room with them. He afterwards told me that the little fellow first took them into the pantry and showed them the stores there, and when he took them into the room he stood in front of them and with appropriate gestures made an eloquent little speech. He told of the large supply of good provisions they had three times a day. Never had to quit eating while they were hungry because the food was exhausted, and at night I roll myself up in blankets and sleep so comfortably right here on the floor. Nothing to make me afraid day or night. The agent and his wife and all the white people are so kind to me. I will never again live with the Indians if I can prevent it. We then accompanied them into the office. After talking to them a short time, I asked them which they preferred, going to their former homes or returning with the Indians? They both said they would like to go to their people.

One of them had his hair combed and dressed before he came to the agency, which indicated that he had " his girl " selected. It was the custom of the Comanche boys to not have their hair cut or combed from the time they commence walking until they approach manhood. One of the first indications of a boy loving a young woman was for him to procure a coarse comb and a small mirror and to go into the woods alone and comb the long and tangled hair that has been wholly neglected for years, except by certain vermin.

Had the one with his hair cut been taken to the agency with Parry-o-coom's boy, he would probably have returned with them, and the little boy might have accompanied him. But the speech of the small boy was, I apprehend, the cause of his leaving the Indians—another case of the overruling providence of God.

I had the pictures of these three boys taken in their Comanche costume, and again a few days afterwards when they were dressed in citizens' clothing. One of them, when shown the picture of himself in Indian dress, had no idea who it was.

These last two boys told of another Mexican who wanted to leave and whom I demanded. But the Indians said I had been " lied to this time sure. Instead of his being a boy he was a grown man and a very dangerous one—one of the greatest raiders among them." I told them to bring him to my office and let me hear from his own tongue what he wanted. When they came again he was not with them. They reported that he had learned that I wanted him, and he was so determined not to go to the agency that he went armed with a revolver ready to shoot any of them who attempted to take him to the agency, and " we are all afraid of him."

" Do you want to hear of some of us being killed by trying to bring that dangerous man to you?" " No," I replied, " I do not want to hear of it, and do not expect to hear of it. But I expect you to bring him here. It makes no difference how dangerous he is, he has to come. You may jump onto him when he is asleep and tie his hands and tie him onto a pony and bring him here. I must see him and talk with him. To-night, when you lie down to sleep, I want you to turn one ear towards Texas and see if you hear your women and children crying.

They will continue to cry then until that man is brought here." They replied: "Your heart is hard." It was no easy matter to talk to those Indians as I did. I thought it right and the Lord sustained me.

The next time they came they had him with them without being tied, but he was dressed like a young warrior, wearing the highly prized pipe-bead breast ornament and other decorations. The post interpreter knew of his coming to the agency and was present when he was brought into the office. He said: "Mr. Tatum, you will not get that man; he is a thorough Indian." It seemed as if the Holy Spirit said to me: " They have been trying to intimidate him," although I had never heard of their resorting to that in any case. A few minutes before he came I heard of a Mexican who had a " Delaware " Indian wife who could talk English, who had gone to the school house to see his children. It occurred to me that the captive might have more confidence in a brother Mexican to interpret than my American, so I sent for him. Before he got there the captive had a good supper. I then asked him about his father and mother, brother and sisters, and if he thought they were still longing to see him and crying about him, to which he gave an affirmative answer. I also inquired about his uncles, aunts and cousins. After keeping his mind on his home associations for a short time, I told him that if he wished to go to his parents and home that

I would send him there. If he would rather "throw away" his father and mother, brothers and sisters, and be a Comanche, he could do that.

"You see a good many Indians here, but don't be afraid of them. You see a good many white people here; don't be afraid of them either. If you wish to go home, say so, without fear of the Indians. If you wish to be a Comanche, say so, without fear of the white people. You shall not be hurt here in my house. Now, what will you say?"

"Meyarrow," ("go home,") he said in Mexican. I had often heard the word, but never before with such a thrill of joy. One word settled his destiny for life, perhaps for eternity. There were two or three chiefs and fifteen or twenty young braves present, who were the very persons to intimidate him. Soon after entering the office the interpreter heard one of the chiefs ask him if he would remain there or return with them. He replied: "Go with you."

After he said "Meyarrow" the Indians stripped him of his ornaments and left. He then told me that as they were coming to the agency the Indians had assured him that if he told me that he wished to leave them and go to his own people they would kill him right there in the office. So if the Holy Spirit had not shown me that they had been trying to intimidate him, I should not have known how to have talked to him. His name was Levando Gonzales, an Indian captive about seventeen years old, and through fear of being murdered by them he would have returned with them. To the Lord be the praise.

Levando Gonzales told of other Mexican captives. When they were recovered they told of others, until, through the help of the Lord, I recovered eleven Mexican boys from the clue which Martha Day gave me. The last one was brought to the agency about two weeks before my resignation took effect, and I began to fear that he would be retained until the new agent took charge, and this might cause a hard beginning for him. I heard of no others among them who wished to leave. The Indians gave me credit of having " the strongest medicine for recovering captives " of any agent that they ever had. In my estimation the " medicine " was the Holy Spirit, who, Jesus said, " will guide you into all the truth."

During the last eight months that I was Indian Agent, through the help of the Lord, I recovered from the Indians seven white captives and twelve Mexicans. Previous to that time I recovered five white children and two women, making a total of twenty-six captives recovered in the four years of my administration, besides some hundreds of horses and mules that the Indians had stolen. By my request, Major Schofield, the commanding officer of Fort Sill, conveyed the Mexican boys to General Augur, of San Antonio, who was the Commander of the Department of Texas, which included Indian Territory. He was to try to find the homes of all the boys, several of whom were stolen from Mexico. He was at Fort Sill and the agency a few months before I left and realized the arduous work in which I was engaged. He and all other military officers with whom I have had business have been very kind and obliging to me, and anxious to assist in every way practicable. Under date of February 7th, 1873, General Augur wrote me: "I regret very much to hear that you are relieved from your agency. While I fully understand that the place has no attractions for you, I can also see that the public service is to be the loser by any change, however worthy may be your successor."

In the latter part of January, 1873, wishing to make a visit to the Indians on the reservation, I went without arms, as I always did when visiting the wild or blanket Indians, unless a small pocket knife could be called a weapon. In the company was an interpreter, my brother-in-law (J. H. Painter), T. C. Battey, a man for cook, and "Kicking Bird" for guide. The first day we went to the widow Chandler's. Her husband, Joseph Chandler, had deceased, and we took a coffin and new suit of clothes for him, as she wished him buried like a white man. He had been a truthful, reliable and industrious Indian. He had rendered me valuable services as interpreter. His influence with the Indians was uniformly good. His home was on the eastern part of the reservation, near the Delawares. The next day we passed

the Keechi Hills, which rise abruptly about two hundred
feet above the surrounding country, showing their rocky
formation.　After visiting Mahway's camp, we passed
on to the Wichita agency.　On the following day we
visited " Horseback's " camp on the Washata.　He was
one of the most reliable of Comanche chiefs.　In the
evening we reached Kicking Bird's camp, on the north
side of the Washata.　He was off his reservation, where
he had gone to obtain pasture for his ponies.　We had
a very satisfactory council with him and his people, and
nine other chiefs who cling to him and to a large degree
accept his council.　They all claimed to want to quit their
depredations on the white people and to live at peace.
" The talk " was continued awhile in the morning, and
then we fell in, " Indian file," and followed Kicking
Bird over some of the rocky foot hills of the Wichita
Mountains.　Before night overtook us we camped in the
mountains alone.　The evening was pleasant for mid-
winter and the moon was brightly shining.　We had a
glowing fire, which added to the wildness of the mountain scenery.　Kicking Bird was asked what the Kiowas
thought of the moon.　He replied: " The moon is the
great white man."　He then looked for a cluster of stars,
which he was unable to see, but said: " They have the
appearance of a man's face, and he is the great Kiowa,
who made us and all this country, with its streams,
mountains and animals.　(We afterwards learned that
the cluster of stars was the Pleiades.)　He was a gigantic

man, and could step across the largest streams. After making the country and a portion of the animals, he went to a large hollow log and with a stick gave it a hard stroke, when out came numerous Kiowa men and women, who ran away from him in alarm. On calling to them, they returned to the great Kiowa, who told them that he was their father. He saw that in some resepcts they were awkwardly formed. After correcting the defects he sent them away. Again he struck the log, and there came forth Kiowas, men and women, correctly formed. To the men he gave bows and arrows. The arrows had flint points, and he taught them how to make them. He gave the women instruments for dressing skins. Soon after making the Kiowas he went to a large flat stone, which, with his gigantic strength, he raised, when out came a large herd of buffaloes. He told the Indians they were made expressly for them. Their flesh was for food. With their skins they could make lodges and clothing." He also said that he afterwards saw the great white man, who had also made a country and people. He told the Kiowas that if the white people ever came to their country they should treat them as enemies and the white people could never exterminate them.

"After a time the great Kiowa and the great white man went up in the clouds, the former to become a cluster of stars and the latter a moon, and are always watching over their works and people." Kicking Bird thought " the great Kiowa gave them bad council about the white people, and he should follow it no longer and should use his influence with others to treat the white people as friends and not as enemies."

" After death they went to a country where there is a lodge prepared for them, and where the game is always plenty and fat and the grass perpetually green. In that happy land there is neither sickness, pain or trouble."

The next day we followed Kicking Bird over some more steep and rocky ridges, and then descended into an extensive valley in the midst of the mountains, in which were camped the remainder of the Kiowas, with Lone Wolf the principal character. The Apaches and several bands of the Comanches were also camped there. They all professed friendship; but we were with the treacherous portion of the Kiowas and but little confidence could be placed in them. The Apaches, with " Pacer " the leading chief, would, I think, have behaved reasonably well had it not been for the influence of Lone Wolf's band of Kiowas.

T. C. Battey greatly enjoyed the grand, the wild and romantic scenery. J. H. Painter, with his finger, made music on a tin pan to the great merriment of the young Indians, some of whom rolled on the ground in laughter while he sedately drummed on the old basin. We had a pleasant and profitable trip. The Indians appreciated the visit of their agent. It seemed to do them good to entertain him in their camps. The next day, on returning to the agency, we met with the four Indian women prisoners sent there by Colonel McKenzie, previously mentioned.

The time for me to leave the agency had nearly arrived. The annoying Quahada Indians had been driven on to the reservation. The New Mexico and Arizona Apaches had been routed out of Texas. The Indians had learned by sad experience what the Commissioners from Washington had told them in council, and the Commisioner of Indian Affairs had told the delegation that went to Washington under Captain Alvord that it would be "war off the reservation, on it peace," and that severe retribution would be the result of their continued forays in Texas or elsewhere. More than one hundred of their women and children were prisoners in Texas. Three of their chiefs had been arrested, and two of them were then in the penitentiary for murder, and three who were ordered to be arrested and not found were displaced by the agent from being chiefs, and at that time the Indians were informed that any chief who thereafter went upon a raid would no longer be recognized as a chief. After that, until the close of his administration, the agent knew of no chief having gone on a raid. They probably did without reporting the fact to him. Displacing chiefs seemed to have a restraining effect. They evidently came nearer realizing than they had ever previously done that the Government could and would control them.

To all appearance the Indians were in a better and

more hopeful condition than they had ever been before. But to my mind the effect on the Kiowas of the promise of the release of Satanta, a daring and treacherous chief, was like a dark and rolling cloud in the Western horizon, and when he should be restored to his people in freedom, it might burst like a tornado upon innocent and unsuspecting parties. Had some other raiding Indians been sent to the penitentiary instead of releasing Satanta, it would have been in accordance with my judgment, but it was not the judgment of my superior officers, or of the Friends' Indian Committee.

My resignation took effect March 31st, 1873. In a subsequent day or two my last quarterly report was made, all the Government property transferred to my successor, James M. Haworth, and, with my wife, I left the Kiowa and Comanche agency for my Iowa home, after three years and nine months' arduous labor for the Government, and on many occasions under severe mental strain when seriously calculating what might be best and right in executing my plans.

My resignation was sincerely regretted by many of the Indians. Kicking Bird said to me: "I am sorry that you are going to leave us. You have had a hard time in trying to get us to behave. Now, as we have concluded to take your advice and follow the white man's road we would like you to remain. No other agent has treated us with the uniform kindness that you have. When you leave you will be dead to me."

A Comanche said: "The white people are very foolish. They send an agent here, and when we all get to loving him he is sent away and then have a stranger to take his place that we know nothing about." In leaving I felt thankful to my Heavenly Father for the good that He had enabled me to perform, but conscious of falling very far short of what I had hoped to accomplish.

My wife, Mary Ann Tatum, was with me at the agency about half the time during my service as Indian agent. Her heart was in the work, and she had great sympathy for the Indian women and children. She made many garments for the little "pappooses," and they were always thankfully received by the mothers. They thought that what she did was a gratuity from the kindness of her heart, while the agent did only what he was hired to do. Her care and her assistance to me were invaluable. With sickness, care and incessant duties, I was sometimes greatly worn. On one such occasion, when there were parties at the office from Texas hunting children and stolen horses, and one thing after another brought before me, until I was nearly exhausted, she persuaded me to go into the bedroom and lie down and let the men wait until I could rest awhile. When she withdrew she turned the key and told my employees that whether the commander of the post or any one else should call to see the agent he is not to be disturbed. I might not have been able to have stood the strain had it not been for her tender care.

I was superintendent of all the agency work, and as often as practicable went to the farm, school, and other places, several miles away—sometimes in the ambulance, but generally on horseback. My wife often went with me, as she enjoyed equestrian exercise, and it did us good. A Mexican Comanche woman whom she taught to make bread, use a cook stove and do other things pertaining to housekeeping, could not refrain from weeping when we were about to start home. Her "mother" was going to leave her. No other woman had ever taken so much interest in her. The Delaware women were also assisted by her; although they were living twenty-five miles from the agency, we occasionally went there. An Indian agency would be greatly lacking in usefulness without the Christian influence of women. The wives of some of my employes also greatly felt the loss of " Mrs. Tatum."

She was very kind and thoughtful in administering or sending suitable food to sick Indians when camped within reach. A sick woman who camped near the agency for some time, felt very sure that her recovery was due to the good food sent her by " agent's squaw." Horseback, a Comanche chief, camped for some time near our quarters to be treated by Dr. Tomlinson for hemorrhage of the lungs. My wife often supplied him with suitable food, but neither she nor any one else was allowed to enter his lodge wearing any red article. " It was bad medicine for hemorrhage."

MARY ANN TATUM

CHAPTER VI.

THE committee of Friends who nominated me were no doubt as much disappointed as I was, that with kindness and fair dealing the Indians would not be brought into subjection and cease their almost continuous depredations in Texas during the spring and summer. They were reasonably quiet in the autumn and winter, when their ponies were too poor for hard riding. Had the kind and honorable treatment that they were receiving by almost every person, except horse thieves and illicit traders, caused a manifest decrease in their depredations,

(165)

the Government could have afforded to bear with them; but when they were evidently growing worse, then firm restraint was the kindness that I thought was needed.

Some of the committee were of the opinion that I was too harsh. They doubted the propriety of having Satanta and others arrested. But no one ever suggested to me what action would probably have had a better effect on the Indians. We were all sadly disappointed that those "spoiled Indians" would not be brought into subjection by peaceable means.

My successor, James M. Haworth, a Friend whose heart was in the work, and wished to do what was right in the sight of God, and what was right and best for the Indians, had no doubt been informed that his predecessor had been too exacting and he should be more conciliatory. The reins of Government were slackened. The chiefs who had been deposed for raiding were reinstated, and other steps were taken to please the Indians. The agent was trying to do what was right and best. It was the sincere purpose of his heart.

Agent Haworth took charge April 1st, 1873. In two months from that time the Kiowas had had the promise of having Satanta and Big Tree restored to them. With the exception of a raid by Lone Wolf and his son, in which the latter was killed, the Kiowa chiefs had restrained their young men from raiding, and they stopped a band of Comanches from going. About the time set for them to see their brethren restored the agent re-

ceived word from Washington that on account of the
Modoc tragedy in the Rocky Mountains the order for the
release of Satanta and Big Tree had been countermanded. The Kiowas had never before heard of the
Modocs, and could see no reason why anything that they
had done should affect them. Neither could Agent Haworth, or T. C. Battey, see why that should be cause for
the Government to break its sacred promise to the
Kiowas. T. C. Battey worte to Agent Haworth that as
he was living with the Kiowas, he knew of their refusal to
join the Cheyennes in a raid on the agencies in that section, and of their restraining their " braves," as well as
some of the Comanches, from going on raids. He
thought that the promise of the Government relative to
Satanta and Big Tree should be complied with. His
letter was forwarded to the Department, and caused the
officers to reconsider their countermand. They wrote
that if the consent of the Governor of Texas could be obtained they would soon have the chiefs returned to their
people.

June 10th. 1873. During the suspense of the
return of the Kiowa chiefs the hundred Comanche
women and children prisoners held by the military in
Texas were restored, to the great joy of all the tribe.
Nearly or quite every band had representatives among
them. Captain McClermont, who conveyed them to the
agency, had difficulty in passing through nearly three
hundred miles of Texas, where there had been much suf-

fering by Indian raids, and where it was the custom to shoot an Indian on sight if possible. In approaching Jacksboro he heard that the white people had congregated there to intercept his train. He therefore sent the wagons around while he drove his ambulance into town, waiting apparently for the train to follow. He found there some thousands of armed citizens, many of them drunk, determined to prevent the return of the Indian women and children to their people. After waiting there for some time, he drove back to see what had detained his train, leaving the drunken mob in anticipation of seeing them. Thus by strategy he conveyed them safely beyond danger.

The Indians manifested very strong attachment by their demonstrations on meeting children, wives, relatives and friends. The Indians reported that ever since they were taken they had been well fed and kindly treated. The chiefs wanted to shake hands with the Captain, and some of them gave him the warm salutation of a Comanche hug. That was the first time that he had ever met an Indian in friendship. He told the agent that he was a convert of the peace policy of managing the Indians. The chiefs seemed to vie with each other in their strong assurance of good behavior. Should any of their young men in future steal horses or mules in Texas they should be taken from them as soon as they were brought to camp, and turned over to the agent to be restored to their owners; and if the Texas chiefs would restore the ponies stolen from them there would be no further occasion of war between them. Captain McClermont was very hopeful that the Comanches would be enemies no more.

During the detention of Satanta and Big Tree the Indians arranged to detain T. C. Battey in the Kiowa camp, where he was acting as teacher, until the prisoners were returned. He had been withheld four weeks without permitting him to know the cause. It was then falsely reported that the chiefs had arrived at the agency. They at once hurried in, and, as T. C. Battey was sick, they took him right to the agent's office before learning that the release of the prisoners was a false report. They then held a secret council to decide what to do. As it was held in the evening, Apache John, who suspected what was going on, had his wife, who understood the Kiowa language, to go with another woman, and secrete themselves behind the lodge and hear what was said. The women overheard the Kiowas arrange a plot for seizing Agent Haworth and T. C. Battey, and fleeing with them to the plains before the soldiers could get after them. White Horse and Running Wolf, two of the most daring, vile and treacherous members of the tribe, with three others to assist them, were selected to perform this nefarious act. The plan was to keep them as hostages until the return of the prisoners.

The plot was reported to the agent by Apache John. He told it to his wife, friend Battey, and one or two others. A few evenings after hearing of it the five Indians went to the agent's office. To show his friendship and docility, White Horse took off the belt containing his revolver, and handed it to the agent's wife. Then, sitting down in an armchair, the agent saw another revolver, and drew his attention to it, much to his confusion. T. C. Battey, being sick, was at the doctor's quarters. The Indians were treated kindly, and no intimation given that their plot was known. After being there two nights and one day, they left for their camps without their prize. The agent gave them beef, coffee and sugar for their homeward trip. They reported to their people that " the medicine of the agent and ' Thomas-sy ' were so strong that we could not touch them." They were evidently under the protection of God, and through an unseen influence He restrained those vile and hostile Indians from molesting them. Praise His name!

It may be proper here to record for the glory of God a somewhat parallel case in my own experience. While acting as agent I took my wife and Lizzie Butler, matron of the school, and the post interpreter, to the Wichita agency, thirty miles north. When we reached there we found Big Bow, whom I had displaced as chief for the reason that he was an accomplice with Satanta on his notable raid. He urged me to reinstate him. I told him that I could not have raiding chiefs. If they went off on raids I could no more recognize them as chiefs. Washington (the Government) was doing a great deal for the Indians in feeding and clothing them. The people in Texas and all the white people help to bear the expense, and it was very wrong for the Indians to be raiding on the people who were helping to feed and clothe them. We had the interview in the evening, and I talked calmly and kindly to him. He left apparently very mad. The interpreter wanted me to grant his request, as we were entirely at his mercy. He thought there was danger of his massacring all of us on our way home. I saw the danger, and after considering it the best I could in the fear of God, I thought it would be wrong to reinstate him, and did not yield to his request.

The morning of our return the agency clerk, by request of the interpreter, H. P. Jones, gave Big Bow and his men a beef. Big Bow afterwards reported that he proposed shooting me in the agent's yard, but thinking that it might cause too much of a consternation concluded to waylay us as we went home and shoot me. But after killing and dressing the beef, and filling their stomachs, he decided to let us go to our homes, and he and his men would go to theirs. The Lord, I believe, by His overruling providence shielded us from the wrath of one of the worst Kiowa Indians. To Him be the praise. (See " Quaker Among the Indians," by Thomas C. Battey," published by Lee & Shepard, Boston.)

The life of Agent J. D. Miles, at a certain time, seemed to be in imminent danger by the hand of an enraged Indian. But the Lord protected him.

It was necessary for the agents to sometimes go to Indian camps to enumerate them and for other purposes, even to the camps of hostile Indians who were in the practice of going to Texas for the purpose of murder and theft. The Friend agents and T. C. Battey, the Kiowa teacher, always went unarmed and without a military or other human guard. Our trust was in the Lord. " Trust ye in the Lord forever: for in the Lord Jehovah is everlasting strength."

It seems remarkable how the Lord has protected the non-combatant Friends from hostile Indians. From the day of William Penn to the present time I believe there is no record of a Friend being massacred by Indians, although their near neighbors have been killed by them. To the Lord be all the praise.

The Kiowas were still in suspense relative to the return of their chiefs. They could not see why it was that the Comanche prisoners could be returned from Texas at the discretion of the United States and that Satanta and Big Tree should be held by the state of Texas. The Governor of that state was making new and impracticable demands. He was acting for the state, and a large part of the citizens, especially in the northern and western portion, had no friendly feeling towards the Indians. The promise of the National Government seems to have been premature. It should not have been made to the Indians until negotiations with the Governor of Texas had been consummated. Much correspondence was going on between the Interior Department and the Govenor on the subject.

At length it was decided to forward the prisoners to Fort Sill, there to be detained in the guard-house until a council of the Indians could be held, at which the Honorable Governor Davis, of Texas, and the Honorable Commissioner of Indian Affairs, Edward P. Smith, were to be present. Meantime the Indians had done but little raiding. Lone Wolf had led a raid in Mexico, where one of his sons was killed, and a few Indians, supposed to be Comanches, had made one or two raids in Texas, where they had killed five citizens, and two Comanches had been killed. The horses that they had stolen were delivered to Agent Haworth.

Governor Davis, on arriving at Fort Sill, refused to have the council except in the post. To this the Indians objected. They said : " It was there that their chiefs were arrested, and it was a bad place." But as he would not yield his point the Indians gave up to having it there.

October 6th, 1873, four months after the time that the chiefs were to have been released, the important council convened. The Governor and Commissioner had not consulted as to what was to be said to the Indians. The Governor had his terms, to which the Indians and the Government must comply. It was enough for the Commissioner to hear them. His terms, as stated by T. C. Battey, in his " Quaker Among the Indians," who was present were: " They must settle down on farms near the agency. Government must put a white man in every camp to watch them and report their behavior to the agent. They must draw their rations in person, instead of from the chief, as heretofore, every three days. At the same time they must answer to the roll-call; place themselves under the direction of the United States Army to assist in arresting all depredating Indians; dispense with the use of their guns, horses and mules; raise cattle, hogs and corn, like the civilized Indians—Choctaws, Cherokees," etc.

In return Satanta and Big Tree, who were present, were to be remanded to the guard-house at Fort Sill, and kept there under the charge of the post commander, to be released on the future good behavior of the tribe, whenever he should be satisfied that these terms are complied with. They were not to be pardoned, but subject to re-arrest at any time upon the misdemeanor of the Kiowas, and returned to the authorities of Texas, saying, in the winding up of his speech, "I will not change these conditions."

The Indians agreed to all the conditions, provided the Governor would release the prisoners immediately without returning them to the guard-house, which he refused to do, and the council closed.

The Indians were greatly excited. A heavy gloom spread over them as well as over the white people. No one knew what might take place. The Indians had their guns, bows and arrows ready for use at a moment's warning. Little was said. Much was felt. Kicking Bird remarked to T. C. Battey: " My heart is stone. There is no soft place in it. I have taken the white man by the hand, thinking him to be a friend, but he is not a friend; Government has deceived us. Washington is rotten."

The agent saw the threatening storm, and urged the commissioner to manage in some way to fulfil the promise to release the chiefs. It seemed evident to some who were acquainted with the Kiowas that they were going to have their chiefs released peacefully if they could; if not, by force. Strong pressure was brought to bear on Governor Davis to induce him to release them. Late in the evening he sent word to the commissioner that he would meet the Indians again in the morning with a more favorable proposition.

The following morning the Indians went to the post with the determination that if the chiefs were brought into the council they should not again be remanded to the guard-house. They had arranged for certain braves to be on their horses in a position to shoot the Governor and the guard when they were ordered to take the chiefs to the guard-house, and two horses were ready for the prisoners to mount and flee. T. C. Battey, while doing all he could to pacify the Indians, and knowing their secret purpose, yet accompanied them to the post, not knowing what might take place, but hoping that the Lord would overrule and that the threatening cloud might give place to sunshine. When they reached the

Fort they learned that arrangements had been agreed upon between Commissioner E. P. Smith and Governor Davis that the chiefs were to be released, but not pardoned.

The commissioner pledged the Government that if the Kiowas again raided in Texas that either they or chiefs of equal rank were to be delivered to the Govenor of Texas to be kept in the penitentiary, and also to procure a roll-call of every male member of the tribe that was over sixteen years of age, with such frequency as to make it impossible for warriors to be absent without its being known. The Comanches were also to be brought under the same regulation as soon as practicable. The Government was also to make an effort to obtain at least five of the recent raiders to take the place of Satanta and Big Tree.

The liberated chiefs embraced the Governor. They then went to the agent's office and had some further talk before returning to their camp life. When the demand was made by the commissioner for five of the recent raiders the Indians told him that more than that number had been raiding, and they did not know which to bring in, and he must give them the names of those he wanted, which he would not do, and there were none delivered. They offered to bring in all of the horses and mules that they had stolen. They also offered to send some of their young men with a squad of soldiers to Texas, and if they found a raiding party to assist in capturing them. This proposition was accepted, the Indians understood, as a compromise. They went to Texas, but found no raiders. About that time some Texas horse-thieves went to an Indian camp and stole nearly two hundred head of horses and mules. The Wichita agent secured the arrest of one of them and recovered a few of the stolen animals.

A month after the release of the chiefs T. C. Battey went with Kicking Bird to his camp, about forty miles northwest of the agency. On their way they crossed a trail of fresh horse tracks, some of them having shoes on, showing that they were just stolen from Texas. It was afterwards learned that they were stolen by Comanches, some of whom belonged to the Wichita agency.

November 30th the agent received a telegram from Washington that the Comanches must in ten days deliver five guilty raiders, and if they failed to do it he was to cease issuing rations to all of the Comanches and withhold their annuity goods. It seemed as if the parties most guilty belonged to the Wichita agency, but no demand was made upon them.

This made hard work for the agent. Nearly all of the Comanche chiefs belonging to the agency had succeeded in restraining their young men from raiding. To him and T. C. Battey it seemed as if it would have been more just and wise to withhold the rations and annuities from the bands whose members had been raiding, and issue to those who were complying with the requisitions of the

Government, and thus punish the guilty and reward good behavior.

As the Comanches were, according to the telegram, to be returned over to the military if they failed to bring in the raiders in ten days, and there being no probability of their complying with the demand, the agent sent a written message to the Kiowas by T. C. Battey and the interpreter to come to the agency before the ten days expired, and avoid being embroiled in any difficulty with the Comanches, and get their annuity goods that were ready for them.

The Indians were far to the northwest, and it took two days to get to Kicking Bird's camp. He and the majority of his people were still farther away hunting buffalo. They went another day's journey to Lone Wolf's camp. The message was delivered to him and his people in the evening. He said that it was a matter of much importance; he must have time to consider it, and would give his answer in the morning.

Lone Wolf was one of the most treacherous and unreliable of the Kiowa chiefs. But bad as he was from the white man's standpoint, before retiring to rest he devoutly went through with the religious ceremony of making "medicine." Between the fire and his bed he scraped the ground and brushed it. After placing some coals of fire on it he sprinkled some cedar leaves and wild wormwood on the coals, which made a dense smoke. As it rose he held his hands in it, rubbed his face and naked body, held some of the smoke up to the Great Spirit, and rubbed some on the ground. They then all retired to rest.

In the morning he wished T. C. Battey to write his answer of about five hundred and fifty words to the agent. In it he said if Indians go to Texas and get killed, I think that is all right. If they kill white people, there I do not want the white people to come upon us here, for this is a country of peace. Catch them there; kill them there. If those foolish young men have killed any of the people in Texas they are dead. Some of those young men have been killed; they are dead. Let it all pass; do not let it make trouble among the living."

He sent word to the agent to " not get excited and act in a hurry. We have killed a great many buffalo, and will come in after a while, heavily loaded with skins and meat. The Kiowas have not been raiding in Texas. They have not been there." He might have added, " We have only raided in Mexico since the arrest of Satanta. I led a party there, and one of my sons was killed."

The following day, on their return to Kicking Bird's camp, they saw some Indians driving ponies, and their Indian guide insisted on going to them, although it would make a few miles further to camp. When they got near they were recognized, and " Thomas-sy, Thomas-sy " was called (their name for Thomas C. Battey). They proved to be a raiding party who had left about four months before, and had been to Mexico, and were now returning with two scalps, a few blankets, and some very inferior mules and ponies. It was dark before reaching camp, and now, as they were with a raiding party, they had to be subject to them. They placed "Thomas-sy" and Caboon, the interpreter, in front, to conduct the raiding party in triumph to their people. Striking up the " song of triumph " they slowly moved forward, occasionally varying the song with the war-whoop and the discharge of firearms. The latter was the signal that they had killed some one. Soon the women and maidens came out with singing and dancing to meet the party. When they found that the leading braves were " Thomas-sy " and Caboon they thought it a grand imposition, and laughed heartily over it. But they soon discovered that in their rear were their long absent raiders, and the singing and dancing were resumed, and they were royally conducted into camp.

It shows with what distinguished honor the raiders were received. Here were the women and maidens treating the heroes, the murderers, with the greatest honor they were capable of bestowing. In this manner the whole camp encouraged the forays of the young " braves." It was the " Indian road " without the gospel of the Lord Jesus.

When the agent's message was interpreted to Kicking Bird he was greatly cast down. He was confident that the Comanches would not take in the raiders. " It was

a new road, one that our fathers have never traveled."
He feared that it would involve the Comanches in trouble, and their trouble would receive the sympathy of the
Indians of the three agencies. If one tribe was involved
they would all be brought into difficulty. " Washington
was strong, but could not kill all the Indians in one year;
it would take two or three, perhaps four years to kill all
the Indians, and then the earth will turn to water or
burn up. It is our mother, and cannot live when the
Indians are all dead."

There were five other chiefs camped with Kicking
Bird, and T. C. Battey made a long, earnest and pathetic
address to them, urging them to take the agent's advice
and move into the agency before the ten days expired,
get their annuity goods and rations, and by that means
show their friendship to their agent, who loved them, and
who would do all that he could to keep them out of any
difficulty that might come upon the Comanches. They had
promised to behave if they could get their women and
children from Texas, and then, when they were restored
to them, they had gone right off to Texas on raids. At
the close of his address the Indians decided to take his
advice, go to the agency, and camp where the agent directed.

As they proceeded to the agency they heard of several
small companies of Comanches who had gone on raids to
Texas. It seemed as if a prominent object might be to
show their defiance. One chief had for years been tell-

ing different agents that had been there that "if Washington don't want my young men to raid in Texas then Washington must move Texas clear away, where my young men can't find it." This was his mode of saying that his young men would raid there as they please, and the Government could not hinder them.

The agent received another telegram to continue issuing rations until further orders, and to issue to the Comanches three-fourths of their annuity goods. Now to continue issuing to them immediately after many of them began raiding would convey the idea to the Indians that the depredations on Texas were the cause of the issue of rations being continued. Such vacillation was bad for the Indians, and added to the labor and perplexity of the agent.

The autumn and early winter of 1873 were unusually favorable for the Indian to procure buffalo robes and meat for drying. With the robes they could purchase many desired articles of the authorized traders, and the hostile Indians purchased of illicit traders revolvers and ammunition.

Evidently as a preparation for more than the usual amount of forays, a Quahada Comanche claimed to have miraculous power to raise the dead, to go up into heaven and converse with the Great Spirit, and to produce from his stomach any quantity of cartridges, and to affect the cartridges of soldiers and white people that they could not injure the Indians, although they might be standing right in front of their guns when discharged. The Indians generally seemed to believe what he told them, and many were afraid to disobey him or to go contrary to his wish through fear of being affected by his " medicine."

The Indian Department was uneasy as to what might be the result. Members of Congress thought it time for the soldiers to stop the raiding, as it had not been accomplished by peaceable means. A portion of " The Executive Committee of Friends on Indian Affairs " went to Washington, and proposed before any change was made for some of them to have a council with the southwestern Indians. Accordingly it was arranged for Dr. James E. Rhoads and Thomas Wistar, members of the committee, with Marmaduke C. Cope, all of Philadelphia, to visit them and see if they could be prevailed upon " to behave " without the harsh measure that was in contemplation. Thomas Wistar and James E. Rhoads had previously visited them a number of times. The former was far advanced in life. He had for many years before visited the Cherokees and other Indians in the southern states, and had visited Indian tribes on the bank of the Mississippi, where St. Louis now stands. Dr. Rhoads was in delicate health. It seemed as though these two dear friends to the Indians would have sacrificed their own lives could it have been the means of so revolutionizing them that they would cease raiding, and have their hearts filled with love instead of hatred and revenge.

At Lawrence, Kansas, they were joined by Cyrus Beede, Superintendent Hoag's clerk, and Wm. Pickerel, of Iowa. Thomas Wistar and Dr. Rhoads pleaded with the Indians as brethren whose hearts were filled with the love of God and love towards them. They told them that unless they ceased their depredations there was trouble awaiting them. They wanted to show them how they might avoid it, and preserve peace and happiness not only for themselves, but for their children. They were reminded of the sacred promise of the Kiowas that if Satanta and Big Tree were released they would cease raiding. The Comanches promised " that if the hundred women and children who were held prisoners by the soldiers in Texas were released they would cease raiding, and would settle down, would send their children to school, and would do as their agent wished." The Comanches were told that they violated their pledge. They have been raiding in Texas. They have killed many people there, and run off their horses and mules. Now they would have to quit raiding or the peace agents that they had been having would be taken from them, and they would be turned over to the soldiers. C. Beede told them that if they were turned over to the soldiers they would find that Washington's hand would be as heavy as his heart had been kind.

The Indians replied that they were sorry that Washington's heart got tired so quickly. They did not get tired of trying to keep their young men from raiding.

DR. JAMES E. RHOADS

They thought that Washington ought to be more patient. One of the young men, addressing the Friends, said: " It matters not what the chiefs said in council with the whites. We, the young men, are the warriors, and shall not listen to them or any one else. We shall do as we please. Washington may be a big chief among white people, but he is not our chief, and he has nothing to do with us. We shall not be controlled by him." After some further remarks made by the Friends the council adjourned about April 5th, 1874.

The agents of the three agencies, the committee of Friends, and the Indian Department had done what they could to bring the Indians to a realizing sense of their dangerous condition. But the Comanches and Cheyennes would not hearken to them. They and one Kiowa chief " smoked the war pipe " together. Neither the Arapahoes or Wichita and Affiliated Bands smoked with them.

Soon after the council, Kicking Bird was misrepresented, or, rather, lied about by one of the chiefs, so as to bring him into disrepute with his people, and he thought that the agent had not treated him right in forwarding a speech of " Big Bow," given in council, to the Commissioner of Indian Affairs, instead of sending his own, which had been given in private. It seemed to him that " the agent had thrown him away," and had taken in his place Big Bow, an accomplice of Satanta in his Texas raid. He could not understand why a speech given in council, on behalf of the tribe, should be more official than his own speech given in private talk. Now, as he was " thrown away " by his tribe and by the agent he was wholly dejected. T. C. Battey had an interview with him in the trader's store. He assured him of the esteem in which the agent regarded him, and of his own friendship, love and sympathy. This was shared by the proprietor and all of the clerks in the store. When he left the agency a few hours before he thought it likely that they would not soon see him there again. "He might forsake the white man's road that he had been following for four or five years."

T. C. Battey proposed that, as a token of the love, friendship and sympathy that they all entertained for Kicking Bird, they make him a present of some things that would be valuable to him, and would, when he looked upon them, remind him that he had warm friends among the white people. The proposition met with a hearty concurrence, and he was asked to select what he wanted of anything in the store. T. C. Battey presented him with a woven coverlet. Other valuable presents were given him. His heart was cheered, and he promised to be back in thirteen days. They saw that it was his purpose to continue " on the good road " that he had for years been following. One of the clerks re-marked that the talk that T. C. Battey gave Kicking Bird that day was worth to the Government $50,000. If it prevented him from joining the hostile Indians, which it probably did, then $50,000 would represent but a fraction of its value. There was no other chief in the three agencies who could manage Indian warriors with as much generalship as could Kicking Bird. This had been proven to some of the army officers before he had taken " the white man's road."

About one month after the Friends' council, in the beginning of May, 1874, the Comanches stole a number of horses and mules belonging to the agency and a larger number belonging to private parties. Animals which had been stolen from a Wichita Indian, and the mules used at the schoolhouse were returned. They also returned some of the most inferior ones that they had stolen. In the beginning of June " the great medicine man " and chiefs with him sent word to the agent " that they should commit no further depredations about the agency, provided the soldiers behaved themselves and did not molest them. But if the soldiers interfered with them they should go to the agency and kill all they could. This word was sent as a fair warning to them. The remainder of the animals stolen from the agency and that vicinity would not be returned until fall to make peace with ! " They were doing much raiding in Texas, where twenty-four Indians were killed, two of whom, Agent Haworth, in his annual report states, were Kiowas, the others being Comanches.

The Comanches, under the direction of the new " miracle working medicine chief," had a " medicine dance " similar to the annual one of the Kiowas. It was probably the only one in their history. The Cheyennes also attended it. There they were told by the " medicine chief " that " he had been up above the clouds, and had conversed with the Great Spirit, who told him that then was the time for them to avenge the death of their brethren who had recently been killed in Texas while raiding. As he, through his great medicine, had so affected the guns of white men that they could not kill Indians, there would be little if any danger of the warriors being hurt." After they were through with the dance the medicine chief led a party on a raid in Texas, where there were seven Comanches and five Cheyennes killed, which was proof of the statement that his medicine was not efficient. At the Kiowa medicine dance strong efforts were made by the Comanches and Cheyennes to get the Kiowas to join them. Lone Wolf and one or two other chiefs, with their people, decided to do so. Kicking Bird positively refused to join them. He was the leader of the friendly and larger portion of the tribe.

For some time previous to this the Indian commissary stores of coffee, sugar and flour had run short, or were entirely exhausted, at all three of the agencies. The " running short " was no fault of the agents. They did all they could to prevent it. Also, there had been a large number of ponies stolen from the Indians, some of them taken to Texas and some to Kansas, and a great amount of whiskey had been bartered to the Indians by illicit traveling traders. Here were three causes to make the Indians dissatisfied, if not hostile.

A large portion of the Comanches, some of the Kiowas, and a considerable number of the Cheyennes decided to go on " the war path," measure their strength with the Government troops, and apparently expecting in the fall to dictate terms of peace.

The authorities at Washington ordered the friendly Indians to go to their agencies, to be registered, and to camp where ordered, and " not mingle with the war element." The first fight was at the Wichita agency, August 22d, 1874. Satanta had gone to the agency and had been enrolled as friendly, but he had left without permission, and he was at the Wichita agency at the time of the fight. He fled to the Cheyenne and Arapahoe agency, and was there arrested. As he had been paroled on his good behavior, he was returned to the penitentiary in Texas. After remaining in prison several years he committed suicide.

The Indians were pursued by the troops under the command of General Davidson throughout the summer with very little fighting, and in the autumn and winter instead of the Indians dictating terms of peace when they wished to quit " the war path " and go to the agency for rations and annuity goods, General Davidson dictated the terms, which were an unconditional surrender. The men were put in prison, the chiefs being ironed. In

October Tab-a-nan-e-ka, the leading chief of the Qua-hada band of Comanches, with several other chiefs and their people, surrendered, giving up their arms, horses and mules, and were put in prison. In mid-winter two of the General's scouts went to a Quahada camp about one hundred and fifty miles southwest of the agency, and induced several other chiefs and their people, number-ing one hundred and eighty-five, to go to the agency and surrender. They gave up their arms and more than seven hundred head of live stock. Colonel McKenzie relieved General Davidson in the winter, and gave back some of the stock to the Indians. Seven hundred and sixty horses and mules were shot or died; one hundred were given to the Tonkawa Indians of Texas, who were guides and trailers for the soldiers; five hundred and fifty were given to white military scouts. The remainder were sold at auction at from three to six dollars per head. At that low price the confiscated stock of the Kiowas and Co-manches brought twenty-two thousand dollars. This sum was invested principally in sheep by the Military Department, which were given in small flocks to the In-dians. The wolves and Indian dogs and other causes soon destroyed them. Some cows were also bought with the horse fund and given to the Indians, which proved to be a good investment.

Agent J. D. Miles, of the Cheyenne and Arapahoe agency, in his annual report for 1874, gives the follow-ing statement: "At the time of making my last annual report a majority of the Cheyennes were hostile and at war with the Government. During the fall of 1874 small parties continued to arrive at the agency and surrender themselves prisoners of war; but it was not until the 6th of March, 1875, that the main Cheyenne village under Gray Beard, Heap-o-Birds, Stone Calf, Bull Bear and minor chiefs surrendered to General Neil, a short distance from the agency, and were promptly disarmed and placed under guard, and their ponies confiscated and sold. A more wretched and poverty-stricken community than these people presented after they were placed in prison camps it would be difficult to imagine. Bereft of lodges and the most ordinary cooking opparatus, with no ponies or other means of transportation for wood or water, half-starved, and very little to eat, and scarcely anything that could be called clothing, they were truly objects of pity; and for the first time the Cheyennes seemed to realize the power of the Government and their own inability to cope successfully therewith."

Of the hostile element thirty-two men and one woman were selected to be punished. The woman was identified by Catharine and Sophia German as having taken part in the murder of their parents, brother and sister, on the Smoky Hill River in Kansas, on the 13th of September, 1874.

On the 27th of April the Cheyennes, except those selected for further punishment, were formally turned over to the charge of Agent J. D. Miles. He personally attended to a registration of the tribe, the adult males by name, the women and children by count, and assured them that they were again at peace with the Government, and so long as they behaved properly they should receive food and protection.

Agent Miles reported that the Arapahoes remained peaceable during the year and friendly to the Government. "They have made some rapid strides in the avenues leading to civilization and further usefulness." The Arapahoe children in school made very satisfactory progress.

The school in the Kiowa and Comanche agency was also in a prosperous condition. The students, however, were almost wholly Caddoes belonging to another agency, as the Kiowas and Conmanches would not send their children there while they were raiding and fighting.

When the Comanches began stealing horses and mules from the agency and vicinity, the matron and seamstress were informed by some Kiowas that the Comanches were contemplating to carry them to their camps. At length a Kiowa told them that the fourth sleep from then was the time set to carry them off. As it was nearly time for vacation they left for their homes in Kansas before "the fourth sleep." That night there were Indians prowling around the schoolhouse, and there was a noise heard at the window that opened into their room, as though parties on the outside were trying to open it. Not obtaining the women, they stole a mule and a pony from near the schoolhouse.

After the Indians had made an unconditional surrender, and the war was closed, it was decided to further punish a certain number of the worst characters. For this purpose there were selected eighteen Comanches, twenty-six Kiowas, twenty-eight Cheyennes, and two Arapahoes. The Arapahoes were doubtless innocent parties who had in no way taken part with the hostile element. They were " cut off " of the line by order of the military officer without investigating charges against them.

These seventy-four prisoners of war were sent in irons to Fort Marion, St. Augustine, Florida, in care of Captain R. H. Pratt, of Tenth Cavalry. In their confinement he gave such of them school facilities as wished to learn. There was also missionary labor extended to them. After three years' confinement Captain Pratt was ordered to return them to their agencies. Twenty-two of the young men wished to remain in the east and attend school. In this they were encouraged by Captain Pratt. He conceived the idea that " in order to get civilization into the Indian, the Indian must be brought into civilization." As there were no Government funds applicable for the education of those Indians, benevolent parties who had become interested in them furnished the necessary means. Seventeen of them were placed in the Hampton School, at Hampton Roads, Virginia, designed for colored pupils, and five more were placed in other schools. Here were some of the incorrigible Kiowas, Comanches and Cheyennes of four years ago, who had been brought under restraint, separated from their tribal influence, and kindly corrected; now, rather than return to their people, they wished to remain in civilization, and to acquire an education and preparation for useful business life.

When on one of my visits to the Cheyenne and Arapahoe agency, in 1878, " Howling Wolf " of that agency, in answer to questions, related to me some of his experiences as follows: " When a young man, while rambling around and raiding with my comrades, I used to sometimes think that I was doing wrong in some things, for I knew a little about God, but I did not think it wrong to raid and fight, which I now believe to be wrong, for I was an Indian and thought and acted as an Indian. I wanted to be a leader and went into sin, for which I was taken a prisoner, and with others sent to St. Augustine. There I learned much more about the Great Spirit, who caused me to realize that I had done very wrong. I wanted to throw away all of my bad deeds. I asked God to take away my bad heart, and give me a good heart. The Great Spirit heard me, and gave me a good heart. Then I felt happy. I often got tired of my confinement, and felt very uncomfortable. When feeling thus I sometimes took the Bible and held it open before me, and that gave me comfort, although I could not read it.

" I threw away my old road, and took the road of the Bible, which I believe is God's road. Now I am holding on to that good road. Since coming here to the school to work I talk to the boys and girls, urging them to take the good Bible road. I also talk to the people at camp about God's road. I urge all the Indians, Cheyennes and Arapahoes, to take the Bible road that they also may be happy."

" May 3d, 1875, Kicking Bird died. Although he was only in middle life he was the leading chief of the Kiowa Indians, and for at least six years previous to his death his influence was always on the side of right. He lived to see the hostile element of his tribe brought into subjection, and all of the Indians in the Indian Territory on friendly terms with the Government, which was a great satisfaction to him.

In 1876 a Comanche broke into a store and stole some goods. Agent Haworth called a council of the chiefs on the subject, and they decided to arrest him, return the stolen goods, and confine him in the guard-house for some months. A Kiowa was arrested by his own people for stealing a horse, and he was put into the guard-house. Another Kiowa was arrested for killing his wife, and was turned over to the agent for such punishment as he saw proper to inflict, with the request that his life might be spared. He was confined for several months, most of the time with ball and chain, working around the garrison in full view of his people. This was a great change from 1874, when they would rather have a war than to permit a few of their people to be arrested for raiding.

In 1876 the Indians of the agency were ready to send their children to school. The house was enlarged so as to admit seventy-two pupils, boys and girls, nearly equally divided. Kiowa, Comanche and Apache languages were spoken. On Sabbath the students and some of the older Indians attended church service.

After the school was opened a young Kiowa told the agent that he wished to go to school. He was informed that he was too late in applying; that the house was full. He said: " Can't you make room for one more. Me want to go to school." He seemed so earnest about it that the agent told him that they would see if there could be room made for him, and to return at a certain time and he would inform him. On his return the agent told him that the teachers had concluded to take him into the school. Now what is your name? " Hant got no name," he replied; " Me throw Kiowa away, and throw name with Kiowa. You give me name." I will call you Joshua," said Agent Haworth. " Josh-u-a," repeated the boy. " That good. But white man has two names. Me want nother name." " Joshua Given, I will name you." " Josh-u-a Giv-en, Josh-u-a Giv-en," he slowly repeated. " That good, that my name." So he entered the boarding-school registered Joshua Given (the name of the agency physician).

The boy made good progress in his studies. From there

he was sent to Carlisle, Pennsylvania, and attended the large Indian school at that place, under the supervision of Captain Pratt. Through the religious influence of the institution he was converted, and as he believed that he was called of God to preach, he studied for the ministry, and returned to his people a minister of the Gospel of Christ.

A number of the Kiowas and Comanches, after the war of 1874 and 1875, were ready to locate and do something at farming and raising cattle. To encourage them in that a few houses were built for them at Government expense.

The great scourge and curse that was resting heavily upon the Indians of the three agencies was the horse-thieves from Texas and Kansas. In 1877 Agent J. D. Miles, in his annual report, states that there were one hundred and sixty horses stolen from the Cheyenne and Arapahoe Indians while they were hunting buffalo, which he valued at four thousand dollars. The white employees who were with them recovered forty-four and arrested one of the thieves. Large numbers were also stolen from the Indians of the Wichita agency and of the Kiowa and Comanche agency. These depredations had been going on for a number of years. It was seldom that any of the horses were recovered.

Agent Haworth states in his annual report for 1875 that the Apaches took no part whatever in the war of

1874 and 1875, but were cultivating some land in the vicinity of Mount Scott, and the horse-thieves made raids on their stock. " I think the estimate of two thousand head of stock—horses, ponies and mules—as stolen from the Indians of this agency not too high."

When horse-thieves were arrested they had to be taken to Fort Smith, Arkansas, for trial in the United States Court. The witness fee was not sufficient to pay the traveling expenses in going and returning. Witnesses therefore, not only had to loose their time, but a part of the expense. Consequently some parties would keep the knowledge of theft to themselves rather than be subject to so great a loss by being witnesses. A white person might steal a herd of horses from Indians,—one hundred, more or less,—and according to United States law the thief, if convicted, could be sentenced to the penitentiary not to exceed one year. The punishment seemed very inadequate.

Agent Haworth managed the affairs as United States Indian Agent five years, when his health failed, and he resigned. In his last annual report, dated August 15th, 1877, he states: " I believe the year has been one of advancement in the road of civilization by the Indians of the agency, many of whom have manifested a willingness to cast aside many of the customs which characterize the wild Indian, and assume in their stead those of the white man, which, as far as we have had means to do with, we have endeavored to encourage." He was very hopeful that they would take good care of the few stock cattle that had been furnished them.

The religious meeting held each Sabbath in the school-house was attended not only by students, but also by a number of the grown Indians, who seemed interested in them, and they wished to learn more of the white man's religion. The following is the Lord's Prayer interpreted into Comanche:

THE LORD'S PRAYER IN COMANCHE.

MATT. VI. 9–13.

Our Father, which art in heaven,
Täh Afpä, pĕrkŭne tōmōvät,

Hallowed be Thy name,
Mōhoits sŭicŭt Uh nänia,

Thy kingdom come,
Pun′ĭht pĕrnĕ′mänärk täm′ŭcrĕckĭn,

Thy will be done in earth, as it is in heaven,
Täh sō′kōnäk Uh pee pŭn′eūne mahän′ĕn, Uh pĕrkŭne hīäōwīte,

Give us this day our daily bread,
Icistse täbä nĕmēmähk nĕmētĕhkärō,

Forgive us our debts, as we forgive our debtors,
Tähn hŏcŏniht nĕmēsutīne, Un hiätänä′sŭtīwīte tähsutī′ne,

Lead us not into temptation, but deliver us from evil,
Tähkesŭäf pit kä tätshockäwīte, käsŭä tähn wēärō,

For Thine is the kingdom, and the power, and the the glory, forever. Amen.
Un simōyĕrōkäwect pŭnicks hĭn nämähcōcŭt, ter hin hanĭt, ĕrie naniavī, känăckämīwitē. Soonēnähän.

P. B. Hunt, an Episcopalian, succeeded Agent Haworth April 1st, 1878. One month after he took charge the prisoners sent to Fort Marion, Florida, were returned, after three years' confinement. The war of subjection under General Miles and that punishment seemed to have effectually subdued the Kiowas, Comanches and Cheyennes, which were the tribes that for many years had given much trouble to the general Government and the state of Texas. Settlers could then locate west of their reservations, which they dared not do previously.

During Agent Hunt's administration the agency buildings near Fort Sill were abandoned, and new ones were erected thirty miles northward, on the south bank of the Washata River, opposite the agency for the Wichita and affiliated bands, and the two agencies were consolidated. The removal from Fort Sill was urged by myself when I was agent, and by Agent Haworth, as well as by special Indian commissioners. For many reasons, some of which have previously been given, the soldiers and Indians should be kept as far apart as practicable when not in open hostility. The Indians should have religious agents who are acquainted with the practical duties of agriculture and horticulture, and religious teachers and other employees. The religion of the Lord Jesus is the only efficient and permanent civilizing influence.

CHAPTER VII.

THE Wichita and affiliated bands of Indians were located between the Wichita and Canadian Rivers, immediately west of the Chickasaw nation; and their reservation extended westward nearly twenty miles, and about ten or twelve miles wide. The Indians thought it a very small reservation for one thousand and sixteen Indians. As far back as the Wichitas and some other of the bands could trace their history they had been cultivating small patches of corn, tobacco and vegetables about the Wichita Mountains and along the Wichita River. A few Delawares had been forced or had drifted from the Atlantic coast to that western region. They were all peaceable, and many of them wanted fields. My predecessors in office, Brevet Major-General W. B. Hazen and Agent Boon, made arrangements for having plowing done for them, which was continued by me until there were eight hundred and fifty acres plowed for them in 1869.

In 1870 funds were furnished to purchase agricultural implements for those Indians, but there were no funds to build them a schoolhouse, which they were desirous of having.   I had urged that as those Indians were advanced in civilization so far beyond the Kiowas and Comanches that they should have a separate agency.   Jonathan Richards was appointed their agent in 1871.   That year he erected buildings and started a school.

In 1872 he erected a substantial saw-mill, with a shingle and lathe machine.   He also prepared for grinding wheat and bolting the flour.   He also erected needed buildings at the agency, and a few houses for his Indians.   They cultivated several hundred acres of corn. Some of them had hogs, and many of them had cattle. Many of them had corn to sell in the fall. Caddo George sold a number of sacks of shelled corn to a trader, who, after paying for the corn, discovered a stone in the centre of each sack, and asked the Indian about it.   He explained it by saying, "White man, him cheat Ingen heep; Ingen, him cheat white man little."   He thought that explanation should satisfy the trader.

Liquor dealers would sometimes barter liquor for ponies in order to learn where they kept their herds, and then they would go afterwards and steal ponies.

The Wichita and some other tribes of that agency had grass wigwams. They made a frame work by sticking some small holes into the ground about three feet or more apart, and then bending them over, so as to come nearly together at the top. On the outside of these were tied smaller poles the proper distance apart. After the frame work was made it was neatly and securely thatched with grass. When completed their lodges would effectually shed the rain and protect the inmates from the storms. The fire for cooking and warming was made in the center. The tents were generally circular, and were from twenty to thirty feet in diameter, with openings for ventilation and light, and with doors on opposite sides of the tent. Between the openings on either side stakes were driven into the ground a few feet from the sides to support their beds, which were about fifteen inches high, made of buffalo robes and blankets. The grass houses had much the appearance of well-built haystacks. I think they generally used buffalo lodges in the winter, as they were a better protection from wind and cold.

In the first three years of his administration Agent Richards expended for improving the condition of the Indians eighty-two thousand, two hundred and eighty dollars. This was exclusive of the annuity goods and rations, which were purchased and transported by other parties. In his annual report for 1873 the agent made the following statement: About the 6th of May Es-sad-a-ma, head chief of the Wichitas, was murdered by a band of Osages. He had obtained a " pass " from the agent to hunt buffalo, and had gone to the plains for that purpose with some of his men. In the chase he became separated from his men, and, falling in with a small party of Osages, after exchanging salutations, apparently friendly, they killed him without any known cause. The Wichitas were thrown into a high state of excitement when the information reached their village, and preparations were about to be made for retaliation. The sympathies of the whole affiliated band was enlisted in a general banding together for a war against the Osages, and in a few days they had the offer of the assistance of the Kiowas and Comanches of the Kiowa agency, and of the Indians of the agency for the Cheyennes and Arapahoes. But information of the murder was brought to the agency as soon as it was known, and a council was called, in which a more moderate course was urged, when it was concluded to endeavor to settle the matter by negotiations and a demand for the murderer.

I. T. Gibson, the agent for the Osage Indians, refers thus to the subject in his report: "A superstitious custom prevails among the Osages of taking the life of an enemy soon after the death of a friend or relative, founded on the belief that the spirit of the departed cannot rest until a sacrifice has been made for them. A son of one of the head men of the tribe went into mourning on account of the death of his wife, and led a party of young men to the plains to seek a victim. They met Es-sad-a-wa, chief of the Wichita Indians, hunting buffalo near the salt plains. They professed to believe he was designed by the Great Spirit for them, and they killed and scalped him; then returned to the reservation, when the customary scalp dance was held, and then the mourning ceased

"The information soon came to this office of the murder of the distinguished chief. The Osages, fearing the consequence of this rash act of their young men, and apprehending an attack from the plains' Indians, collected together for defence. This greatly impeded the operations of those who were endeavoring to plant their crops. The chiefs and leading men severely condemned the act, and sent a letter to the Wichitas, offering satisfaction. A delegation of thirty-eight Wichitas visited this agency soon afterwards, and accepted from the Osages money, ponies, blankets, guns, etc., to the amount of fifteen hundred dollars as compensation and satisfaction."

Here was an instance of the averting of a war between Indian tribes by the intervention of the peace agents of the contending tribes. Had the Plains Indians joined the Wichitas against the Osages it would no doubt have been a disastrous war to all of them, and very especially to the Osages.

Agent Gibson records: "A similar mourning party soon afterwards killed a white man on the plains, but was also mortally wounded himself. This custom of the Indians has all the sacredness of a religious duty, and

I apprehend that more victims have been sacrificed by them than was heretofore supposed. Information can now be had through the employees at the different stations and confidential Indians, of the formation of these parties, which require several days' ceremony to perfect, and by persuasion, gifts and threats all of them have since been broken up."

At a subsequent time I was visiting the Osage agency when a " mourning scalp " was desired. An Indian discovered a substitute. He claimed to have found a stone the shape of a man's head, with something grown on it similar to hair. I was in the station when he brought in the highly prized stone head, and the Indians assembling to take part in the " scalp dance," I was anxious to see the substitute, and waited an hour or two, as he would not exhibit it until they were about ready to commence the dance. At length he carefully and devoutly removed the covering as though it was very sacred. There was then brought to view a stone taken from the creek, upon which long green moss had grown. In some parts of that agency the bed of the creeks presented a very green appearance by the long moss grown on the stones and waving in the clear water.

In the estimation of the Indian here was a stone so near the shape of a man's head upon which moss was grown that it was to take the place of a human scalp in the long accustomed " scalp dance " for a deceased loved one. After seeing the substitute I was ready to leave without seeing the dance, thankful that some lifeless thing had been found to take the place of human sacrifice. But how sad that a tribe of people should be living near the centre of the nation with such heathen customs. Since that time, about 1878, some of the Osages have been converted and have abandoned their heathen ceremonies.

Agent Richards was very fortunate in obtaining the services of Dr. Fordyce Grinnell for agency physician. He was skillful in his profession, and he and his wife were gifted of God for personal religious work with the Indians, besides the part they took in church services held at the agency. About fifteen or twenty of the Indians were converted, principally through their instrumentality. They gave satisfactory evidence that through repentance for past sins and prayer to God for forgiveness, and faith in Christ as the Saviour, they had been accepted of Christ as his followers. The agent, his wife, and all the Friends connected with the agency, were thankful for the change of heart that had taken place.

At this point a grave difficulty was presented. What shall be done with these uncouth Christian Indians? The agent and his wife were educated, refined Philadelphia Friends. It would hardly seem consistent to take these Indians, some dressed in citizen's clothes and some wearing blankets, into church membership with those living in the City of Brotherly Love, although equally, so far as appeared, the children of God. In addressing them we could call them "brothers," because we were all created by the same Supreme Being, and his love alike extended to all, and the " precious blood of Christ " shed for the redemption of blanket Indians as well as the college student or quiet Quaker.

" The Associated Executive Committee of Friends on Indian Affairs," who had the oversight of all the work as well as the nominating of agents, had made no provision for taking care of the lambs after being born into the fold of Christ. They rejoiced in the evidence of spiritual birth, but there was no provision at that time made by the committee or by any of the Yearly Meetings of Friends by which these Indians could receive the fostering care of the church. They seemed to be orphans, and they felt it.

At length a white man went there, claiming to be a Baptist minister, and he offered them membership in his church, and they unhesitatingly accepted him and his offer, the only one that had been presented to them of being taken into church membership. Agent Williams, successor to Agent Richards, sawed lumber and shingles for them, and they put up a plank building for a meeting-house. Slabs with legs put into them were their seats. They moved on smoothly for a time, until their preacher stated in one of his sermons that there was no definite experience in the Christian religion, and people would not know until death whether they were ordained for heaven or hell! This was so different from the teaching they had heard from Friends, and contrary to their experience, that they at once forsook their minister, and would go no more to hear him preach. He left them again to be orphans. After a time the Baptist Church sent them an Indian minister, a spiritually-minded man, who taught as the Friends did, that the Holy Spirit not only convicted a man for sin so that he knew it, but when his sins were pardoned he made that equally clear in a happy experience.

Agent Richards seems to have been very successful with his manual labor boarding-school. He enlarged the building as the children who wished to attend school multiplied. In 1875 his report states: "When the school building is completed there will be accommodation for all the children of the agency, and the house and the ar-arrangements, which are for a manual labor school, will be substantial and of first-class order. The school has been eminently successful, and the desire shown by the adult Indians for the education of the children has very much increased, and the advancement made by the students has been constant, and in some instances peculiarly marked and rapid."

In 1874 the agent had an orchard planted of nearly five hundred trees " of the best varieties of apples, cherries, pears and peaches, for summer, fall and winter use; also he planted grape-vines, blackberry and raspberry plants, rhubarb and other things of similar kind which are so desirable at such an institution."

The sixth annual report of Agent Richards, dated September 1st, 1875, was his last report. He was a faithful and energetic agent. Under his administration there was a marked advancement in civilization, and some of his Indians were converted to Christ. His resignation took effect March 31st, 1876.

A. C. Williams, a Friend, was his successor. During the summer of 1876 there was a council convened for the Indians of that agency to consider the adoption of a constitution submitted by the Okmulgee council of the civilized Indians. After considering it for three days they decided that they did not know enough about constitutions, laws and politics to meddle with them, but would wait until their children were educated, and then they could take hold of them. The agent reported that the school had been in successful operation during the past year, except the usual summer vacation. The number of names on the roll was one hundred and three. Philadelphia Friends were very helpful in furnishing supplies and helps for the school from its beginning.

Agent Williams reported that " religious services had been held weekly without any intermission during the past year, generally attended by the agency employees, and frequently by some adult Indians. The school children also receive daily religious instruction in addition to the weekly Sabbath School exercises." He also reports that his Indians " sold to the traders buffalo robes, deer skins and firs to the amount of twenty thousand, four hundred dollars." The maturing crop of corn was estimated at forty-five thousand bushels, and a good supply of vegetables was grown.

He, as well as his predecessor, had for years been greatly annoyed with white men dealing in whiskey and stealing horses. More than a hundred horses and mules were stolen from the Indians during the year. A part of them were recovered, and two of the thieves were arrested and convicted. He, with all of the Indian agents who had served in that part of the territory, felt the pressing need of a court nearer than Arkansas where criminals could be tried.

There were a few families of Delaware Indians living in the northeastern part of the Kiowa and Comanche reservation, and belonging to that agency, who were living on little farms that the Kiowa agent had plowed for them, and he had also supplied them with lumber for flooring and other purposes in building their loghouses. They were independent farmers, having no chief and needing none that the Kiowa agent could see, each family being independent, as are the farmers in the states. Agent Richards seemed to see the subject differently, and encouraged them to join the Caddoes and come under their chief, and return to the tribal and clanish habits of other Indians. He also encouraged them to abandon their farms and houses, and move onto the Caddo land and commence anew, which they declined to do.

To the writer this advice seems to have been a mistake. It would, in his estimation, be much better to dispense with all of the chiefs as the Indians become civilized, and each family be independent, as the Delawares were on their farms, living far enough apart to have their stock and effects to themselves, and subject only to the laws of civilization. After the Kiowa and Wichita agencies were consolidated Agent Hunt enumerated the Delawares separately.

In September, 1878, Agent Williams was relieved by the two agencies being consolidated, and P. H. Hunt, the agent of the Kiowas and Comanches, had charge also of the Wichita and affiliated bands. He appears to have made a good and efficient agent. Soon as practicable he had a schoolhouse and other buildings erected at the new site for the agency, on the south bank of the Wachita River. The schoolhouse was well patronized by Indian children, and affairs generally moved smoothly and satisfactorily, with the exception of the pernicious horse-thieves. He authorized the Indians to immediately follow the horse-thieves, and capture them and their ponies without waiting for a detachment of troops. That plan seemed to work well. When the thieves saw the Indians in pursuit they would abandon the stolen herd and flee. They overtook a stolen herd " on Peace River, in Texas, about one hundred and fifty miles from wheie they were taken, and captured them."

In his report for 1879 he states: "No minister of the gospel has been stationed among the Kiowas and Comanches, but they have been several times during the year visited by missionaries. The Rev. Mr. Murron, Major Ingalls and Mr. Lawrie Tatum have each visited the agency in the prosecution of their good work. Rev. John McIntosh, a Creek, has been working faithfully among the Wichitas and affiliated bands, and the result of his labors has been very gratifying. There is a small church building on the reservation, and in several of the camps arbors have been erected, and every Sabbath a religious service is held at one of the places with a very large attendance. There is a church organization which numbers fifty members, and additions are being made nearly every week."

As Agent Hunt was an Episcopalian, the consolidation of the two agencies severed the official connection of Friends with those two agencies, but not the interest for the welfare of the Indians. Some had been converted through their instrumentality, and very many had been benefited by them, and some of them had caused great anxiety, care and solicitude of agents, employees, the committee, and Government officials at Washington.

The commissioner's report for 1897 does not give the census of the Kiowa agency.

The number of Indians in the consolidated agency in 1879 and 1895:

	1879.	1895.
Kiowa	1138	1037
Comanche	1552	1507
Apache	315	226
Caddo	543	498
Wichita, Waco, Towaconie, Kuchi and Delaware	569	453

Captain Frank D. Baldwin, of the United States Army, acting Indian agent of Kiowa and Comanche agency, in his annual report for 1897, states that the Indians of that agency dressed in citizens' clothes, except a few of the old men, who still adhered to their blankets. That year there was more than the usual supply of rain, and they had bountiful crops of " corn, wheat, oats, kaffir corn, millet, sugar cane, and nearly every kind of vegetables." The Indians were paying much attention to stock-raising, which is an important industry for that drouth-afflicted country. Arrangements had been made by which the Government bought their beef cattle so far as needed, but they were frequently overreached by white people buying their young stock before it came to maturity at prices below its value. The agent thought that they had nearly thirty thousand head of cattle.

They cut and delivered all wood required by Government and traders; also hay and wood for the quartermaster's department at Fort Sill. One hundred and twenty-seven thousand dollars was paid them for their labor during the year. They have near two million acres

GROUP OF APACHES AT THE INDIAN INDUSTRIAL SCHOOL, CARLISLE, PA.

Of all the Indians Carlisle has undertaken, no tribe presented a more hopeless outlook than the Apaches from Arizona, who have long held a most unenviable reputation as the outlaws and Ishmaelites of the Indians. Carlisle's experience with the Apaches is that they are as susceptible as others of civilization. They are unusually active and valuable as workers.

of their land leased for grazing, at ten cents per acre a year.

One hundred and seventeen new houses were built during the year. The Government furnished the lumber, and the Indians put them up or paid for it. The agent thought that it would require about one hundred more to furnish each family with a house.

There are three boarding schoolhouses in the agency, all crowded to their utmost capacity, and another in contemplation, which, when completed, will give capacity for all the children of the agency to attend school. There are missionaries laboring with them, and many of the Indians attend church service.

CHAPTER VIII.

Brinton Darlington, a "Friend," was Appointed Agent of the Cheyenne Arapahoe Indians—He Went into the Service from a Sense of Religious Duty—The Arapahoes Peaceable—But One Depredation of Cheyennes in 1871—Great Influence with All of His Indians—Deceased May 1, 1872—Funeral Services —J. D. Miles His Successor—He Eulogized Agent Darlington —Boarding School—Cheyennes on "Warpath"—Decrease of Buffalo—School Boys Cultivate Two Hundred and Thirty Acres—Indian Freighters, a Grand Success—Cheyenne Boarding School House Built in 1879—Cattle Herd Belonging to School Children—Senator Kirkwood's Visit to Agency—Surprised at the Success of Civilizing Indians.

THE Cheyenne and Arapahoe Indians were assigned to Brinton Darlington. From a brief memoir published of him the following is extracted: " For several years he was impressed with the belief that some service would be required of him as a Christian missionary among some of the Indian tribes. The duty grew into the cherished desire of his heart. And when at length the door was opened into that field of labor by the Government of the United States to the Society of Friends, he was ready to offer himself to enter it, though it should be to lay down his life there. His heart glowed with interest and love for the red man, and though feeble in health, and greatly dependent upon the comforts and affections of his home life, he welcomed privation, hardship and toil, in order to discharge the debt of love which the Lord had

(220)

laid upon him. The important and difficult agency for the Cheyennes and Arapahoes was assigned him.

" He left home to enter upon the duties of his office in the spring of 1869. On his way he was strongly urged to accept military escort to the interior of the Indian Territory by some who represented the dangers of the journey to be very great. Unmoved, and adhering to the principles of peace, he unhesitatingly and decidedly declined the offer. He soon won the respect and confidence of the Indians under his care. Wild and warlike chiefs yielded to his gentle sway and followed his council.

"Amid the arduous duties, responsibilities and trials of his position, his character was eminently manifested as a man of prayer in all his Christian life; his trust was in the Lord for defence, for support, for direction and for success.

" While living in a tent he wrote of his experience as a strange mixture of a deep exercise of mind at times, and at others a serenity and calm that might truly be termed ' perfect peace. Although,' he continues, ' my privations have been considerable and baptisms many, yet I never was engaged in any service in which I have experienced sweeter peace than I have been permitted to enjoy in this land, and I desire to be enabled to resign all into the Lord's care and keeping, who has been so merciful and good to me hitherto, and trusting that he will not forsake me in this lonely and desert land.' "

Agent Darlington located the agency on the north bank of "the north fork of the Canadian River where the military road from Fort Harker to Fort Sill crosses that stream." During 1870 he had a saw-mill erected and some buildings constructed. In his report for that year he states: "The Arapahoe Indians have remained at peace, and not a single instance has come to our knowledge of any of them committing any depredations within the past year. All of the leading men among them have said repeatedly to me that they will never again make war upon the whites." They were ready to locate and go to farming, and he had two hundred acres plowed, and a portion of it was planted with corn, beans, pumpkins, etc., but not being furnished with means to fence it, only a part of the crop was secured.

In his third annual report, dated August 26th, 1871, Agent Darlington states: "It gives me great pleasure to report considerable advancement in the objects connected with this agency since my last report. We know of but one instance of any depredation being committed since our last annual report. The last winter's hunt realized a bountiful harvest of excellent robes." A number of the Arapahoes were ready to raise corn and other produce. "Big Mouth" was the leading chief in farming. He had "twenty-five acres of corn, of which he is justly proud."

Some of the young Cheyenne warriors attempted to go to the Ute country for revenge, but the agent succeeded in stopping them and returning them to the agency. He started two small schools, one for each tribe, before the mission school building was erected. He was very hopeful of rapid progress of his Indians towards civilization. He seems to have had great influence with the chiefs and other Indians. The mental and physical strain on him was more than he could stand. His health gave way, and he peacefully passed away May 1st, 1872, aged 68 years.

In the memoir, previously referred to, it is stated: "As the time of his release drew near his spirit seemed to perceive the shadow of the coming event, as he intimated that future earthly prospects were veiled from his view—his work was done, and words were not needed to assure his friends that the seal of Divine acceptance was upon him. The hands of loving children ministered to his latest needs, and amid the mourning of a little group of Friends and the tears of his Indian people he was laid in his lonely grave in the Indian Territory.

Many of these wild, and until lately warlike tribes, were at the agency on the occasion of his funeral, and spontaneously presented themselves at the appointed hour, filling every available portion of the house, and gathering around the doors and windows. When the meeting for worship commenced one of the chiefs, without any prompting, spoke a few words, when every sound was hushed, and the entire assembly continued in silence till Joseph D. Hoag, for whom the Indians en-

tertained great respect, spoke to them through an interpreter, alluding to the great loss which they had sustained
in the death of their agent; the sacrifices he had made
for their sakes, the valuable council he had so often given
them, and the love he had manifested for them, as well as
the benefits which they had received from following his
advice.   There was then given from the whole company
their usual earnest (vocal) sign of approval, and one of
the leading chiefs briefly responded.

Previous to the coffin being closed the whole body of
Indians passed through the room and quietly viewed the
corpse, many of them dropping silent tears as they
passed.   Most of the leading men went to the grave,
into which they looked seriously after lowering the
coffin, and then quietly remained until the interment
was finished, when they dispersed to their several lodges
or homes."

J. D. Miles, the agent of the Kickapoo Indians in
Kansas, was transferred to the Cheyenne and Arapahoe
agency.   He was a much younger man than Brinton
Darlington.   He took his amiable wife and some young
children with him to the agency.   Her heart, as well as
his, was in the work.   She was very helpful in advising
and instructing Indian women, and in many other ways.
He took charge the 1st of June, 1872.   In his annual
report, dated August 28th, 1872, he states: " Since last
year's report considerable progress has been made in the
avenues leading to the civilizing and Christianizing a

portion of the two tribes that constitute the inhabitants of this reservation, presenting proof conclusive to the most obstinate mind that Indians can be civilized, and by receiving justice and proper moral restraint at the hands of their fellow-men they can resist the allurements of the war-path, and settle down into the peaceful pursuits of buffalo hunting and farm industry. For the accomplishment of this end the Indians and the department are indebted to the late Agent Darlington for his untiring efforts."

The sale of buffalo robes was almost the only source of income to the Indians. Agent Miles, following the example of his predecessor, authorized the traders to take goods to the hunting camps and exchange them for buffalo robes. In his annual report he says: " To refuse them the regularly licensed traders, who are responsible men, is but to hold out inducement to illegal traders who swarm on the Kansas and Texas frontiers, and introduce annually large quantities of whiskey, powder and guns, and other illicit articles of trade especially prohibited by the department."

Although the Indians at their hunting camps might barter a few thousand buffalo robes to the traders, who transported them in wagons, they generally retained as many as they could well take to the agency. It was a novel sight to see them returning from a successful hunt. Numerous horses and mules were laden with bulky loads of robes and dried buffalo meat, securely tied on their backs, and then the animals were usually turned loose and were permitted to slowly move along the trail, some Indians in front and some following the caravan.

It was evident that buffaloes were rapidly diminishing in numbers. This year (1872) the Indians had to go further than usual to obtain a supply. Some of the Arapahoes saw that they would be under the necessity soon of raising cattle and grain to take the place of buffalo hunting. Many Indians of that tribe had commenced cultivating the soil, and the number increased in 1873. The Cheyennes said that they would not " take the corn road " until they saw how the Arapahoes succeeded.

In 1873 Agent Miles had the boarding schoolhouse filled with Arapahoe children " to its utmost capacity, sometimes as high as seventy scholars being present; but as the hands leave the agency the children go with them, and having no restraining power, we are compelled to abide in patience and watch the school dwindle away day by day, until, at the present time, but sixteen scholars are left. Those who have attended have made commendable progress, and we have faith that in the end our efforts will be crowned with success."

Under the head of " civil law " the agent wisely states: " I am of the opinion that the sooner these Indians are made amenable to the civil law and are held personally responsible for their acts as individuals, the better it will be for all concerned, and especially for the efforts that are being put forth to civilize and Christianize them." He especially urged the importance of being furnished " in some way with a police force to operate against Indian outlaws, white horse-thieves and whiskey-peddlers."

In 1874, the year of the outbreak of the Comanches and Kiowas, as stated in Chapter VI., the agent reports: " Three hundred lodges of Cheyennes, estimated to number one thousand, eight hundred, are absent without leave, and are supposed to be hostile. He gives a sad account of the murder of a number of his employees and some " freighters," committed, he had cause to believe, by Cheyennes and Kiowas. The Arapahoes voluntarily formed a police guard to watch the agency from sunset until daylight. But notwithstanding their vigilance an Indian rode into the agency in the night and " assassinated the doctor's son while he was attending upon a comrade who had the misfortune to get a leg broken."

It seemed as if their lives and the Government property was in danger. He had asked the previous year for a police force, which was not furnished, and the only resort that he now saw was to ask for United States soldiers to perform police duty in protecting the Government property, as well as their lives. The presence of soldiers generally warded off danger, for the Indians would much rather fall upon unsuspecting and unarmed parties than to face the soldiers, unless their numbers were greatly superior.

In regard to schools his report states: " We have maintained school in our mission building almost uninterruptedly during the past year, with very good success. We have found it impossible to induce the Cheyennes to send their children to school, being deaf to all the arguments that we have used in its favor. They say that schools are well enough for Arapahoe children, but Cheyennes do not have to go to school to learn to hunt buffalo; and when told that the buffalo would soon be gone, and the school was intended and designed to teach them how to live without them, they replied that they do not desire to live after the buffalo shall become extinct."

The rations for his Indians was the same as given in Chapter IV., but he recommended that the one and a half pounds of beef net per ration, or three pounds gross, be raised to two pounds net per ration (a ration is food for one day). He also recommended that the half pound of flour be reduced to one-fourth pound per ration, and one-fourth of cornmeal be added. The beef ration seems very large, but the Indian had been accustomed to living almost exclusively on buffalo meat, with a very scant supply of wild roots and fruit in their season. Very different from the food of civilized people.

In 1876 the Indians realized the rapid decrease of the buffalo herds, and a number of the Cheyennes and Arapahoes purchased small herds of cattle from the sale of their buffalo robes and ponies. The agent employed a Cheyenne and an Arapahoe for assistant herders, who were competent and faithful. As the Government cattle had to be " night-herded " for a time, and having no funds for hiring it done, six Indians of each tribe did the herding at night without pay. Some of them were men who a few years ago would go to the Government herd, shoot one or two, take some choice cuts, and tauntingly leave for their camps.

THE MANUAL LABOR AND MISSION SCHOOL.

This school contained one hundred and twelve scholars, and it was under contract with J. H. Seger " on the basis of six dollars and fifty cents per month for each scholar, the Government furnishing such rations and annuity goods as are furnished the Cheyennes and Arapahoes of this agency. The boys cut and hauled the wood for the mission and agency, and plowed, planted and cultivated in a systematic manner one hundred and twenty acres, being ' the school farm,' which was all planted to corn, excepting ten acres, which was planted to potatoes, melons, beans, and an almost endless variety of vegetables, all of which yielded a bountiful supply for the mission table and school children."

The boys, as in the previous year, were to have the corn they raised on the school farm, and half they raised on the agency farm (of one hundred and ten acres); the balance for feed for agency stock. They invested the principal part of their corn money in cows and calves. Each boy milked his own cow, and thus furnished the school with milk. That year (1876) the Cheyennes placed thirty-three children in school with the Arapahoes, the first time that they had sent any children to that school.

The traders always succeeded in getting their goods and supplies transported when needed, but from some cause the Government supplies of annuity goods and provisions transported by Government officials, other than Indian agents, were often months behind time. Annuity goods due at the three southwestern agencies in the fall were sometimes not delivered at the agencies until mid-winter or in the spring, which caused much annoyance to the agents and dissatisfaction and suffering of the Indians. The rations would sometimes run short, and then only a portion of what was due the Indians could be granted them. Sometimes the agents would borrow of each other when they were from thirty to seventy-five miles apart, or from traders or the military department.

Agent J. D. Miles conceived the idea of having his Indians do the freighting for the agency. In 1875 there were five hundred and twenty-three thousand, one hundred pounds of provisions and annuity goods transported from Wichita, Kansas, to the Cheyenne and Arapahoe agency, one hundred and sixty-five miles, at the rate of one dollar and fifty cents per hundred pounds. He requested from the Government in 1876 forty wagons and fixtures, eighty sets of double harness, eighty plows, forty axes, forty whips, twenty spades, one thousand pounds of rope, twelve dozen boxes of axle-grease, at a total cost of six thousand, four hundred dollars, and one thousand, three hundred and sixty dollars for forage, shoeing and repairs. The total being the amount that was paid for freight the previous year.

His plan was for the Indians to do the freighting for the Government, using their own mules and horses, and take wagons, harness, plows, etc., for their pay, and in the spring they would have teams that had been used, and harness to hitch to the plows, and they could thus go to farming on a much larger scale than they had previously done, using their energies in a way that would be beneficial to themselves and to the Government. His plan for using those blanket Indians, some of whom two years before had been on " the war-path," for Government freighters, he states, was " considered very novel by some and impracticable by others, yet from its first inception it has been regarded by me as being entirely practicable, being backed by a foundation of right and supported by a wholesome inducement and opportunity to engage in some commendable industry."

His " estimate " was not honored the first year that it was made, but in 1877 it was filled, and the wagons and Government supplies for his agency were shipped to Wichita, Kansas, the nearest railroad station, and the agent was instructed to carry them to his agency.

"The Cheyenne and Arapahoe Transportation Company" was composed wholly of Indians, and as they set out from the agency with one hundred and sixty of their best horses and mules, bound for the city of Wichita, in charge of J. A. Covington and Wiliam E. Malaley, employees and wagon masters, it was a unique "company." Their arrival was a novel sight to the citizens of Wichita. Crowds of them were soon at the depot. Some of them offered to assist in "setting up" the wagons. But the trainmasters would accept of no help except from the Indians. Awkward as they were at first, they soon learned how to put a wagon together. In three days they were ready to hitch up and pull out the train of forty four-horse wagons, hauling sixty-five thousand pounds of supplies. Here were some green Indians driving four-horse teams equally green and awkward. After circling around on the prairie, until the teamsters learned how to hold the lines and guide the teams, the wagonmasters had them to drive through the principal streets of the city of Wichita to gratify the curiosity of the people—a unique scene. On their way to the agency, although they had quicksand streams to cross, they arrived there with very few casualties, "with everything in good order and condition." In a few days the Indians started back for forty more loads. That year the supplies were all delivered on time. Then the Indians were the happy owners of wagons, harness and

plows, paid for by their own honest labor. The enterprise was a grand success.

The next year " The Cheyenne and Arapahoe Transportation Company " was supplied with new wagons and
harness, and another company of Indians did the freighting and paid for the wagons and harness, etc.; but there
was some dissatisfaction, for the reason that other Indians had wagons, harness and plows issued to them without working for them, to which Agent J. D. Miles called
the attention of the Commissioner of Indian Affairs.

In 1879, Agent P. H. Hunt, in his annual report,
states: " The new undertaking—the freighting of supplies from the railroad by the Indians—has been thoroughly successful. Soon after the fifty wagons and one
hundred sets of harness were received two trains, one
from Fort Sill and one from Wichita, were on the road
to the railroad. The Indians entered into the new work
very eagerly, and all who applied could not be supplied
with wagons. The wagonmasters report good order
maintained throughout, and the trips have been made
in good time, and the supplies were delivered at the
warehouses in good condition."

The enterprise of using Indians and their horses and
mules for the purpose of freighting, suggested by Agent
J. D. Mills in 1876, and put in successful practice by
him in 1877, was soon adopted in many other agencies.
In 1879 Commissioner E. A. Hayte reported that in
1878 and 1879 the Sioux Indians transported near four

million pounds of freight about one hundred and fifty miles—from their old agency to their new one—by being furnished with four hundred and twelve wagons and six hundred sets of double harness. He reported that in several other agencies the Indians were freighting Government supplies. " One thousand three hundred and sixty-nine wagons and two thousand five hundred sets of double harness are now employed in the service, with excellent results in all cases."

During the summer of 1879 Agent Miles had a boarding schoolhouse put up near Caddo Springs, a mile or two north of the agency for the Cheyenne students, " at a cost to the Government of eight thousand dollars, besides cost of transportation of the material. About three hundred and fifty children can now be accommodated in the two boarding schools." With an hydraulic ram he had a stream of good, clear water thrown from the spring into the school building on the hill. He had two excellent schools. The students were not only taught book lore, but the boys were taught to farm, to garden and the care of stock, and the girls were taught to sew and to cut and make garments and do all kinds of housework. He was careful to have religious teachers, and a Christian influence pervaded the schools.

" The cattle herd belonging to the Arapahoe school was the property of individual scholars and other children of the tribe, and they went on constantly increasing in growth, numbers and value." Each child had his

CHEYANNE SCHOOL AT CADDO SPRINGS, INDIAN TERRITORY

individual brand. The calves were branded before they were weaned, so there was no difficulty in identifying the ownership of each animal. In addition to the natural increase, the children had the school superintendent, J. H. Seger, to purchase " yearling heifers " with their earnings. In 1879 he bought one hundred head of them. There were then in the herd nine hundred and seventy head, valued at nine thousand one hundred and eighty dollars. The agent and school boys were very much elated with this enterprise. It was giving the latter a valuable training in an important industry for that part of the country.

Through jealousy, or some other cause unknown to the writer, the agent was ordered by the Department to close up the herding business by having the children take their cattle to their parents, or dispose of them in some way, and not have them kept in connection with the school. Thus was suspended, in the estimation of the writer, without cause, a very important adjunct of the school.

There was no missionary or ordained missionary stationed at the agency up to 1869, but religious meetings were held twice each Sabbath, which were attended in the mornings by many of the camp Indians. The cardinal principles of Christianity were taught by the agent and some of his employees, and there is cause to believe that some of the older Indians, as well as the school children, were converted to Christ. Some Mennonite missionaries afterwards labored with the Indians of that agency with good results. They had schools there for the children, sustained at the expense of their church.

It was reported in Washington that J. D. Miles had an interest in a cattle herd, which was considered of such grave importance that it should claim the time and attention of the United States Senate. Was it likely that a Quaker agent had an interest in a cattle ranch? After being discussed in that august body, a committee was appointed to go to the Cheyenne and Arapahoe agency and investigate the facts of the case and report. Senator Kirkwood, of Iowa, was placed on the committee. He subsequently told me of his trip to the agency. After making the journey on the cars from Washington to Wichita, Kansas, nearly fourteen hundred miles, he then took the old-fashioned stage coach to travel one hundred and sixty five miles to the agency. As he went jolting over the unmade road, thinking how he would accost the agent and what he should say to him, the thought occurred to him, " I have stock in a bank in Iowa, and is it any worse for a United States officer to have stock in a cattle herd than in a bank?" He could not see that it was, and in debating the subject in his own mind he concluded, before arriving at the agency, that he was on a " fool's errand."

On he went, thinking that if the agent was neglecting his official duties, and letting them run at random while he was spending his time with the cattle herd, there might be cause of censure. For a long distance he saw no habitations but prairie dog towns, and occasionally a homely stockade stage ranch with dirt roof; then he came in full view of the stately Cheyenne school building, that would have looked creditable in Iowa City, the home of the Senator. Passing on a mile or two further he came to the little village of Darlington, where was the agency, and another large school building, with many children playing on the school grounds, "who seemed to be tamed and well behaved." Grown Indians, too, he saw dressed in citizens' clothes and docile, and harmless as white people, and some of them at work. He was greatly surprised. He had imagined that it would be about as easy to tame a herd of wild buffalo as to tame wild Indians. He saw his mistake.

He found Agent J. D. Miles to be a courteous, energetic, upright business man. He had an interest in a cattle herd which was very lucrative, but it did not interfere with his official business as Indian agent. The honorable Senator was unable to inform the agent wherein it was more improper to have stock in a cattle ranch than to have stock in a bank. He returned to his seat in the Senate hall a wiser man for his visit to the Cheyenne and Arapahoe agency.

John D. Miles was a very efficient and successful Indian agent, and honorably and economically served the Government in that capacity for fifteen years and two months.

The Cheyenne and Arapahoe Indians commenced taking allotments in 1891, and in 1897 there were three thousand three hundred and thirty-two allotments. There were seventy-four new dwellings put up on them during 1897, and many had previously been erected. The effect of allotment in that agency has been such that the Kiowas and Comanches, in 1898, preferred to not attempt it in their agency.

In the Cheyenne and Arapahoe agency there were three boarding schools in 1897, which were attended by three hundred and forty-five pupils. The Mennonites had two schools, with ninety-nine scholars, and there was one day school with sixteen pupils, making a total of four hundred and sixty scholars being educated at the agency.

Number of Cheyennes and Arapahoes in

	1879.	1897.	Decrease in 18 years.
Cheyennes	3593	2089	1504
Arapahoes	1903	1005	898

CHAPTER IX.

SAC AND FOX INDIAN AGENCY.

THIS agency was assigned to Thomas Miller, a
" Friend " minister, in the fall of 1869. During the
winter, quite advanced as he was in years, he removed
three hundred and eighty-seven of his Indians from their
reservation in Kansas to their new reservation of seven
hundred and fifty square miles west of the Creeks and

north of the Seminoles. One chief and about two hundred people refused to leave their Kansas homes. Agent Miller had land plowed for the Indians, and they assisted in making rails and in fencing their fields. Their little fields aggregated one hundred and fifty acres. They were planted in corn, pumpkins, squashes, beans, etc., and made a good crop, and the women dried much of the corn and some of the vegatables. The Government did not furnish them with provisions, but the Indians who were living on their reservation had annuity funds paid them.

John Hadley made the report for 1871. He reported that more of the Indians had moved there from Kansas, making the total number of Sac and Foxes four hundred and forty-eight. He reports a good saw mill erected, " to which is attached a pair of burrs for grinding corn, and a shingle machine, which are found of great service here." In 1872 the agent reported much sickness, and one-tenth of the Indians died during the year. He had a small school for the Sac and Fox Indians and another for the " absentee Shawnees," who were attached to his agency, and were located on the south side of the North Fork of the Canadian River. There were several hundred of them, and they raised a comfortable living by farming when there was rain sufficient to make a crop.

John H. Pickering reported as agent in 1873. The Sac and Fox boarding house was in successful operation. A farm was attached to the school and the boys assisted in farm work and in gardening. They assisted on one occasion to plant some peach seeds. The following evening they digged up what seed they could find and ate the kernels. They would rather have that much " goody " then than to wait three or four years for a crop of delicious peaches. The Government built a few houses for the chiefs. Nearly all of the other Indians of the agency lived in log houses of their own construction. The Shawnees " numbered nearly seven hundred." They were improving faster without any annuity funds than the Sac and Fox Indians did with sixty dollars annually for each member of the tribe.

Agent Pickering reported, in 1874. that " the Kickapoos, from the border of Texas, are now in this agency. They were ready to raise a subsistence from the soil, but they were very averse to sending their children to school, or listening to the gospel. It was many years after that before they yielded to either.

Many of the absentee Shawnees wore citizen clothes, as well as the Pottawatomies. The other Indians of the agency generally wore blankets, except the half-bloods. About twenty of the Shawnee children attended a day school. Their homes were so scattered that few of them could attend. The agent urged that a boarding school be provided for them. There were near two hundred men in the tribe, who cultivated one thousand and twenty-two acres of land. Of the Sac and Fox Indians the agent states: " Their religion is principally a traditional antagonism to civilization, and an individual who patronizes the school, or follows the customs of the whites, is stigmatized as a traitor to their Great Spirit. Consequently we get but few of the full-blood children to attend school except orphans."

The annual report for Sac and Fox agency for 1876 was made by Levi Woodard as agent. A boarding school-house had been erected for the Shawnees, and three hundred and fifty-four acres were assigned by the Secretary of the Interior for the Manual Labor School. There were eighteen scholars, half of whom were day students.

Number of Indians in Sac and Fox agency in

	1876.	1897.	Change in 21 years.
Sac and Fox	433	495	Increase, 62
Absentee Shawnee ...	661	483	Decrease, 178
Mexican Kickapoo ...	375	255	Decrease, 120
Citizen Pottawatomie .	250	780	Increase, 530
Iowa, removed from Nebraska since 1876		86	

It is probable that the increase of the Sac and Fox and Pottawatomie Indians was caused by some members of the tribe moving into the agency from Kansas.

Friends had the management of the Sac and Fox agency nine years. During that time the Indians progressed in civilization, and some of the children in school learning. A few members of different tribes had been converted, and the affairs of the agency were moving smoothly and harmoniously. As the work of the agency was constantly increasing, Agent Woodard applied for authority to appoint a much-needed clerk, which was granted. He then appointed his son, O. J. Woodard. Commissioner Hayt refused to confirm that appointment, for the reason that it was not for the best interest of the service for an agent to have relatives employed. The Commissioner informed the agent that he had appointed J. Hertford to the position of clerk, and on his arrival the books and accounts were to be turned over to him. This was done. He proved to have no ability for the position. He could not prepare for transmission to the Department the simplest forms; books were not properly kept; accounts were behind, and the office became in a very unsatisfactory condition in the course of a few months, when J. Hertford was granted by the Commissioner leave of absence for three months—two with pay and one without. He left with no provision for a substitute to act as clerk.

The agent alone was responsible to the Government for all mistakes and mismanagement of the clerk. His son, O. J. Woodard, therefore took up the office work and corrected and brought up the months of Hertford's back records. After a month's absence J. Hertford wrote that he was going to Europe and would not be back. Agent Woodard then appointed his son for clerk, which was approved by Commissioner Hayt, to take effect at the expiration of Hertford's " sixty days with pay." About this time the Friends' Executive Committee visited Commissioner Hayt and endeavored to show him that it was not right to impose an incompetent clerk upon Agent Woodard, when the agent was responsible and not the Commissioner for the mistakes or failures that he might make. They told the Commissioner that Agent Woodard would certainly not serve with J. Hertford as clerk. The Commissioner told the committee that Mr. Hertford had gone to England and was not likely to return to the agency.

After the unpleasant affair seemed to be amicably settled, Commissioner Hayt wrote Agent Woodard that J. Hertford was to return to his agency as clerk, and must be placed on the pay roll when he arrived. When he reached there the agent refused to again accept a man who was so incompetent and so thoroughly unfit for the position. Soon as possible John McNeil was sent there as inspector. He spent three days of private examination of nearly or quite every individual about the agency, seeking to find cause for the removal of Agent Woodard, but he signally failed. On the fourth day he formally dismissed O. J. Woodard as clerk, and demanded that the agent should accept Hertford as clerk. The agent replied that his experience with J. Hertford was such that he would under no circumstance have him in any capacity at the agency, whereupon the inspector suspended Agent Woodard for insubordination and placed

J. Hertford in charge as acting agent, greatly to the chagrin of the Indians and employees.

The agency for the Osages, called Neosho agency, in 1869, was in southern Kansas. " A domain three hundred miles long by thirty in width, being about one thousand six hundred and fifty acres for each member of the tribe "—vastly more than they could utilize. Their agent, G. C. Snow, who had been agent for seven years, in his report for 1869, gives a sad account of the failure of the Government to comply with treaty stipulations in paying their annuities. Exorbitant prices had been paid in New York for inferior blankets and other goods, costing the Indians more than good material purchased of the traders. In some instances committees of Congress had refused to recommend the appropriation of funds to pay the interest due them, so that the schools and other work of the agency were greatly crippled, and much suffering on the part of the Indians was the result. They and the Cheyennes were enemies, and they were afraid to go to the plains to hunt buffalo, which greatly added to their privations.

Mahlon Stubbs, who had been nominated by the Friends, was agent, in 1869, of the Kaw or Kansas Indians, who were a band of the Osages, but in some respects appeared to be further advanced in civilization. The agency was at Council Grove, Kansas. A number of stone houses had been built for them, but they preferred to live the most of the time in their buffalo lodges.

They numbered about five hundred and twenty-five. They appeared to be very destitute, largely owing to difficulty between them and the Cheyennes, and therefore they were afraid to go to the buffalo country to hunt.

In 1870 Agent Stubbs went, with some of his Indians, to the Cheyenne and Arapahoe agency, and had a council with the Cheyennes and made peace with them. They could then hunt buffalo without fear of being molested. They soon purchased some plows and harness, and had more than the usual amount of land under cultivation. The school increased in size and interest. Some of the white people who were settling around them visited the school and complimented the children on their progress, which was very encouraging to them. In 1871 they were preparing to move to the Indian Territory and did not have much heart in their work. White people were more and more occupying their reservation. In 1872 they moved to the Indian Territory, but too late in the spring to put in a crop.

In 1872, I. T. Gibson, a Friend, had been appointed agent of the Osages, and had them removed to the Territory, on a tract of land that they bought of the Cherokees, being the part of their reservation west of the ninety-sixth meridian, bounded on the north by Kansas. There were about one hundred and sixty acres for each member of the tribe. A large amount of it was very rocky—unfit for cultivation—but there was sufficient good, rich land that they could utilize in farming. The most desirable portion was adjoining the Cherokees, and there they commenced making improvements. In less than a year " the ninety-sixth meridian was resurveyed and officially established about three and a half miles west of the line made by former survey." This threw much of their improvements off their reservation, which was very discouraging and disgusting to the Indians, who immediately went to the plains to hunt buffalo, thinking that the Government had perpetrated an intentional fraud upon them.

The agent promptly reported the facts of the case to the Department, and George Howland, Jr., of Massachusetts, and Thomas Wister, of Philadelphia, were appointed a commission to investigate and endeavor to settle the difficulty. The former went with Agent Gibson " to the plains in the latter part of winter to communicate with the chiefs, who came into the agency, where we were joined by Commissioner Wister and Superintendent Hoag. A council was convened on the first of March and a fair conclusion obtained, which was satisfactory in the main to the Osages." Their improvements were to be paid for by the Cherokees. (Indian Commissioner's Report for 1873.)

The agency was then located in the central part of the reservation. Many of the Indians were ready to go to farming, realizing that the buffaloes were fast decreasing and that they could not long depend upon them for food and robes. Two thousand acres were planted in 1872 in corn and various kinds of vegetables.

Soon there were some ten or fifteen hundred white intruders locating on their new reservation, and as the agent had no police force he could not remove them. United States troops, by order of President Grant, put them off of the reservation. The agent urged that a legal tribunal be located in the Territory. In 1873 the Indians were divided into settlements. "Each division was placed in charge of an efficient farmer and his assistants, who reside at a station most central and convenient for the Indians under his care, where are kept oxen, plows, wagons, and other farming implements, for general use in that division. The agent visits each station as often as practicable to see how the work is progressing and to advise with the farmers and chiefs as to their necessities and future operations. The method has worked admirably, bringing all the Indians to some extent under the influence of the agent. Those divisions are being provided with necessary buildings for the employees at the station, none of which are nearer the station at the agency than fifteen miles, and some of them are fifty miles from each other."

To encourage the Indians in civilization, the agent paid, he says, " fifty-eight blanket Indians, who refrained from going on the buffalo hunt in the fall, two dollars and fifty cents for each hundred rails split by them and built up into a good ' staked and ridered ' fence, inclosing prairie suitable for cultivation. I promised to break all they would thus inclose for their own use. It was necessary to pay them in order that they could obtain means to support their families; otherwise it would have been necessary to issue rations to them, which would have destroyed all incentive to labor. They split and laid up in fence eighty-one thousand rails, thus supporting their families and acquiring skill in labor. But what is still better, they have now a spot of ground they call home, which they prize very highly, and have no thought of again returning to the chase."

In the spring Agent Gibson had about eleven hundred acres of new prairie plowed for the Indians. Two thousand two hundred acres were cultivated by two hundred and nine families. "As their moccasins, which, during wet weather, are scarcely any protection to the feet, but, by being constantly wet, endangered pulmonary disease," he employed a shoemaker, who, with some Indian boys, made boots and shoes for many of them. He put up a good saw mill, and Indians assisted in sawing lumber. Of his numerous white employees every one was "expected to perform missionary work." Their Sabbath meetings were well attended by employees and school children and some camp Indians. At the last one previous to making his report "fifty-four persons took part in the spiritual exercises of the meeting."

Soon after Superintendent Hoag had taken charge of the office, he learned that the L. L. and G. Railroad

Company had negotiated with the Osage Indians for their large tract of land for eighteen cents per acre, and the contract was then pending before Congress. He at once held a council with the Osages on the subject, and the Indians, learning that they were likely to be overreached, desired other arrangements made. The superintendent reported the facts of the case to the Commissioner of Indian Affairs, which resulted in President Grant withdrawing the bill from the Senate. A bill was afterwards passed providing that the Kansas Osage lands were taken in trust by the Government to sell at one dollar and twenty-five cents per acre. This was doubtless the result of the care of Superintendent Hoag.

Agent Gibson, in his report for 1873, states: "In June two prominent Cherokees, C. N. Van and W. P. Adair, were in the camps of the Osages several days counseling them to sign an order on the Honorable Secretary of the Interior for the sum of three hundred and thirty thousand dollars, as payment of a claim for alleged services rendered the Osages in procuring the defeat of the treaty made by the Osages with the L. L. and G. Railroad Company; also for procuring the passage of the act whereby the Kansas Osage land was taken in trust by the Government to sell at one dollar and twenty-five cents per acre. I interviewed these Cherokees to ascertain the nature of their services. Not obtaining the desired information, I requested them to desist importuning the Osages, interfering with the business of the chiefs at the agency, and that they give me an opportunity to investigate their claim, and if it was just I had no doubt the Government would authorize the payment of it. This was met with an implied threat, in that if I would let them alone they would let me alone.

I openly advised the chiefs in council not to sign any agreement, nor commit themselves to any amount, until the officers of the Government could ascertain whether the Cherokees had performed any service for them. Several chiefs refrained from counseling with them afterwards; but through persuasive influences that were generally believed in camp to be improper, several of the chiefs were induced to sign such an order after the Cherokees had reduced the sum to two hundred and thirty thousand dollars. No member of the little Osage tribe of any position signed the order, thus preventing the document from having any binding force on the tribe. A half-breed of known integrity has left on file in my office an affirmation stating that fully one-half of the names affixed to the paper were not present, and many of them have since informed me, after hearing their names had been attached, that they had not author-ized any one to do so, and that it was done against their will. After the Cherokees left the agency, the half-breeds' proceeded to get up a remonstrance, which the most of the tribe appear to have signed." They urged that the merits of the claim be investigated.

There was probably little attention given to the earnest and apparently just appeal from Agent Gibson and his Indians. The Cherokees were very persistent in pressing their claim at Washington, and it was eventually paid. A United States officer, who was in a position to understand the merits and demerits of the case, in talking to the writer about the payment of that claim, said: " The Osages have plenty of funds without it." He apparently thought that in paying it there was no justice, but it was done to get rid of the clamor of the Cherokees.

In 1874, as the Indians did not raise a subsistence, on account of drought and grasshoppers, about five-sixths of them went in the fall to the plains to hunt buffalo, and returned in the spring with about eleven thousand buffolo robes and a large amount of dried meat and tallow. " About seventy-five families of the civilized full-bloods are living in comfortable hewed log houses, with from five to twenty acres of improved land to each family. Nearly all of the half-breed families have good houses and farms, with from twenty to one hundred acres in cultivation, and are self-supporting." When the full-bloods " have ten acres or more inclosed and under cultivation, a wagon, plow and harness is to be given to each of them." That year twenty persons were entitled to wagons, etc.

Those who had fields usually wanted houses and wells, and they could get lumber at the agency sawmill for floor-

ing, shingles, etc. Wheat was raised, and the agent prepared for making flour. The Indians assisted in the
shoe and harness shop, smith shop, wagon and cabinet
shop, carpentering, and running the saw and grist mill.
"The agency buildings, comprising church, schoolhouse,
commissary, agent's and physician's offices and council
room, dwelling houses for agent, physician and blacksmith, are completed as per contract." These were generally, if not all of them, substantial structures of stone.
Very good building stone was near. The agent reported:
" The school building is designed to accommodate seventy-five pupils, and the necessary officers and teachers,
with all the comforts of home. The course of instruction
is on the manual labor system. The school farm contains
one hundred acres. About eight acres were planted in
fruit trees and vines, and cultivated in vegetables, the
boys doing the most of the work under the care of an
industrial teacher. The girls are taught all the duties
of housekeeping, and they are also under the instruction
of an industrious teacher."

" The religious and educational interests of this tribe
have had the special care of Iowa Yearly Meeting of
Friends. Men and women of ability and deep, active
piety have been furnished to occupy important positions
as regular employees and for unpaid missionary labor.
Friends of Philadelphia, and those of Iowa, have furnished us with several boxes of goods and clothing for
distribution among the destitute. Friends of Philadel-

phia also sent us a box containing books for the library, and papers, charts, cards, pictures, etc., for the Sabbath School, which are invaluable to us. . . . To insure success in settling and domesticating uncivilized Indians, the best of men must be had as employees—men of ability and of pure life and conversation, overflowing with love for their kind, magnetic, patient and hopeful; in brief, large-hearted, generous Christians." . . . "Profanity, intemperance, card-playing and kindred vices are not tolerated among the traders or employees. Consequently we have no quarreling, fighting or carrying weapons of defence. About seventy-five white men are in the service, five of whom are ministers, and many others are active working Christians of different denominations. Persons who do not take sufficient interest in promoting morality and religion by attending Sabbath School and religious services are discharged if such should, by mistake, be employed." This shows the great care that a Christian Indian agent exercised to promote the best interests of the red brethren in charge.

In the fall he bought one hundred head of oxen, ready to do a large amount of fresh " breaking " of prairie for his Indians the next spring and summer. But the plowing force was not equal to the demand. The agent states: " I believe all the heads of families would have selected claims and held the plow or driven the oxen while breaking their fields " had there been enough teams. For improving the stock of domestic animals that the Indians had he bought some high grade hogs, cattle and horses for breeding purposes. He had two trusty employees—B. K. Wetherill and Edwin Andrews —to accompany hunting parties to the plains to see that they behaved and were properly treated. The " plains Indians " were on the " war path," but the Osages exerted their utmost influence with them for peace. They have never fought the Government since their first treaty. Under the influence of Agent Gibson they made peace with their Indian enemies, the Pawnees and Cheyennes.

When the agent learned of the " plains Indians " being at war against the Government, he dispatched messengers to his Indians who were out hunting to immediately return to the agency. A party of Cheyennes had wantonly murdered some people in Kansas, which may have been the cause of about forty white men visiting a hunting party of Osage men, women and children, and murdering four of the men who went to meet them, when the rest of the party jumped on to their ponies and fled under a shower of bullets, leaving sixty horses and mules, all of their provisions and other property, which were stolen or destroyed. " The murderers rushed to the Governor of Kansas, and he mustered them in as State militia, dating the papers back so as to legalize this cruel massacre!" Neither the Governor of Kansas or Department at Washington took measures to restore the stolen animals, or to make redress, and some of the relatives of the murdered Indians could scarcely be restrained from going to the vicinity of the tragedy and taking vengeance on innocent parties. The agent used his influence to restrain them and to get Congress to make reparation. He states: " Several attempts have been made by small war parties, composed of their friends, to leave the reservation for the purpose of retaliating. On one occasion Chief Che-sho-how-kah offered his own life, after giving his favorite horse and his chief-money to the relatives of the deceased, to prevent them going to take revenge "— a rare instance of self-sacrifice.

The Kaw Indians purchased of the Osages about one hundred thousand acres of the northwestern part of their reservation. Agent Stubbs moved them there and erected some stone buildings for school and dwelling houses. " The new buildings are substantial and commodious. The school was promptly opened, with an attendance of fifty-four pupils, who are deeply interested in their studies." " Western Yearly Meeting of Friends " contributed three hundred dollars for educational and religious purposes. The Indians worked with energy to improve their lands, which they now regard as their permanent homes. The agency was merged into the Osage agency, I. T. Gibson being agent, and Mahlon Stubbs retained as principal manager of " the Kaw station," which was located in a beautiful grove about thirty miles west of Osage agency. (See Report of August 1st, 1874.)

In 1875 the two tribes raised about twenty thousand bushels of wheat and fifty-six thousand bushels of corn. On the school farm there were two thousand five hundred bushels of small grain and two thousand bushels of corn. "The pupils did most of the work on the school farm." There were five hundred and thirty-eight families, of whom four hundred and seventy-eight have fields; two hundred and fourteen had houses; one hundred and seventy-seven had orchards aggregating twenty thousand fruit trees; three thousand eight hundred and seventy-six acres were under cultivation, and three thousand acres of new ground were plowed.

After six years of faithful, energetic and efficient service, I. T. Gibson resigned. Every department of his agency work seemed to be successful, and the Indians at all stations made commendable progress, except one or two bands, who were reluctant to abandon their nomadic life.

Cyrus Beede was appointed agent of the Osages and assumed charge February 21st, 1876. The Indians returned from the winter's buffalo hunt " utterly unsuccessful, destitute and half starved." The appropriation for the fiscal year had been so near exhausted that the school was closed some months earlier than usual, and the agent could not render the accustomed assistance to the Indians who wanted to commence farming. The two bands who refused to farm appeared now to be ready, but no assistance could be rendered, which to them semed hard and unreasonable. Those who had fields could help themselves. An unprecedented freshet swept away the fences and crops of many of the Indians, and the school farm was submerged with water, and wheat shocks were washed away. The water rose fifty feet above the ordinary level of the creek at the agency. It was a trying summer for a new agent to commence business, with less appropriation of Osage funds than usual.

Agent Beede instituted self-government to a greater extent than had previously existed among the Osages. In addition to the Governor and counselor that they formerly had, they accepted his proposition that "a business committee of five leading men be appointed, representing both parties, to be associated with the Governor, who should be chief counselor in the transaction of all necessary business with the agent and Government." Their salaries ranged from three hundred to five hundred dollars per annum.

Agent Beede continued in office three years. During that time the Indians steadily advanced in civilization. He was crippled in the efficiency of his service by more limited appropriations, and by an act of Congress limiting the number of employes at Indian agencies. The interest on their large fund held by Government was ample to carry on the agency, and some of them needed the assistance of skilled labor to teach them how to farm. All that the Osages needed, and through their agent asked for, of the Government, was permission to use the interest, and, if needed, some of the principal of their large sum held by the Government. The agent was greatly annoyed by whiskey dealers and horse thieves, and he justly made the universal complaint of Indian agents in the Territory of the great hardship of going two hundred miles to Fort Smith, in Arkansas, to attend court. The "Osage Government" seemed to give satisfaction. It placed more responsibility upon the Indians and was a valuable training to them.

E. A. Hayt, Commissioner of Indian Affairs, removed Cyrus Beede from the office of Indian Agent without just cause, in the estimation of the Committee on Indian Affairs who nominated him. The committee was satisfied with his administration and greatly regretted his removal.

Laban J. Miles succeeded Cyrus Beede as Indian Agent. In his report for 1879 he states: "The Osages number two thousand one hundred and thirty-five, of whom two hundred and sixty-five are mixed blood. In 1872 Agent Gibson reported the number three thousand nine hundred and fifty-six, of whom two hundred and seventy-seven were mixed bloods. They both gave the number in each band, which indicates correctness. This shows a decrease of one thousand eight hundred and twenty-one in seven years. There were three hundred and sixty Kaws in 1879, of whom sixty were mixed bloods. They had decreased, the agent states, "about one-half in seven years, caused mainly by a contagious disease with which the tribe is largely infected." During the seven years the Indians had changed from the nomadic to settled habits, which is generally a trying period on the health of the Indians, and they usually decrease more rapidly at that period.

For many years the Methodist Church has had a missionary at the agency (Pawhuska), and he was still laboring there in 1898; but the Indians of that agency are largely under the control of the Roman Catholic priests.

In 1879 there were in the agency four hundred and seventy-seven Osage children attending school—a part of them at the school off of the reservation; eighty-two not at school; fifty-nine of the sixty-three Kaws were attending school.

Number of Indians in Osage agency in

	1879.	1897.	Change in 18 years.
Osage, full blood	1870	900	Decrease, 970
Osage, mixed-blood	265	829	Increase, 564
Kansas, or Kaw, full-blood	300	105	Decrease, 195
Kansas, or Kaw, mixed-blood	60	103	Increase, 43

The Osage Indians have funds held in trust by the Government amounting to eight million four hundred and forty-one thousand dollars, the annual interest on which is four hundred and twelve thousand dollars. Funds not needed for agency expenses are paid to them. The

Kansas, or Kaw, Indians have like funds amounting to one hundred and eighty-eight thousand seven hundred and thirty-two dollars, on which the Government pays nine thousand four hundred and thirty-six dollars in interest.

Agent L. J. Miles states that " The old custom of living in a ' common mess ' (eating together) is a great obstruction to the advance of the Osages in civilization." A family may be industrious and raise a good crop, having plow, harrow, wagon, etc., which they even loan to a neighbor Indian with great reluctance. After the industrious man has his crop raised it is then " common," and the indolent neighbor and the one to whom he would not loan a plow and other implements, that he might raise a crop, may come and camp by his cornfield when it is suitable for roasting ears and help himself, as though it were his own, and go to the table and eat what the industious Indian has raised. He detests the idea of being stingy with his provisions, and the indolent fare about as well as the industrious. This trait is not peculiar to the Osages, but seems to be a common characteristic of all tribes in their uncivilized and semi-civilized state. As they advance it becomes more and more discouraging to the industrious class to have the fruit of their hard labor consumed by the indolent and improvident.

In 1879 they had one thousand, four hundred and seventy-one acres of corn and three hundred and thirty-eight acres in wheat. They had one thousand, four hundred and thirty cattle and four thousand, four hundred and eighteen hogs. Their agency is in " the drouth belt," and that year their crop of corn was much shortened for want of rain. The agent reported: " The school has been kept up during the year with a greater average attendance than in any previous year. To accomplish this it has taken arduous labor, as children seem to prefer freedom at home. They have to be brought from the camp, and even then the parents often reluctantly give them up. But few of those who were in school a few years ago retain the citizen's dress and comparatively few speak English. The children learn well while at school, and could they be kept regularly there a few years most of them would become good English scholars." The Kiowas " have a boarding school well attended by nearly all the children in the tribe of suitable school age."

Agent L. J. Miles faithfully served the Government as Indian agent a number of years. After he was relieved to make room for a politician, the Osage Indians, without prompting from him, petitioned to have him reappointed their agent, which was done, showing the high estimation in which he was held by the Indians. There is cause to believe that some of the Indians of that agency were converted through the instrumentality of Friends, but having no church organization or special missionary there, the Methodist Episcopal Church sent a missionary to the Osage agency and organized a church.

CHAPTER X.

THERE were several small agencies in Kansas. J. D. Miles was appointed agent for the Kickapoos in 1869. In his report for 1870 he says they numbered two hundred and ninety-six. There were some schools, and a Bible School organized in their log church building in Boone County. The chiefs were leaders in intemperance. In council, when talked to on the subject, they claimed that when in Washington the great father (Andrew Johnson) gave them the example, and they should not be censured for doing as he did. It was checked by applying the law to those who sold to the Indians. In 1871 buildings were prepared for a boarding school, as the day schools were not satisfactory.

J. D. Miles, as stated in a previous chapter, was transferred to the Cheyenne and Arapahoe agency, and B. H. Miles was appointed agent of the Kickapoos. He states in 1874 there was an almost entire failure of their crops by drought and grasshoppers. The mission school was well attended, and " the two churches are regularly kept up with about one hundred and thirty-one members." The whole number of the tribe was two hundred and eighty-eight. In 1895 it was two hundred and thirty-one.

The Kickapoos were merged into the Pottawatomie agency, under Joel H. Morris, who was appointed agent of the latter tribe in 1869. A considerable number of this tribe had become pretty well civilized. They had well improved farms, and seemed reasonably industrious; many of them had some education, and it appeared to the authorities and to some of the Indians that they were capable of attending to their own business without the assistance of an agent. A number of heads of families and single men therefore complied with the law and became citizens. They had warrantee deeds for their farms of one hundred and sixty acres for each head of a family; also wagons and implements necessary to carry on farming in good shape. A portion of the tribal fund was held by the Government.

Agent J. W. Morris states, in his report of 1871, that of the nine hundred and six who had become citizens " many of them have large, fine stone and frame buildings for residences, barns and granneries," and well fenced fields. " Many of these are men of moral influence in church and state. I regret to state that this is not the case with quite a large number of those who have thrown off their tribal relations. These now declare their act in becoming citizens to have been a premature one; they in their sober moments say that they were intoxicated with the idea of becoming citizens of the United States, and exercising the right of franchise! They have squandered their land and money in gambling, drinking whiskey, and other evil habits, and are now thrown on their own resources, as poor as the poorest."

The Pottawatomies still had funds in care of the Government, and, seeing how affairs were going with many of them, they purchased a tract of land, about thirty miles square, of the Creeks, and a number of "The Citizen Pottawatomies," as well as some who were not citizens, moved there to start anew. One of them told me when visiting there in their new home how some of the white people took advantage of them. In one instance a lawyer asked a citizen Indian if he had all the money he needed. " I have more than I need at present," said the lawyer, " and can let you have five hundred dollars, and you can pay it back to me when you sell your crops. You may sign a couple of papers, stating how much you get of me and when it is to be paid." "All right, I will take it," said the Indian. The illiterate Indian signed the papers, receiving the money, and he and his family had a good time spending it. When his crops were sold he needed the proceeds for the support of his family, and a foreclosure of mortgage swept the farm away from the Indian! A legal fraud without redress.

Another Indian was told that he must pay tax to the treasurer of the county. He replied that he had never bought anything of that man, and he would not pay him money. His farm was sold for tax. A single man boarded at a hotel and " lived sumptuously every day " until his funds were exhausted. Many of them found to their sorrow that there was a vast difference between helping to sustain the Government and the Government helping to support them. The law now provides that when Indians take allotments of individual farms they are inalienable for twenty-five years. So they cannot be swindled out of their homes for that length of time. The " Prairie Band," still under the care of the agent, numbered four hundred and fifteen in 1871, with some members of the tribe in Wisconsin and some in Mexico, who were expected to return to their agency, as they had no other home.

Mahlon H. Newlin reported as their agent in 1874, and states that " a mission schoolhouse had been erected by my predecessor. . . . We have a promising school of obedient and intelligent children. . . . Every head of a family of this band has a farm or cultivated field, generally improved by houses and orchards, and always by substantial fences." Many of them were strictly temperate, but a few were addicted to drinking, which was a great annoyance to the sober Indians and agent.

In 1876 the prairie band of Pottawatomies numbered four hundred and eighty-two. In 1897 their number was five hundred and twenty-two, an increase of forty in twenty-one years. The Government was owing the tribe six hundred thousand dollars, the interest on which was more than sufficient to pay for their school and other agency expenses. The balance not needed for that purpose was paid to them. They usually passed the principal part of their cash to the " trader " to pay their indebtedness at the store. Agent Newlin also had charge of the Kickapoo, Chippewa and Christian, Sac and Fox, Iowa and Munsee Indians, all of whom lived in the northeastern part of Kansas and southeastern part of Nebraska. The aggregate number, exclusive of the Pottawatomies, was five hundred and eight. In 1897 their number was five hundred and seventy, an increase of sixty-two in twenty-one years. They have five hundred and eighty thousand dollars in care of the Government, the interest on which is ample to support their boarding schools and other agency expenses. All the Indians in that agency have taken allotments of land.

Agent Newlin reported, in 1876, that each tribe had a boarding school, and the children made good progress in their studies, in cleanliness, and in behavior. The

Moravian Church had charge of and supported the Chippewa and Munsee school. " The resident missionary manifests great interest in the religious and moral elevation of these Indians. They have adopted the language and customs of the white race; they reside in comfortable dwellings, have finely cultivated farms and orchards, and by their industry and business capacity they obtain all the necessaries and many of the luxuries of life."

Since 1858 the Kickapoos have " had the advantages of missionary labor by different denominations of Christians. About one-third of them have accepted the teaching of these missionaries. Every Sabbath in their churches the native preachers preach to their people. They have no idea of sectarian views."

In 1877 the last prejudice and superstition of the Pottawatomies against taking medicine prescribed by a physician, and living in houses like white people, disappeared, and their ragged appearing old bark houses gave place for good log or frame buildings, warmed with stoves or fireplaces. M. H. Newlin was dismissed as Indian agent by Commissioner Hayt without just cause, in the estimation of the Executive Committee of Friends.

Dr. Reuben S. Roberts was appointed agent of the Shawnees in 1869. These Indians had long been under the care of Friends, who put up a boarding schoolhouse on their reservation in Kansas, and sustained a school at the expense of the church. It was under the immediate care of "Indiana Yearly Meeting of Friends," but Baltimore and Ohio Yearly Meetings assisted financially. "The Minutes of Indiana Yearly Meeting" for 1855 show that the committee in charge of the Shawnee school had at their disposal three thousand and ten dollars, and there have been during the past year twenty-nine children in the school,—ten boys and nineteen girls, —twenty-two of which were Shawnees, three were Wyandottes, two Sacs, one Munsee, and one Kansas. . . . The Bible School has been kept up. . . . The Indian girls have made their own garments, and have spun yarn and knitted all the socks and stockings used in the family; and the boys have assisted in cultivating the vegetable garden."

The Yearly Meeting Minutes of 1856 state: "The school has continued during the past year under the care of our friends, Jeremiah A. Hadley and wife, as superintendents, and Martha Townsend as teacher, and has averaged about thirty-five children. . . . The school continued in a prosperous condition until the 20th of Eighth month (August) last, when a body of armed men, eighteen in number, came to the establishment, took all the horses and saddles on the premises," and threatened to shoot the superintendent, and "told him this was only a beginning of what he might look for if he did not leave the place." Some of the Indian children had previously been taken away from the school by their parents, who feared that one of the pro-slavery mobs that were then infesting Kansas would maliciously visit the institution. It was not likely that the Indians would allow any of their children to remain there. The superintendent and employees therefore left for their homes in Indiana, leaving the premises in care of a hired man and his wife, who were not afterwards molested by the mob.

The report further states: "At the time that our worthy predecessor, William Penn, formed a treaty of friendship with the Indians, they were a numerous and powerful people, the undisturbed possessors of the rich country we inhabit, but they have been reduced to a small number, and have been driven back from the Atlantic coast to the far west. . . . When Friends commenced their labors among the Shawnees at Wapakoneta, Ohio, . . . they were in a wild state, enveloped in darkness and superstitution, having little or no knowledge of the Christian religion. . . . Now many of them have comfortable dwellings and well cultivated farms. . . . A considerable number of them have embraced the doctrines of the gospel." As Friends had no church organization there they joined the Methodist and the Baptist church.

In 1852 an Indian named Kiko joined in membership with Friends, who appears by the "Minutes of the Yearly Meeting" to have been the only Indian taken into membership during the forty years that Friends supported a school for them. This school was discontinued in 1862. The Shawnees received a large money annuity from the Government, which enabled them to live in much idleness and dissipation, and they cared less for school than in former years. Money annuity appears to have been an injury to them, which was probably always the case with Indians. Those Indians succeed the best who rely wholly on their own exertions for subsistence.

Dr. Reuben L. Roberts was appointed by the Government Indian agent of the Shawnees in 1869. In his first report he states: " With the exception of a few who have good and cultivated farms and bountiful crops the present season, the Shawnees as a tribe are not at present very prosperous, having been long looking for and expecting the privilege of selling their entire allotment of lands preparatory to a removal to the Indian country (Territory), in consequence of which their agricultural business has been much neglected. I regret to say that the Shawnees have entirely withdrawn their support of the schools especially designed for their benefit; hence but few of them are now receiving school learning." The Shawnees had executed an arrangement with the Cherokees whereby they were to become merged with the latter tribe when they moved into the Cherokee country. There their tribal relations would be changed, and they would become officially Cherokees. In 1870 Agent Roberts reported that a number had effected sales of their lands and had removed to the Cherokee country, and " there are yet five hundred and twenty-seven of the

Shawnees remaining on this reservation, nearly all of whom express a desire to move to the south." In 1871 the agent reported that the Shawnees had about all gone to the Indian Territory. Some of them, in order to continue with their brethren, have left " well cultivated farms, with comfortable and attractive residences, to undergo the fatigue and hardship of a new country." " Black Bob's Band " went to the Quapaw agency with a band that had previously gone there. The agency was discontinued.

James Stanley was appointed agent of the Miamis, etc. His Indians had nearly all moved to the Territory, and his agency was also soon discontinued.

Hiram W. Jones was appointed agent of the Indians of Quapaw agency in 1871. It was located in the northeastern corner of Indian Territory, with Missouri on the east and Kansas on the north; hence was of easy access to liquor traders in both of these states. The next year he reported: " This agency comprises the following tribes, viz.: Quapaws, numbering two hundred and forty; Confederate Peorias, Kaskakies, Wias, Piankeshaws, one hundred and sixty; Ottawas of Blanchard's Fork, and Roche de Bœuf, one hundred and fifty; Eastern Shawnees, ninety; Wyandottes, two hundred and twenty-two, Senecas, two hundred and fourteen, making a total of one thousand and seventy-six." There were also about forty Miamis, and seventy-five members of Black Bob's band of Shawnees, recently removed to the agency, but not located. Many of his Indians were well advanced in civilization and wore citizen's clothes and spoke the English language. Some of them were largely mixed with white blood.

Agent Jones states in his report for 1873 that all of his Indians "worked well in farming." The boarding schools were well supplied with children. The Senecas were "bitterly opposed to schools" in 1872, but were then "decidedly favorable" to them." All who attended made commendable progress in their studies. Besides the Wyandotte, Seneca and Shawnee boarding school, the Ottawas and Quapaws each had a school. Of the latter Asa C. and Emeline H. Tuttle had charge. He was a Friend minister, and his wife was not only an efficient school teacher, but a good personal worker. They previously had charge of the Ottawa mission school, where they had won the hearts of parents and students, and a number had been converted through their instrumentality. The agent had farms opened at each of the mission schools, to make them so far as practicable manual labor schools.

The work was largely crippled by an act of Congress, the agent reports, "by which the salaries of employees are limited to six thousand dollars, which compels us to abandon their (Peoria and Miami) schools entirely, the children thereby not only loosing the time, but forgetting to a great degree what they had previously learned." In that agency there were three boarding schools besides the Peoria day school, and the Peoria Indians had ample funds to carry on their own school, but that unwise law of Congress prohibited it from being used for that purpose. Two other boarding schools had to be suspended before the close of the year for the same cause. That law was a great hindrance to the work in several agencies. In some of them the whole expense of the agency was paid with the interest on funds which the Government owed the Indians, but the schools and other work was crippled by that unjust limitation. Agent Jones had an orchard of from one hundred to three hundred and eighty fruit trees planted on each of the mission farms for the benefit of the schools. There was a Sabbath school at each schoolhouse and one at the agency.

In the fall of 1873 there were one hundred and fifty-two Modocs turned over to his care, with no funds to start them to farming or gardening. He therefore plowed twenty acres of the agency farm for them in the spring of 1874, which they planted and cultivated, principally with the hoe. " They worked well and attended their crops well." Their children were placed in the Quapaw school.

The Modocs report that when the Government was trying to get them to leave their country in Southern Oregon, which they had possessed from time immemorial, Captain Jack and his band refused to go to the country of the Klamath Indians. They remembered that years before some state soldiers collected a band of Modocs for peaceful council, as the Indians thought, but when the soldiers got them into their possession they killed all of them! In retaliation for that, when General Canby and some Commissioners convened Captain Jack and some of his warriors for council, they set a similar trap for the officers and massacred them, and then fled to the " Lava Beds." After a hard struggle for soldiers and Indians the latter surrendered, and were taken to the Quapaw agency for the Friends to manage under the banner of " the Prince of Peace."

In 1875 the agent reported that " the mission school under the care of A. C. and E. H. Tuttle has had an enrollment of ninety, with an average attendance of seventy, during the past year. The advancement made by the pupils is very satisfactory. This is especially the case with the Modoc children, whose application and regular attendance has been exceptionally good. The Ottowa mission school, under the care of Pelatiah and Caroline E. Bond as teacher and matron, has had an enrollment of forty-five during the past year, with an average attendance of twenty-nine. The Seneca, Shawnee and Wyandotte mission school was under the care of Henry and Anna B. Thorndike as teacher and matron. The enrollment was one hundred and twenty-three, with an average attendance of seventy-three. The progress of the students in all the schools was commendable, and religious service was held on Sabbath days at all of the schoolhouses. Henry Thorndike was largely gifted of

God for personal religious work. He has been the instrument in the hand of the Lord in the conversion of many people by his private talk in regard to their salvation. A number of his Indian pupils, there is cause to believe, were converted through his instrumentality.

In 1876 Agent Jones reported all of the schools were in a prosperous condition, and the Indians of the various tribes were progressing in farming and in civilization. Of the Modocs, so recently brought in contact with civilization, he reports: " They are now, and have been for some time, living on the products of their own farm labor. They are earnest and diligent in sending their children to school, and are much interested in their progress. They attend religious meetings, and evince, by their orderly deportment, an earnest desire to be instructed in the way of life. During a residence of nearly three years in the agency not a single Modoc has been intoxicated." The other Indians were becoming more temperate. Two hundred and seventy-eight scholars had, during the year, attended the three boarding schools and two day schools. There were about twenty of school age who had not attended school. " Religious meetings were held at all the schoolhouses, which were attended and participated in by the Indians in considerable numbers."

In 1879 Agent Jones made his seventh and last annual report.

Number of Indians in Quapaw Agency in

	1879.	1897.	Change in 18 years.
Quapaw	235	239	Increase, 4
Peoria and Miami. . . .	197	269	Increase, 72
Ottawa	135	167	Increase, 32
Seneca	242	312	Increase, 70
Modoc	103	52	Decrease, 51
Eastern Shawnees in 1895	88	90	Increase, 2
Total	1000	1129	

Agent Jones states: "Taking all the tribes together their condition is very encouraging. They have worked well during the year, and have made fair additions to their improvements. . . . The Indians have broken one thousand, two hundred and eighty acres of new land; have made rails and put up seven thousand, two hundred rods of new fence, and have built forty-one new houses during the year. They have four hundred and fifty log houses, seventy-one built of frame, and one brick house. The educational interests have been in a prosperous condition during the year. Total enrollment at the schools, one hundred and sixty boys and one hundred and fifty girls. . . . The prospects for schools were never better than they are for the coming year. . . . The Quapaw and Modoc school will be under the charge of A. C. and E. H. Tuttle, and the Seneca, Shawnee and Wyandotte school will be in charge of C. W. Kirk and wife; the Peoria school under charge of G. M. Lindley, and the Miami school under charge of M. H. Stoner for the ensuing year. With this able company of teachers and superintendents I hope for great results. . . . The religious interest among the Indians of this agency is an encouraging feature of the work."

The Nez Percé prisoners, numbering eighty-six men, one hundred and sixty-eight women, and one hundred and thirty-seven children, were transferred to the care of Agent Jones. The writer had been appointed general agent of the Friends' Committee to visit the agencies under their care, and I met with those Indians. In the report to the committee is the following: "The Nez Perce Indians have, I think, been unfairly dealt with. There is no doubt but they surrendered to General Miles with the promise on his part that they should be allowed to remain with their people in Idaho. But the General was overruled in his promise, and they were removed from west of the Rocky Mountains to this agency. Three Christian Nez Percé Indians have left their tribe and families in Idaho, and come to this agency to benefit their people, all of whom have been employed by the agent. They are James Ruben, interpreter; Archie B. Sawyer, teacher (he is an ordained minister), and Mark Williams, a farmer.

" On Sabbath days a religious meeting is held in the agent's house, where, on the day we attended, which was cool and rainy, there were seventy Nez Percés and ten Modocs, besides a number of white people. The Indian women sat on the floor on one side of the room as closely together as possible. The men sat on chairs or on the floor on the other side of the room. Archie Sawyer spoke in his native language, with ease and fluency, and the three joined in singing the praises of God. The Bible, a hymn-book, and some other books have been printed in their language. The three men appear to be good, earnest Christians. A. B. Sawyer informed me that about forty years ago a Presbyterian missionary went among their people in Idaho, and by the blessing of God many of them had embraced the Christian religion, and had become members of the Presbyterian church. In addition to the Government School there is now a day school of higher grade, taught by a lady, where a few of the young men are preparing for preachers, teachers, etc. This school is sustained by the Presbyterian church."

A. J. Chapman appears to have accompanied the Nez Percé Indians from Idaho, and was employed by the agent for interpreter. But finding him a very immoral man, the agent discharged him. Commissioner Hayt then employed him as superintendent-farmer for the Nez Percé Indians. (They already had a farmer employed by the agent.) Mr. Chapman made the Indians believe that if they would give him money enough he would take them back to their country. By this false representation he extorted from them a few hundred dollars. He advised " Joseph," the head chief, to not allow the children to attend school or religious service. He was living in open adultery with an Indian girl. When all this was reported by the agent and by General McNeil, an inspector, to the Commissioner, he ordered that the money should be refunded to the Indians, but did not discharge him. The agent and inspector thought they had not the authority, as he was employed by the Commissioner." (Report of general agent to Indian Committee of Friends, 1879.)

Agent H. W. Jones had been very successful in his administration as Indian agent. When he assumed the office a large number of his Indian men carried revolvers, and as they could easily obtain liquor in Kansas and Missouri, drunkenness among them was very common; and if an Indian shot another Indian the United States law did not take cognizance of the crime, but allowed the Indians to settle it in their own way. Through the influence of Agent Jones, and his religious employees, the revolvers had largely, if not wholly, disappeared, and drunkennes had largely decreased. The Senecas' gambling " dog-feast " was discontinued.

" The Executive Committee of Friends on Indian Affairs " had been requested by President Hayes to continue their services in the Indian work, as they had under President Grant. They had met with no difficulty in the transaction of their business in connection with the

Commissioner of Indian Affairs until the appointment of E. A. Hoyt for Commissioner. The following is an abstract from the minutes of "The Executive Committee" of May, 1879:

"The sub-committee was continued to see the Commissioner and call his attention to the following points, viz.:

"1. The agreement with President Hayes, made May 2d, 1878, says: 'That in case any cause of complaint should arise against any person appointed under such nomination (i.e., by the Associated Executive Committee) that the Executive Committee shall be informed, so that innocent parties might have full opportunity to explain and shield themselves against unjust reproach without unnecessary exposure." Agent H. W. Jones was dismissed without such information to the committee of charges against him, or opportunity on his part to reply to them.

"2. The charges made verbally against H. W. Jones are now alleged to have been wholly false, and some evidence given to show that this is the case. We believe, until further proof is given to the contrary, that the charges are false.

"3. On the 19th of December, 1878, the Commissioner gave us the assurance that in future agents nominated by us shall have the appointment of all employees, with our approval of them. Since that date A. J. Chapman, who had been discharged by Agent Jones from the position of interpreter for the Nez Percés, by instruction of the department and on the ground of alleged immoral conduct, has been appointed by the Commissioner as a superintendent of farming for the Nez Percés, irrespective of the above-mentioned assurance. There is, we believe, ample testimony to show that A. J. Chapman is grossly immoral. We ask that he be discharged.

" 4. We ask, also, that no appointee of the department be retained in agencies under agents nominated by us, who shall in the judgment of the committee prove a positive hindrance to the work of solid improvement of the Indians." . . . " Notwithstanding the favorable report of Dr. Nicholson about the Quapaw agency, it was understood that United States Inspector McNeil had been sent to this agency to make a full investigation of its condition. On reaching there Lawrie Tatum (general agent of the committee) found Inspector McNeil had just finished his investigation, and procured from him the charges and replies. It appeared from these that Agent Jones was exonerated."

The sub-committe had further interviews with Commissioner Hoyt, which were not satisfactory. The last one was on May 17th, 1879, when it is stated he " left upon the minds of the committee the impression that he proposed to do as he might think proper in any case, quite contrary to our understanding of the agreement with the President, and the Commissioner's former assurance as to appointment of employees." The committee,

Benjamin Tatham, of New York city; Dr. James E. Rhoads, of Philadelphia, and Murray Shipley, of Cincinnati, then called upon President Hayes, who, they report, " received us with kindness, and we informed him that after careful consideration, we were decided that it would not be wise for us further to co-operate with the Government in the management of Indians under Commissioner Hoyt; that we now resigned on behalf of the Society of Friends all further responsibility for the Indian work, but wished to assure him of our appreciation of the kind consideration which we had always received from him, of our desire for the prosperity of his administration, and our high regard for him as Chief Magistrate of our nation. The President said that necessarily he was not acquainted with the details of the action of the department; expressed his regret that we felt that it was our duty to adopt the course we had indicated." He accepted the resignation!

Thus closed the official connection of Friends with the Indian Department of the Government, after ten years of faithful service, in which the Indians under their care, as well as those under the care of agents nominated by committees of other churches, received an uplift such as they never had during any previous decade of the nation. The civilization and Christianization of the Indians has since been advancing in the agencies that were under the care of Friends, as well as in others, notwithstanding in some instances unregenerate and wicked men have been appointed agents. But missionary labor has been carried on by various churches in many of the agencies, which has been blessed of God.

Dr. James E. Rhoads, of Germantown, Philadelphia, was probably the best informed and most influential menber of the Friends' Indian Committee, and the one on whom the Commissioner called for a nomination in the Central Superintendency. From an address delivered by him before Friends of Baltimore Yearly Meeting, on "Progress in Indian Civilization," printed in "Friend's Review," Sixth month 14th, 1894, the following extracts are taken: *

"From the first settlement of this country by European immigrants two attitudes have been assumed by different portions of the white race towards the native Indians. One group has looked upon the Indian as a heathen and inferior race, who might be defrauded in trade, robbed of their lands, and slain if they resisted or retaliated. The other has been composed of those who, like the early Roman Catholic missionaries of Canada and the northwest, or Brainerd, Eliot, and men of New England, or the Moravians and "Friends" of Pennsylvania and New Jersey, have patiently sought to befriend the Indians, to teach them the truths of Christianity, and bring them to the enjoyment of the best fruits of Christian civilization. . . .

"Probably never more than five hundred thousand

*Dr. James E. Rhoads was removed to his heavenly home in 1895.

GROUP OF PRINTERS AT THE INDIAN INDUSTRIAL SCHOOL, CARLISLE, PA.

Students must be fairly well advanced in their school work before they can enter the printing office.

in number within the region occupied by the United States and its territories (excluding Alaska), the Indians were estimated three hundred and fifty thousand in 1872; but the more accurate census of 1890 shows that they number a little under two hundred and fifty thousand. This diminution has been largely due to their access to alcohol, and to certain forms of diseases, like smallpox, measles, and epidemic influenza, introduced among them by the advent of Europeans. But even when treated with uniform kindness and justice, as on the Island of Nantucket, they have diminished in the presence of white civilization, unable to resist its temptations and the physical strain it imposes in the struggle for livelihood. . . . The area of land occupied by this quarter million of Indians was, in 1890, nearly as large as that of France or Spain.

" In earlier days, through the agency of the army, and since 1832, through that of the Civil Bureau of Indian Affairs, the National Government has carried on its relations with the Indian tribes. For a long period they were treated as quasi-independent nations, but in 1872 Congress forbade the making of treaties with them, and ordered that all subsequent relations with them should be established by enacted laws.

" The Indian Bureau is one of many sub-divisions under the Department of the Interior; it has its headquarters in Washington, with a Commissioner of Indian Affairs at its head; also there are legal advisers and a corps of clerks, and a Superintendent of Indian Education. It directly influences the Indians through fifty-nine Indian agents, who are apopinted by the President, and who reside among the various tribes and bands of Indians. . . .

"The name of Indian agent had become almost the synonym, in popular estimation, of fraud and dishonor. But now men are chosen for their high integrity and personal devotion to the welfare of the Indians, and although these men were sometimes lacking in business ability and in force of character, the honesty of the service was greatly increased, and the best interest of the Indians was more largely secured. For almost twenty years past the Indian service has been as free from fraud as any branch of the Government.

"The Central Superintendency, comprising the Indians in Kansas and the wilder tribes in the Indian Territory, numbering seventeen thousand in all, was placed under the charge of Friends. Enoch Hoag was made superintendent, and under him there were nine agents. Of all the millions that passed through their hands not fifty dollars, perhaps not one dollar, was dishonestly used, though mistakes of judgment doubtless occurred. At one time there were, besides the general superintendent and agents, nearly one hundred teachers, clerks, farmers, smiths and other employees who were "Friends," engaged in the Indian service. . . .

"In 1867 there were but three thousand, five hundred

Indian children enrolled in school; the number rose to six thousand in 1872, and now there are over twenty thousand out of the thirty-five thousand to be educated. In 1877, at the urgent solicitation of " Friends," Congress, for the first time in our history, made an appropriation for Indian education not demanded by a treaty stipulation. That year the churches added two hundred and fifty thousand dollars for Indian education, beside the sums expended for the support of missionaries. But in 1892 the appropriations for education were two millions, two hundred ninety-one thousand, six hundred and fifty dollars, and the churches were still giving over a quarter of a million for the same purpose. The Government school for negroes at Hampton, Virginia, stimulated by the remarkable success of Captain R. H. Pratt in training his adult Apaches and other Indian prisoners in the fort at St. Augustine, Florida, and at his suggestion, took Indians under its excellent training, and soon afterwards the Carlisle Indian School was established by Captain Pratt, who has done so noble a work for Indian civilization. Everywhere the churches were stimulated to seek the conversion of the Indians to Christianity; missions and schools were multiplied and enlarged, and thousands of Indians were added to the former converts of the Christian faith.

Difference or hostility towards the Indians as a race has been changed into a permanent desire for their civilization, partly through the closer relations into which the churches were brought with the Indians, but more largely through the wise and efficient labors of the Women's National Indian Association and the Indian Rights Association. . . .

" In 1885, Indians committing crimes against the persons or property of other Indians or whites, were brought under the jurisdiction of United States and State Courts, and they received corresponding protection from these courts.

" Senator Dawes, after long and most serious discussion, secured the passage of the law giving lands in severalty to Indians prepared for it, conferring upon them a gradual introduction into civilization, and making possible the sale of their surplus goods by their consent and for their benefit. Many thousands of Indians now hold their own allotments of lands, and seem permanently settled upon them. . . .

" It is safe to say that many hundreds of Indian children and adults have been led by Friends to a new life and character through a living faith in Christ, so that in the four Monthly Meetings of " Friends " in the Indian Territory we have a membership of over four hundred Indians. Corresponding blessings have accompanied the loving ministrations of other churches. There are now (1894) twenty-five thousand, two hundred and eighty-five members of churches among the Indians; but this leaves a large number out of the quarter million who are ignorant of the Gospel, and for years to come whatever missions the Christians of the United States sustain, those among the Indians should be steadily extended till all are Christians in name and fact."

The Indian agents generally, if not universally, had difficulty in settling their accounts with the Government. The accounts were made out in quadruplicate; one copy to be retained by the agent, and three were sent to the superintendent at Lawrence, Kansas. He retained one and forwarded two copies to the Commissioner at Washington, who transmitted one to the Treasury Department. After the accounts passed under the critical inspection of the Commissioner of Indian Affairs and the Interior Department and their numerous clerks, and were found to be satisfactory, they were passed to the office of second auditor of the Treasury Department. Having satisfied that officer and his clerks, they were placed in the hands of the second comptroller of the Treasury, where the examination was more critical, if possible, than either of the other offices. When found correct the Indian agent was allowed credit for his expenditures and his accounts were settled.

In my accounts, the three thousand dollars appropriated to erect a boarding schoolhouse of sufficient capacity to accommodate thirty students and necessary employees, was reported as insufficient, and I estimated for one thousand dollars more to complete the building, which was placed to my credit, and eight hundred dollars of it was used for the purpose.

I had an interpreter for the Comanche language, and " estimated " or petitioned for funds to have the Caddo language interpreted by the same person who interpreted the Comanche language. The funds were forwarded, and four hundred dollars were used for that purpose. About two years after the funds were used for both purposes, the Commissioner wrote me that there were no Government funds applicable to either of the above items, and the twelve hundred dollars must be refunded. My commission commanded me to obey the instructions of superior officers. I obeyed their instructions by using the funds for the purposes for which they were placed to my credit. Suit was instituted against me for not refunding the amount. Before the date occurred for the lawsuit, a proposition was indirectly forwarded to me that if I would pay one hundred dollars and costs of legal action my accounts would be cancelled and the lawsuit should be withdrawn. The proposition was accepted, and my accounts, covering several hundred thousand dollars, were settled.

Agent J. H. Pickering had funds placed to his credit for building a schoolhouse. In the fall, when the house was completed, he drew on the funds to pay for it, but to his surprise the funds had reverted to the United States Treasury. A regulation had been made by the Interior Department that unused funds should at the close of the fiscal year (June 30th) revert to the Treas-

ury.   Neither he nor any other agent had been informed
of the regulation.   He therefore had to pay for the
schoolhouse from his personal funds.   Subsequently he
was relieved by an act of Congress.

On one occasion the duplicate accounts of Agent
Beede were transmitted to the Indian Bureau, where
they were allowed to remain until examined by the
Indian office, and then one copy was forwarded to
the Treasury Department.   The Second Auditor suspended one voucher of thirty-two thousand, five hundred
dollars because the Indian office had forwarded the
wrong copy.   Both copies were precisely alike, except
that one was marked " Duplicate."   Agent Beede from
his distant home had to correct the mistake of the Indian
Commissioner, which could have been done much sooner
and equally well without writing to Agent Beede, but
would not have been according to " red tape."

These events are given as specimens of the hardships
to which Indian agents have been subjected in settling
their accounts.   One of my friends, who has long lived
in Washington, and who has known what has transpired
in the Interior Department, informed me that of the
many lawsuits that he had known against Indian agents
they had all been decided in favor of the agents.   The
instruction contained in the " commission " of the agents
has sometimes proved a valuable testimony in Court, as
it orders them to obey superior officers.   If funds are

placed to the credit of an agent to be used for a specific purpose, and after being used for that purpose it is discovered that there was not proper authority for forwarding the funds, the agent has the shield of his " commission."

CHAPTER XI.

Elkanah Beard and Wife First Missionaries—Can "Friends" be Saved Without Missionary Work?—Franklin Elliot Succeeded E. Beard at Shawneetown—A. C. Tuttle and Wife Did Missionary Work While Teaching a Government School—Afterward Employed as Missionaries—J. Hubbard, Missionary—Epoch in "Friends" Church—Ninety Indians Taken Into Church Membership—"The Lord's Supper"—The Six Nation Indians—"Monthly Meeting" Established—Frank Modoc Recorded a Minister—Skiatook Meeting and School—Iowa Indians—Kickapoo Indians—Pryor Monthly Meeting—J. Hubbard, a Cherokee Indian—Chilocco School—Number of Meetings and Ministers—Grand River Quarterly Meeting.

THE first ministers engaged by the Executive Committee of Friends on Indian Affairs for definite and continued missionary work with the Indians in Central Superintendency were Elkanah and Irena Beard, in 1878. They were located at Shawneetown, in the central part of Indian Territory, near the Shawnee and Pottawatomie Government boarding school. Religious services were held at the schoolhouse until the Friends' Meeting House was built near there. In his first annual report to the committee, in 1879, alluding to the sixty scholars who attended school and religious services, he states: "Quite a number of the children say they have given themselves to the Lord Jesus. . . . Some of them unsolicited have asked to be 'made Friends.' We think, however, it is yet premature to attempt an organization."

He put up a " double log-house," each part twenty feet square, two stories high, with a hall between them ten feet wide, which was roofed, and in which was the stair-way. In closing his report he wrote: " The question is not, Can the Indian be saved? but, Can Friends be saved if they do not attempt to support at least one mission for the aborigines of our country ? "

The next year E. Beard and wife were at the Cheyenne and Arapahoe agency. In his report in 1881 he states that the Episcopalians were educating a Cheyenne to do missionary work there, and that they wished to leave the field and return to their home in Indiana.

The Executive Committee of Friends published a short manual of " Doctrines of the Friends' Mission Church." It did not sever those who joined it from any church, nor attach them to the Friends' Church. It appeared to answer a good purpose for a time.

Franklin Elliott and wife were stationed at Shawnee-town in 1880, and they made their first report in 1881. F. Elliott states that a church organization had been effected with the Pottawatomies with twenty-eight members, some " faithful workers being among them."

Jonathan and Lydia Ozbun were located at the Osage agency, and organized a " mission church " for the workers, expecting it to be a " nucleus to which to gather those who may become interested." He had labored for some time among the Kiowas, with quite hopeful results. Some of them, he believed, were converted, but while he was absent from them a short time at the agency a minister of another church went to the Kaw station and organized a church and then departed. As he did not remain there or send a missionary, it seemed to only frustrate the work of Friends, and the organization was not sustained.

A. C. Tuttle and wife were engaged at the Ottawa school in about 1870. They found the Ottawas in a very degraded condition and sadly intemperate, but through their faithful labors drinking was largely reduced, and order was restored. Some of the Indians were converted, and they started a "mission church." When the Quapaw and Modoc boarding schoolhouse was built they were transferred in charge of that school, and continued to have charge of the Ottawa meeting. My wife and I visited them and the Quapaw and Modoc school in 1879. In my report as general agent of the committee is the following: "The scholars are more thoroughly taught the Scriptures than white children usually are, even in Christian communities. Two gentlemen were once visiting the school, who, after hearing the children answer many Bible questions, were asked if they wished to question them. 'No,' they replied, 'we do not wish to ask them any questions, and we would rather they would not ask us any.'"

One evening six or eight of the boys asked permission to go into the sitting room to talk with us on religion. They were all desirous of living Christian lives. After they retired six of the girls were invited into the room. I asked them definite questions about their conversion and religious life. They had all been converted, one of them about two months before, and four of them under the influence of Henry Thorndike and wife, while pupils of theirs. Several of them lamented their unfaithfulness in performing religious duty. Three of them prayed while we were together that evening.

On February 23d, 1879, we attended meeting with Asa and Emeline Tuttle in the Ottawa meeting-house, which is a stockade building, erected, I believe, by the generosity of New England "Friends."* The house was full and the people listened attentively to the word preached. Many of them had been converted, and several expressed a desire to have a change of heart. At the close of the meeting there was a marriage of a white man, Mr. Jennison, and an Indian woman, Catherine, daughter of Chief Judge Wind. Some years before she had been converted, but was then regretting that she had not lived nearer the Saviour. While attending school she said to A. and E. Tuttle, as they were about to leave for a few days, " Don't you run off, for if you do I shall never be anything but an Indian squaw." She, in common with many others, realized the import-

---

*Stockade buildings are made by planting logs in an upright position into the ground, close together, permitting them to project as high as the story is to be, and then placing a plate on the top, on which the roof rests. It is a very common mode of building where trees grow short.

ance of the school learning and the religion of Jesus, by which their aspirations were raised to something higher than to be an Indian Squaw.*

After the marriage the wedding party and others partook of a basket dinner. All appeared to enjoy the repast. The pastry made by the Indians was decidedly good. After partaking of the meal we were called together for a temperance meeting, which had previously been arranged for by the Indians. There were several new signers to the pledge, and the blue ribbon which had been provided was in demand. At the close of the temperance meeting there was a funeral of a young Indian who had been converted some years before. The living were reminded to " be ye also ready." Thus closed a Sabbath day's work.

By the next year—1880—A. C. Tuttle was engaged by the committee to devote himself to missionary work. In his report of the Modocs he states: "The people are an example to all that visit them, willing to confess the Lord and plead for his cause. At our last Sabbath evening meeting we had twelve living testimonies by way of exhortation and prayer, and a most affecting rehearsal of the dear Lord's condescension in visiting the sick and afflicted in time of trouble. . . . It may safely be said that the predisposition of the Indians of this agency is decidedly for ' Friends ' and their work. The efforts of Charles W. Kirk are being abundantly blessed at the

*I received a letter from her in 1895 when she was still an earnest Christian.

Wyandotte, Seneca and Shawnee Mission. Not much religious influence is being exerted outside of ' Friends' ' organization." Lizzie Test was the principal teacher under Dr. Kirk. She was apparently called and qualified of God to teach the Indians and to direct them to Jesus, whose blood was shed for the redemption of all men.

Jeremiah Hubbard, of Timbered Hills, Kansas, made a religious visit to some of the Indians in Quapaw agency, and sent an appointment for a meeting to the Seneca nation. The chief, Joseph Spicer, sent him word to not come there; they had their own religion, and if he did not want to lose his scalp he had better stay away. Thomas Smith and he went there with Nicholas Cotter as a pilot and interpreter. They drove to John Winney's, a full-blood Seneca, his wife being a Wyandotte, who attended school in Ohio, and she could talk English well. They had a small but favored meeting at J. Winney's house. This was the first religious meeting ever held in the Seneca nation by a minister of any church, as they were strongly prejudiced against Christianity. They were not disturbed or molested in any way. J. Hubbard was impressed that the Lord had further service for him in that as well as in other tribes in the Quapaw agency.

He afterwards attended a meeting of the Executive Committee of Friends, at Richmond, Indiana, held in May, 1880, and told the committee that there should be made a more special effort than Friends were making to get the Indians converted, and then take them into church membership, establish meetings among them, and set them to work. He told them that he knew of no other church organization so well adapted to the Indians as "Friends." Up to this time, at the various agencies, there had been scores of Indians converted, and some were converted in the schools which had been held for fifty years or more among the Shawnees and at Tunesassa, New York, and only two that I have any trace of had been taken into the "Friends'" church! J. Hubbard saw that there was something more needed; it was seen also by the committee. He believed that it would be right for him to do evangelistic work among them if the committee would sustain him in working as he believed the Master called him to work, which was to preach salvation through Christ; and all who accepted the message and were converted, if they wished to join "Friends," he believed should be encouraged to become members. The committee was satisfied with his plan of work, and engaged him to spend one week in each month in evangelistic work among the Indians.

He then brought the subject before Timbered Hills Monthly Meeting, Kansas, to which he belonged, and obtained its approval of his religious work among the Indians, with the assurance that they would receive into membership those who gave satisfactory evidence that they had been converted, and who wished to join in membership with "Friends." The action of the com-

mittee, and of Timbered Hills Monthly Meeting, in connection with Jeremiah Hubbard, formed an epoch in
Friends' Church.

J. Hubbard now started to work in the field in which
he believed the Lord called him. Many of the Indians
had already been converted through the faithful labors
of the Friends, who for years had been laboring among
them as Government employees, but under the influence
of the Holy Spirit. With the plain, happy, cheerful
teaching, preaching and talk of " Jerry Hubbard," others
were brought to repentance of their sins and surrendered
to Christ, their Saviour. In the course of a few months
he took the names of ninety Indians to the Monthly
Meeting who wished to become members of the Friends'
Church. Praise the Lord for His blessing!

After going to the Seneca nation a number of times,
the council appointed an Indian to kill J. Hubbard. But
somehow the Lord got hold of the appointee and converted him. Then, instead of being a deadly enemy to
Jeremiah Hubbard, he became one of the strongest
friends that he had among the Senecas. During one of
my visits to the Indians, Joseph Spicer, the chief who
sent word to J. Hubbard forbidding his going to their
nation to preach, sent word to us to come to his house and
hold a meeting, and he would have the room prepared
for the occasion. This was a surprise to J. Hubbard, as
he had seen no yielding in this chief or his wife, except
that he had attended one of our meetings. Some chairs

were placed for us, and benches for the congregation. Three of his neighbors, who apparently did not wish to be seen attending a Christian service, were there grinding their axes! J. Spicer and wife were evidently pleased with the meeting, and their house was afterwards one of the places for holding regular religious services. It was believed that he, his wife, and two daughters were converted; the women were taken into membership, and he gave evidence of dying in peace some years ago.

It was not unusual, when Indians were converted who had been married according to their custom, for them to wish to be married again according to the Christian ceremony. J. Hubbard and other ministers were frequently called on to consummate such marriages. The committee had marriage certificates printed, and the missionaries were furnished with them.

There was a law of Congress providing that no persons other than Indians, licensed traders, or employees of the Government, should go into business in the Territory for pecuniary profit. This prohibited our missionaries from being self-supporting, other than to have a garden, orchard, and enough cows and horses for the use of the family. They could make themselves useful, however, in showing the Indians how to farm and garden, as well as talking about the interest of their souls. But they had to be supported by the committee.

It was very common, when a meeting was held at the house of an Indian, for the family to provide for the whole congregation to remain and eat a meal together. With some of the Indians this seemed to the missionaries somewhat burdensome, especially when frequently repeated at the same house. Those meetings and the repasts were very like the meetings and social meals that the apostle Paul and early Christians called " The Lord's Supper." A royal preparation was made by Matthias Splitlog, a Seneca, on an occasion when J. Hubbard and others were to have a meeting in the large room prepared for the purpose over his store. " He killed a beef, provided fifty pounds of butter, twenty dozen eggs and other food in preparation for the meeting, so that no one need go hungry. We had a very good meeting; the power of God was felt in our midst, to the building of us all up in the hope of the gospel. Oh! what a blessed thought, that when we meet in the name of the Lord, then He is in the midst of His people to bless. Thomas Stanley spoke to us for awhile to our help and encouragement, as he is very much at home with the Indians."*

Thomas Stanley was one of the grand friends of the Indians. He has traveled hundreds, if not thousands, of miles afoot, and being consciously with Jesus, from his home near Americus, Kansas, to various agencies, to visit the Indians and encourage them in their spiritual life, and in showing and assisting them in farming, horticulture, etc., he has probably done more than any other person in encouraging Indians to plant fruit trees, and

*Page 13. " Grand River Monthly Meecing of Friends, Composed of Indians," by Jeremiah Hubbard.

informing them how they could be procured. J. Hubbard frequently spoke of his valuable assistance in the work among the Indians.

On February 29th, 1881, at a meeting appointed by J. Hubbard and J. M. Watson at John Winney's, who had formerly been chief of the Senecas, "J. Winney arose in a very dignified manner and said: 'My people we came here long time ago, seven hundred strong, and now we only number about two hundred strong. What is the reason of all this? I believe I know. Because we do not do as Great Spirit wants us to do. Now, I want my people to turn; go with me and be Christians. I turn; I go.' He turned about and gave me his hand, and at the same time gave his heart unto the Lord, and with his mind fully made up he yielded all into the hands of the Master. He said: 'If we turn the Lord will love us. This way all new to me, but I feel in my heart it is right, this way to do; and the Great Spirit says right.' His wife, Lucy Winney, told me she was now ready to make the start also." ("Grand River Monthly Meeting," page 20.) With the assistance of friends of Indiana, J. Winney afterwards built Bethany meeting-house.

Agent Jones, in one of his reports, stated that there were representatives of all "The Six Nations" in his agency. From John Winney, probably the oldest Seneca in Indian Territory, I learn that in the long, long ago, before Christopher Columbus reached America,

Ta-cah-na-we-tah, a Seneca, who loved his people and peace more than he loved war, originated " The Council Fire " of the Iroquois or Six Nation Indians, consisting of the Senecas, Cayugas, Mohawks, Oneidas, Onondagas and Tuscaroras, when they agreed to bury their tomahawks and scalping knives and be one people. From that time they have ever been brotherly and never have been vanquished. Ta-cah-nah-we-tah prophesied that they would eventually be lost in another people, who would take the country. A considerable number of the Six Nation Indians are living on small reservations in the State of New York, but the main body of them is living in Ontario, Canada, where there were, in 1876, three thousand one hundred, and they were slowly increasing in numbers.

A house was built for school and meeting purposes by the committee, near Bluejacket, in the Cherokee nation, in 1881, where a number of the Shawnees were living who were formerly under the care of Friends in Kansas. Several of them had joined Friends. Application was made to the Cherokee Council for permission to have the use of another small tract of land, upon which to build a house for a missionary. The council was willing to grant the petition provided Friends would obligate themselves to board and educate at least ten Cherokee children. It was not thought wise to enter into such an obligation, and the house was not built and the work was thus largely frustrated.

In 1882 there were established four " Preparative Meetings of Friends "—Ottawa, Wyandotte, Modoc and Seneca—and they constituted a Monthly Meeting called Grand River, with one hundred and thirty-three members, ninety-three of whom were received during the year—i. e., between the times of making the annual reports to the committee, which was in the spring. Twenty-one of these members were white people, thirteen of whom had married into the Indian tribes.

In less than three years after the first Gospel meeting was held in the Seneca nation enough of them had been taken into membership to organize a " Preparative " Meeting. In 1884 the committee, under the supervision of J. M. Watson, built Seneca meeting-house for them, described by Lucy Winney as " a very comfortable and pleasant one in every way, well finished in and on the outside." In nine years after the desperate scenes in the lava caves of Oregon, many of the Modocs had been converted, principally through the influence of A. C. Tuttle and wife, and had joined the peace church of Friends, and a " Preparative " Meeting had been organized of Modoc Indians. Praise the Lord for His power to save, and give eternal life to pagan and savage warriors, as well as college students, and who can give to all the lamb-like Spirit. Ottawa Preparative Meeting was also the fruit of Asa C. and Emeline H. Tuttle.

Jeremiah Hubbard was engaged by the committee to spend the whole time in the Territory as a missionary, and there was a dwelling-house built for his use near the meeting-house that the Government had built some years before, nearly half a mile from the Wyandotte boarding schoolhouse.

As Friends believed that the baptism with the Holy Spirit, and not of water, was taught by Christ as belonging to His dispensation, it seemed appropriate to the missionaries that some public demonstration should be made to show that converts were taken into church membership by some other means than by water baptism. It therefore became the custom, after the Monthly Meeting decided to take Indians into membership, to " give them the right hand of fellowship," in the Monthly Meeting, or at the close of a Sabbath meeting.

At the Monthly Meeting held July 22d, 1882, the reporter stated: " One new member by letter and eight by request were added. It was a time of joy to many, especially on account of a very aged woman—a Seneca —whose tottering footsteps told of need for a home beyond this life. A recess of five minutes was given for the members to take the new ones by the hand, and then all knelt down before the Lord, and our friend, Lizzie Test, led in solemn prayer for the strengthening of the church, and for His blessing upon those whose names were just enrolled."

" Seneca Preparative Meeting of Friends, held the 25th of January, 1883. Seventeen present—eleven adults and six children. Opened by Sister Margaret

Ward reading the one hundred and thirty-seventh Psalm, followed by singing number sixty-two of Gospel Hymns; then prayer by Sister Ward. She also spoke of the great privilege of reading of God out of His own book, and encouraged all to faithfulness, that we may wear the crown that is laid up for His children. Sampson Smith and James Armstrong testified and praised the Lord that they had the privilege of mingling again with God's children to tell of his great love for mankind, and both expressed a desire to keep in the way. They are rejoicing that they have found the way that gives peace to their souls. Other testimonies were given of God's mercies to the children of men. Matilda Whitecrow said: ' I joined the Friends about a year ago, but I have not said anything before. I now want to say that I am glad I did, for I feel better. I can think of my God now every day, when before I did not. I would not go back to those times. I have forsaken all, and do desire to go on in this way of holiness.' This has been a refreshing time. No business coming before the meeting, we solemnly conclude."

" Signed, "LUCY A. WINNEY,

Clerk for the day."

The foregoing is a sample copy of the Preparative Meeting minutes, obtained by the writer during one of his visits to the mission stations.

"Steamboat Frank," a Modoc, was acknowledged a minister of the Gospel of Christ by Grand River

Monthly Meeting, held May 24th and 25th, 1884. He appears to have been the first Indian recorded a minister in the Friends' church. In ten years after he had been a desperate fighter in the caverns of Oregon he was an humble follower of the Lord and a minister of the Gospel of the Prince of Peace. " If you can make Quakers of them it will take the fight out."—President Grant. He afterwards carried the Gospel message to his brethren, and also to the Klamath Indians, in Oregon, a number of whom gave evidence of being converted, and six of them requested admission to membership in Grand River Monthly Meeting. He also preached the Gospel in a number of meetings in Iowa and Kansas. He felt so strongly the need of more thorough knowledge of English, and of the Bible, that he was sent to Oak Grove Seminary, in Maine, for further instruction. Before he was through with his studies he was taken with consumption and died. His name was changed to Frank Modoc, the name by which he was generally known in the East. When I last heard him it was difficult to convey his thoughts in English, but in his mother tongue he seemed to speak with fluency and power. He was faithful unto death, which occurred June 12th, 1886, aged forty-five years. His funeral sermon was preached by his spiritual father, A. C. Tuttle.

The following was written June 26th, 1884, by Huldah Bonwell, a Philadelphia Friend, who spent some time in Quapaw agency: " I feel it a privilege to be with and have the privations of these people, and particularly do I feel it a privilege to hear their deathbed testimonies. Four of those whom I waited on this spring made a peaceful end, waiting for the coming of Him who hath washed them and made them clean. One old Seneca woman whom we do not know to have been in a meeting-house, and who appeared to be a confirmed pagan, was taken sick this spring. She asked the people who were about her to go to the Christians and get some of them to come and see her, as she wished to talk with them; but the pagan Indians would not let her wish be known. Then she said: 'Mind I tell you now, Christianity is right and paganism is wrong,' repeating it many times. Still her people let her die without seeing those she asked for. . . . May Friends everywhere be stirred up to our duty to pursue the work of missions to the Indians and others to whom the Lord calls us to carry His glorious Gospel. Deeply do many feel the need of wisdom for this, and they desire that all shall be done decently and in order; but let us see to it that fearfulness about ways and methods do not deter us from bearing the message to those in darkness and ignorance, and in whose hearts the Lord perchance has put a thirst for a knowledge of His salvation." ("Grand River Monthly Meeting," page 52.)

In 1882 Ervin G. Taber was engaged as a missionary at the Cheyenne and Arapahoe agency. He found so much hindrance to his work that he remained but a year or two. Agent J. D. Miles did what he could to further his work.

Jonathan Ozbun's work at the Osage agency, with a station extending thirty miles eastward to the Roger settlement, and thirty miles westward to the Kaws, was not very promising. The committee thought that the funds to sustain the last two missionaries would do more good to put into the buildings at White's Manual Labor Institute, Indiana, in preparing to take Indian children there for education.

Franklin Elliott did efficient service for six years at Shawneetown, where he organized a Monthly Meeting with fifty-four members and superintended the building of a neat meeting-house. He resigned his position that he might take his children where they would have the benefit of a school. Dr. Charles. W. Kirk and wife resigned their position at the Wyandotte, Seneca and Shawnee school, and they were afterwards engaged as missionaries at Shawneetown, about two hundred and fifty miles southwest of the Quapaw agency. He reported that there were but nineteen members living within six miles of the meeting-house, but the teachers and school children from the Government school made a good-sized congregation. Of the members he reported: " A number appear to be growing in grace and seem likely to make strong men and women in the Lord, while others are kept alive by the nursing care of the church."

John F. Mardock had been laboring as a missionary

in Osage agency, principally at the Kaw station, and
although there had been a few converted, the prospect
for building up a church did not seem promising, and he
was removed to Skiatook, in 1885, in the western part of
the Cherokee nation, near to the Roger settlement, in
Osage agency, where there had been missionary work
done by James K. Ozbun and others. The work at
Skiatook seemed promising. Buildings were put up for
school and meeting and dwelling house. In 1888 the
average attendance of the school was about twenty-five,
taught by Elizabeth Shields. The school and meeting
continued to grow in size and importance. It seemed
best for J. F. Mardock to take charge of the missionary
work among the Iowa Indians, in 1889, and J. M. Watson, wife and daughter, were located at Skiatook. It
seemed that J. M. Watson was called and qualified by
the Head of the Church for missionary work, and his
daughter Eva called " by the same Spirit " to superin-
tend and teach the Skiatook School. Eighty acres of
land were furnished Friends for the mission by J. G.
Brady.

Philadelphia Friends have liberally sustained her in
furnishing funds for enlarging the buildings, and to pay
additional help as the school has enlarged. In 1896 the
report of the committee states: " At Skiatook there are
thirty-four Indian members. John M. Watson and wife
and their daughter, Eva Watson, reside here. The latter continues in charge as principal of the excellent

school, which is steadily increasing in size and usefulness. The present enrollment is eighty-eight. Nearly
three-fourths of the scholars are Indian children. An
average of thirty-two pupils have boarded at the school
during the current year, most of whom are Indians.
[It is understood that the white students pay board and
tuition.] . . . There are about three hundred and
thirty Indians within a radius of ten miles from this
centre, of whom about one-half are Cherokees, one-
fourth are Shawnees and the remainder are Osages.
Occasional meetings are held at two or three out-sta-
tions. The young people at Skiatook have for several
years succesfully maintained a Christian Endeavor Society, which has been helpful to its members and to the
meeting." J. M. Watson's wife, Eliza Watson, died
August 26th, 1898, aged seventy-three. "She hath done
what she could." A great loss to the school and mission
station.

In my visit to the Indians in 1895, J. F. Mardock
took me in his wagon to several agencies. We went to
see the Iowa Indians in the western part of Sac and Fox
agency. They told us that many of the Indian families
in Nebraska, where they formerly lived, had good frame
houses, with cook stoves and furniture, cultivated
farms, and were doing well. They were urged to take
allotments of one hundred and sixty acres for each head
of a family, or else move to Indian Territory. About
half of them preferred going to the Territory, where they

were assured that a tract of land fifteen by sixteen miles
would be asigned to them, and where they would have
no white neighbors to annoy them. They had been there
a year or two and we were the first ministers to visit
them. They were glad to see us and to hear preaching
again as they had been accustomed to hearing it in
Nebraska.

J. F. Mardock afterwards felt drawn to these Indians,
and located with them after leaving Skiatook. They
"heard him gladly." In 1890 Superintendent Kirk reported: "John F. Mardock's labors among the Iowas
have been greatly blessed. Meetings have been held each
Sabbath morning and evening. The attendance, though
not large, is regular and slowly increasing. He and his
wife employ all their time here. One of the best features of their work is the visiting from lodge to lodge,
when needed, ministering to the sick and praying with
all. The Lord is wonderfully giving him the hearts of
these people. Several profess conversion. About thirty,
including the children, have recently applied for membership in the Friends' church. . . . During 1890 the
Board of Commissioners appointed to treat with the
tribes in the Indian Territory have succeeded in securing
the consent of the Iowas to the allotment of their land
and to the sale of surplus lands, which doubtless leaves
them but a step from citizenship in Oklahoma Territory." The committee has secured a few acres of land

and built a meeting-house and a dwelling for the missionary.

The country was soon occupied when opened for settlement, and J. F. Mardock took a homestead near the mission that Friends had for the Iowas; and in addition to preaching to the Indians, he preached at Carney and Oak Grove, and organized meetings composed wholly of white people, and they were transferred to the care of Kansas Yearly Meeting. J. F. Mardock still has charge of Oak Grove meeting, and has other appointments. As the allotments of the Indians are twenty miles away from J. F. Mardock's home, Charles E. Pearson is the missionary in charge of the Iowa Indians. They number ninety-five, twenty-five of whom are Friends. In 1897 their number was eighty-six.

The Mexican Kickapoos have been the hardest to reach with the Gospel and education of any of the Indians to whom Friends have attempted to carry the Gospel. The Government put up a schoolhouse for them about 1876, but no children have gone there to school. Elizabeth Test believed it right to teach them, and after much effort succeeded in getting some orphan children to board with her at Shawneetown, whom she taught. The Indians, seeing the good effect, at length permitted her to put up a tent at their camp and to teach some of the children. The Lord blessed her labors, and the hearts of the Indians relented in their superstition enough to allow of the building of a house, where she and Lina B.

Lunt have faithfully labored to elevate those benighted Indians. Rachel Kirk has lived there since 1895 and assisted in the work. Thomas W. Alford, a Christian Shawnee, has also rendered valuable help as interpreter and otherwise. Par-thee, one of the prominent Kicka-poos, was converted in 1894. In March, 1896, in the report of E. Test and L. B. Lunt, they state: " Par-thee sometimes walks eight miles and back to hear the teach-ing about Jesus. He usually testifies, and sometimes earnestly exhorts in the meetings. He says that he often talks to his people, and believes by and by they will ac-cept the Son of Righteousness into their hearts." E. Test writes me that she believes that three other adults have been converted and probably more. One of them said that he had watched the missionaries, and by their lives was convinced that it was good to follow Jesus, and so far as he could understand he had accepted Him as his Saviour.

Many of the first settlers in Tecumseh, near Shaw-neetown mission, were hard-hearted people. William Neal, an English Friend, thought it right to labor among them as a missionary. He had been a street missionary in London. A few Indians attended his meetings, and crowds of white people. The first church building in the town he put up with a little assistance by the committee. A number were converted, and he had large and interest-ing meetings. Wiliam Neal and wife did good service there. " Tecumseh Meeting " was transferred to the care of Kansas Yearly Meeting of Friends.

In the limits of Bluejacket Monthly Meeting, John B. Bishop has been laboring for a number of years, holding meetings regularly in three stations in course—Divar, Pryor and Dog Creek. In May, 1896, the Quarterly Meeting authorized the establishment of a Monthly Meeting, embracing the three meetings, to be known as Pryor Monthly Meeting of Friends. The membership of these meetings numbered one hundred and three, of whom fifty-one are Indians. He writes that there are openings for other meetings in the vicinity, if ministers would go there who are called and qualified by the Head of the Church.

Jeremiah Hubbard has retired to that vicinity and has taken a claim as a Cherokee Indian. His grandmother was one-fourth blood Cherokee, and he is onesixteenth Cherokee. He has put up a two-story house, with the upper story seated for a meeting room, where meeting is regularly held. Although not as actively engaged in missionary work as formerly, his heart is in it still. In 1898 he was Quarterly Meeting superintendent of evangelistic work in Grand River Quarterly Meeting.

In visiting the Indian stations in 1885, I went to the Chilocco Government Industrial School, which was under the superintendency of H. J. Minthorn, M.D. It is located in Indian Territory, joining the southern boundary of Kansas. The tract of land assigned to it consisted of eleven thousand five hundred and twenty acres, equal to four by four and a-half miles in extent. Four thousand acres were fenced for pasture and one hundred acres were under cultivation. There were two hundred students at the school. It was then new. It has since been enlarged. The following is from my diary:

"Had meeting with the children and others at Chilocco for three evenings, and on Sabbath had meeting in the school room at eleven o'clock, and then gave the employees a Bible lesson on the ordinances at two o'clock, and another meeting at three. It seemed to be very manifest that there was a deep religious feeling at work in many of the scholars. After preaching a short time I called for the singing of the hymn, "Who is on the Lord's Side?" Then to answer the question by all standing who had been converted. There were probably twenty besides the workers who arose. I then asked all who wished to become Christians to arise, when there were about twenty more stood up. I then asked all who were standing to kneel down where they were, and after a season of prayer I asked those who wished to become Christians to remain on their knees and the others to take their seats. These were urged to pray for themselves. A number of them told me that they were made happy in the Lord, and there was cause to believe that they were converted. Eleven years afterwards I asked Laura Minthorn if those children proved their conversion by their subsequent life. She said they did while they remained there, and after going to Carlisle Indian School, in Pennsylvania, they were active members of the Society of Christian Endeavor.

Conversion, or the new birth, is of the Lord, and it is a miracle of grace. But the Lord generally uses instruments to bring it about. Jesus told the apostles to " make disciples of all nations." In the case of the children referred to, it seems a little like driving a nail through some boards to hold them together. One person holds the nail steady and gives it a tap with a hammer, another gives it a stroke, and another, or one person, may give it several strikes, until it is driven through. Then it requires a different kind of a stroke to clinch the nail. The Lord used me to do the clinching. The Doctor and his wife, and perchance other Christians, did the main part of the work—" a nail in a sure place." To the Lord be the praise.

Since the employment of missionaries, in 1878, the Executive Committee has had a number of missionaries and school teachers called, there is cause to believe, of God, who has largely blessed their labors. Probably more than one thousand Indians and seven hundred white people have been converted from the evil of their ways through their instrumentality. Many of them remain firm and steadfast, and a number of them have died in the triumphs of a Saviour's love. Jeremiah Hubbard has written me: " I do not call to mind one Indian who has died belonging to Friends' church but what

made a peaceful end and left a good testimony for God."
In 1898 Friends had twenty-three missionaries and nine
teachers employed in Indian Territory and Oklahoma.
In addition to these there are a number of native helpers
who render efficient service, among whom are Smith
Nichols, a Wyandotte, and Samuel Clinton, a Modoc Indian, both of whom are recorded ministers of the gospel.

In 1898 there were six Monthly Meetings, composed
of twelve Preparative Meetings, representing twenty-
three meetings for worship. Religious service was held
at several other places, and there are more locations
where the missionaries are desired to go and cannot.
There were eleven series of meetings reported that year,
resulting, it was believed, in one hundred conversions,
and the strengthening of believers. Sixty-seven were
received into membership. The average attendance of
meetings on Sabbath days was about fifty-four at each
meeting. There were fifteen Bible Schools, with an
average attendance of thirty-five. There were thirty in
the Bible Schools who could not speak English, and
eleven native officers and teachers.

The above-mentioned meetings, with Timbered Hills
Monthly Meeting in Kansas, constitute Grand River
Monthly Meeting of Friends, which belongs to Kansas
Yearly Meeting of Friends.

Since many of the Indians have taken allotments, and
the balance of the country has been opened for settlement, the reservations are largely filled with white set-

tlers. Some of the benefits that are expected to be derived from allotment of land to Indians is to bring them in close contact with civilization; to break up their tribal relations; to be subject to civil law; to make them citizens, and that they may contend with others in the struggle of life. When the Indians take allotments, and the remaining portion of the country is settled, it will bring them into civilization. It will be vastly better for them if their white neighbors are Christians, and extend to them a helping hand, instead of being unregenerate and evil-disposed towards them. The missionaries are expected to make the Indians their special work, and also to labor for the conversion of their white neighbors, and when they give satisfactory evidence of a change of heart, and approve the doctrines of Friends, they are encouraged to take them into church relationship. In 1895 five meetings that were organized by the missionaries were transferred to Kansas Yearly Meeting, as there were but few Indians belonging to them.

The church membership in the twenty-three meetings in 1898 was one thousand, one hundred and twenty-five, of whom five hundred and eleven were Indians and six hundred and fourteen were white people.

The following are the names and addresses of the missionaries in 1898 with the names of tribes under their care—

George N. and L. Ella Hartley, Tecumseh, Oklahoma, *Pottawatomie and Shawnee.* Also Superintendents.

Charles E. and Alice Pearson, Fallis, Oklahoma, *Iowa.*

Elizabeth Test, Lina B. Lunt and Rachel Kirk, McLoud, Oklahoma, *Kickapoo.*

Philander and C. M. Blackledge, Burnett, Oklahoma, " *Big Jim's Band* "—*Shawnee.*

D. Amos and Rhoda J· Outland, Otoe, Oklahoma, *Otoe.*

John M. Watson, Hillside, Indian Territory, *Cherokee and others.*

John B. Bishop and wife, Foyil, Indian Territory, *Cherokee.*

William P. and Abbie. C. Haworth, Miami, Indian Territory, *Ottowa.*

J. E. and Olive W. Sargent, Seneca, Missouri, *Seneca.*

Edward C. and Amy D. Cook, Seneca, Missouri, M*odoc.*

E. M. and Eunice A. Pearson, Wyandotte, Indian Territory, *Wyandotte.*

CHAPTER XII.

WHITE'S MANUAL-LABOR INSTITUTE, INDIANA.

INDIAN TRAINING SCHOOL.

THIS institute, with seven hundred and fifty acres of fertile land, and a similar one in Iowa with one thousand, four hundred and forty acres of second-class land, were founded with funds bequeathed by Josiah White, a Friend, of Philadelphia, to Indiana Yearly Meeting, to purchase land and erect buildings, etc., and then the proceeds of the land were to pay for carrying on manual-labor schools for white, black and Indian children who might need homes. The Executive Committee of Friends on Indian Affairs, in anticipation of taking a

(326)

much larger number of Indian children to that institution than the farm could support, made arrangements with the trustees of the institute to erect buildings in preparation for a Government Indian School. The Commissioner of Indian Affairs agreed to pay annually one hundred and twenty-five dollars for transporting, educating, board and clothing for each of sixty Indian scholars. The committee expended in addition, in building a "girls' home," seven thousand, nine hundred and sixty-two dollars, and for other improvements the sum of seven hundred and seventy-six dollars.

Twenty-six Indian children were taken to the institute on March 26th, 1883. This was increased to forty-seven before the committee met here in May, 1884. The Indian Committee authorized the erection of shops for carpenter work, and blacksmithing, etc., that some of the boys might learn trades. Broom-making was subsequently added. In the summer half the boys were detailed to work on the farm, garden, in the shops, etc., in the forenoon, and in the afternoon they attended school and the other half were at work. In the winter they all attended school, and did the " chores " mornings and evenings. By 1888 the enrollment was eighty-five, and an average attendance of seventy-one. The Government at that time paid one hundred and sixty-seven dollars annually for sixty students. The minutes of the committee state: " In all that effects the training of the children the year has been a prosperous one. There seems to have been no abatement in the excellence of the measures used heretofore to develop in the scholars those habits of diligence, system and self-dependence so necessary for their future welfare. . . . Eleven pupils have been sustained beyond the number allowed and partially paid for by the Government. . . . ' The Indian Aid Association of Friends,' of Philadelphia, has made a donation of two hundred and fifty dollars towards the maintenance of the eleven pupils above referred to, and they propose to contribute one thousand, six hundred and fifty dollars towards the transportation and support of ten pupils beyond the number (sixty) allowed by the Government." This beneficence was continued in after years.

The minutes of 1890 record the prosperous condition of the school. In addition to regular religious service they had a Christian Endeavor Society. "There have been a few conversions. More than half of our pupils are professed Christians. A number take part in prayer meetings." In 1895, O. H. Bales, who had been superintendent of White's Institute during all the years that the Indians had been there, states that the school was divided into three grades. The lower one had the usual Geography, United States History, Grammar, Arithmetic, First Part Algebra, Civil Government, and Bookkeeping. In the Graduating Class, Rhetoric, Second Part Algebra and Latin. Nearly all the students in the advanced grades will have completed their studies the

THE SUSAN LONGSTRETH LITERARY SOCIETY OF THE INDIAN INDUSTRIAL SCHOOL, CARLISLE, PA.

This society, bearing the name of one of the first and most honored friends of the School, has existed for more than ten years. Including, as it does, the best character and talent from some 300 girls, with a comfortable and tastefully decorated room for its meetings, it is an influence for good, mentally and morally, which cannot well be measured. All the societies emulate each other in furnishing the School most pleasing entertainments.

close of the term, June 30th, 1895. At that time it ceased to be an Indian School, and the children returned to their homes or to other schools. One girl went to Earlham College.

1n 1896 the superintendent, W. A. Mills, informed me that the whole number of Indians who had been to the institute was two hundred and sixty-one, from eighteen tribes. There was cause to believe that two hundred and forty-five of them were converted, thirty of whom joined Friends, and two hundred and fifteen joined other churches. Of these converts he wrote : " Some have married and settled down in homes of their own. Others have obtained positions, such as assistant seamstress, laundress, cook or matron, carpenter, etc., in other schools out west at good wages. Some taught schools, thus leading useful lives. Some are still at school in other places, from whom we hear good accounts."

Of the unconverted ones he wrote: "A few have returned to their old habits, seemingly worse than ever, going from bad to worse. They had some bad white blood in them.

" We have good reason to believe that our work with the Indian children was a success, as the lives of most of our pupils will attest. Miss Gertrude Simmons (a Sioux Indian), who won second prize at the oratorical contest at Indianapolis, Indiana, in 1895, was a pupil here for eight years or more. She represented Earlham College at the contest. She is now (during vacation) giving music lessons to obtain money to go back to Earlham this coming fall (1896)."

Friends, with other Protestant Christian churches, ceased to ask the Indian Department for funds to carry on their respective schools, for the reason that Congress, in granting those subsidies for sustaining denominational schools, bestowed the major part on the Papists. Friends were refused funds to support more than sixty scholars at the White's Institute, Indiana, and they supported a part of the time ten or fifteen from private sources.

In 1892 Congress appropriated for eight churches to carry on schools similar to White's Institute one hundred and sixty-one thousand, three hundred and seventy-four dollars, and for the one Roman Catholic Church, three hundred and ninety-four thousand, seven hundred and fifty-six dollars. The next year the Methodist Church asked for no funds, and in subsequent years other churches have been dropped, or their expenditures have been greatly reduced, until Congress, for the fiscal year of 1896, appropriated for Protestant Churches five thousand, eight hundred and eighty-five dollars, and for the Roman Catholics three hundred and eight thousand, four hundred and seventy-one dollars. (See "Report of the Commissioner of Indian Affairs, 1895," page 13.) Senator W. B. Allinson, of Iowa, wrote me, January 6th,

1899, that some years ago Congress passed a resolution to gradually reduce appropriations for sectarian schools, and this year ' ends the whole matter.' "

"INDIAN SCHOOL UNDER PRIVATE CONTRACT."

About 1882, while Indian Schools were being conducted by various churches or private individuals, Benjamin and Elizabeth B. Miles, Friends of West Branch, Iowa, made arrangements with the Commissioner of Indian Affairs to take some Indian children to that small town, and carry on an " Indian school under private contract." The Government agreed to pay one hundred and sixty-seven dollars annually for transportation, clothing, boarding and educating the children. They commenced with eleven Indian ·children under their care, who were principally Osages. The number was soon increased. They found that their quarters were too contracted. The boys needed to be on a farm, where they could learn to work and earn a part of their support, as the amount paid by the Government was insufficient to cover the expenses. In 1884 the trustees of White's Iowa Manual-Labor Institute reported to Iowa Yearly Meeting: " We have leased for a term of three years, from Eleventh month (November) 1st, 1883, a school building, barn and four hundred and eighty acres of land, to Benjamin and Elizabeth B. Miles, granting them the privilege of educating Indian children in connection with the eleven white children then in the institute. They are to board, clothe and educate the eleven white children for the use of said land."

In 1885, B. and E. B. Miles reported to the trustees of the institute that recently " sixteen Osages and ten Omaha and Winnebago children had been received. . . . Our present number of Indian children is seventy-two. A few others are expected to enter the school soon. The Government has reduced the price for the support of these from one hundred and sixty-seven dollars to one hundred and fifty dollars per capita per annum, which will straighten us financially in the work. But we have decided to go forward, believing we shall be able to provide comfortably for the children, irrespective of receiving remuneration for our labor. . . . The boys have worked faithfully through the crop and harvest season, and the girls have fully equalled them in houshold industry, and they have made commendable advancement in their growth in grace."

In 1886 seventy-five Indian pupils had been in school during the year. Two of the large boys had been employed for a time by farmers, and had performed their duties satisfactorily. Other boys had been useful on the farm, and the girls had been well taught in household work. The instruction and example of the superintendent, matron and teachers, as well as the labors of ministers, had been much blessed, and forty-seven Indian and two white pupils applied for membership in Chestnut

CAPTAIN R. H. PRATT
Superintendent of Indian Industrial School, Carlisle, Pa.

Hill Monthly Meeting of Friends, which was about two miles from the institute, and where the pupils and others connected with the school usually attended religious service.

The school remained in a prosperous condition until the 27th day of May, 1887, when the building was destroyed by fire. The school was broken up. Nearly all of the pupils were sent to the large Indian school at Lawrence, Kansas. The building was brick, and the walls remained standing with but little damage, and the trustees of the institute roofed it as soon as practicable.

CHEROKEE INDIANS OF NORTH CAROLINA.

Barnabas C. Hobbs, LL.D., a minister and educator of Indiana, was appointed by the Government as agent of those Indians which lived in North Carolina. They were regarded as civilized, and were wearing citizen's clothing, and supported themselves by farming. Agent Hobbs found that the schools and all other Government matters connected with those Indians were loosely and badly managed. He made his first report in 1882. The Cherokee Training Schoolhouse near Whittier, N. C., was erected about 1881, by Friends of Western Yearly Meeting in Indiana, largely through the instrumentality of Agent Hobbs, and by means of funds bequeathed by a benevolent sister to trustees " to be used in Indian education and civilization."

In the minutes of the Executive Committee for 1885 is recorded: " Barnabas C. Hobbs gave interesting information respecting the work in which Friends of Western Yearly Meeting have been engaged for four years among the eastern band of Cherokees in North Carolina. They expend six hundred dollars yearly in addition to the funds supplied by the Government." The record for 1886 states: " There are five day schools and one boarding-school, with an enrollment of two hundred and seven pupils, and an average attendance of one hundred and fifty. The Friends have saved enough from Government appropriations to build a dormitory for the boys of the boarding-school and a home for the teachers.

Friends own buildings to the value of one thousand five hundred dollars. The schools are well managed, and exert a valuable moral and religious influence. . . . The stock, implements, furniture and school appliances, supplied by Friends, have amounted to one thousand dollars. These Indians appear now to be further educated, more industrious, and in better circumstances financially, and a larger portion of them are church members than the white population in the surrounding mountains."

DOUGLAS ISLAND MISSION, ALASKA.

This mission was organized by Kansas Yearly Meeting of Friends.

In 1886 Elwood W. Weesner believed that he was called of the Lord to go to Alaska, and labor with some of the Indians there as a missionary. After receiving the approbation of his Monthly and Quarterly Meeting, the Yearly Meeting encouraged the proposition by appropriating three hundred dollars for the expense of the journey.

He went to Douglas Island, Alaska, about three thousand miles from Lawrence, Kansas. The island is a gold-mining point, where about two hundred Indians were employed by one firm at two dollars per day. He walked over the island to see the people and to ascertain their needs. The Indians worked well as hired hands, and he saw about seventy-five children of school age. Girls were sometimes sold to evil-minded men, who would live with them as long as they wished and then would send them off without home or friends. There was no school on the island.

It is not an agricultural country, and the only means he saw towards self-support was in preserving some of the large quantities of fish, by canning, smoking and salting. Notwithstanding there was an unusual abundance of rain, the climate was healthy. He reports: " No malaria or fever. Most of the sickness among the natives was caused by exposure and ill treatment. They all live in log or frame houses, and dress in citizens' clothes. Many of them are very filthy in their habits and mode of living. Generally two or three families live in the same house. There are a few, who have had the privilege of some education and knowledge of white men's ways, that are living in good houses, neatly furnished. Timber being abundant, and our building site being near a saw and planing mill, the cost of erecting buildings will not much exceed that of other States and Territories."

He rented a house and started a day school, but the Indians moving from place to place hunting work caused irregularity in the children attending. In 1889 the committee reported that he was assisted by his wife and by Silas and Anna Moon. "None of these workers have received any compensation from the committee, except their support and quarters, but a salary of seven hundred and twenty dollars is allowed by the United States Government for the school on Douglas Island, which had been equally divided among the two families as some compensation for their faithful services."

The school was opened in their own schoolhouse in the fall of 1888, under the care of Anna Moon as teacher. The average attendance was but fifteen. Charles H. Edwards, a minister and educator, went there to assist in the mission. "The total receipts from all sources were three thousand two hundred dollars, which was not quite all expended. Their possessions were one acre of ground, one good school building with accommodations for about fifty day scholars, one dwelling house, with quarters for fifteen children and for the necessary employees; a wood shed and other outbuildings." The Women's Foreign Missionary Society contributed their funds towards the support of the girls' home on Douglas Island.

Several destitute children were taken into the family,

among whom was a girl of thirteen years who was about to be sold to a white man. She proved to be a valuable help in the house. They had seven boys and eight girls in the home. The girls assisted in the house and the boys to get wood and other work. During the year 1890 the enrollment, including the day scholars, was ninety, with an average of twenty. They also had a night school for white miners, which was well patronized; also religious service for miners on Sabbath evenings, in addition to the service at the schoolhouse in the morning.

In 1892 they put up an addition to the building, twenty by forty feet, and two stories high, which cost eight hundred dollars. They report: "Soon after we commenced this work, Abby J. Woodman, of Danvers, Massachusetts, who has heretofore been a very liberal contributor to the mission, offered to secure funds to build a boys' dormitory or dispensary, provided the first addition was completed, which offer we accepted. The Government officers at Washington appointed a teacher and sent one there who was not at all satisfactory." They state: "We filed an urgent remonstrance at Washington against having any more political appointees given in charge of the school this year, and on our recommendation Dr. Connett was appointed teacher. The day school opened on September 1st, with thirty-eight in attendance. The Bible School and meeting have averaged sixty-five for the last six months, and the attendance has been as high as one hundred."

In January, 1892, C. H. Edwards, who had been appointed by the Superintendent of Indian Schools for Alaska to teach in another part of the Territory, " met his death at the hands of M. Campbell, who was engaged in smuggling whiskey and whom Edwards was endeavoring to secure, in order to turn him over to the authorities. Although C. H. Edwards was not then connected with our mission, the workers there and the committee felt his death to be a severe blow to the cause."

Women's Foreign Missionary Society of Oregon " sent Frances Liter, a minister and member of Kansas Yearly Meeting, to Douglas Island as field matron. She has been actively engaged in visiting the natives, and her efforts have had a very perceptible effect on our work. Wilmington Yearly Meeting, in 1895, decided to adopt Alaska as their field of labor. We hail with joy these offers of assistance in the work from our sister Yearly Meetings."

The Woman's Foreign Missionary Society of Kansas Yearly Meeting reported, in 1892, that they had raised for the mission eight hundred and thirty dollars, and they had engaged Sibyl J. Hanson, of South Dakotah, to assist in the mission. That year, with the enlarged building, their enrollment was one hundred and one Indians from the various tribes of Southern Alaska. " Conversions in the school-room were not uncommon, and their influence for good was most positive, awakening, as they did, in the minds of others the importance of the religion of Jesus Christ, and its power to help in everyday life." The board having charge of the work consisted of five women nominated by the Missionary Society, and five men, all appointed by the Yearly Meeting.

In 1894 the report of the Yearly Meeting states: " There are now thirteen children in the home, between the ages of five and fifteen years—four boys and nine girls. They are bright, active children of much promise. . . . Oregon Yearly Meeting called Frances Liter from the field and established a mission of their own on Kaak Island, with Silas and Anna Moon and Fannie Liter as missionaries. . . . Sibyl Hanson, having married and gone to a different field of labor, is succeeded by Jennie Lawrence, of Chester, Indiana. . . . Dr. J. E. Connett returned to his home in Illinois, and his place was supplied by a lady teacher," who was selected and employed by the Government. " Charles and Mary Replogle, our present superintendent and matron, are earnest, consecrated workers, doing with their might what their hands find to do for the temporal and spiritual welfare of their charge."

A number of the Indians had been converted and the missionaries " organized a Monthly Meeting, March 8th, 1894, with forty-two members in good standing. Most of these are living a life as near the cross as is possible with their limited information. We have two young men who desire with their whole heart to be ministers, but have not sufficient education. It would be a noble work to send these young men to a Bible School for a year at least. We have held regular services on Sabbath mornings and every Wednesday evening at the church," and occasionally other meetings have been held.

The report for 1895 states: " The past year has been one of steady, healthy Christian growth of our work on Douglas Island. Charles N. and Mary Replogle, the superintendent and the matron of the mission, are performing faithful service, and the Christian influence of the mission, through its workers, is felt throughout the island and surrounding country. The personal Christian work of the missionaries among the natives on the beach, and the white miners, is bringing souls to God." They reported forty-nine church members.

On account of the Government employing a teacher for the native school who was not a Christian, and who had no sympathy in the work, the committee thought it best to not accept of that kind of help. " The matron, Mary Replogle, took charge of the school, which numbered fifty students, who are doing good work. The children are anxious to learn, and more interest is taken this year than ever before by those on the beach to become acquainted with books."

William V. Coffin, Francis A. Wright and Hannah E. Sleeper, members of the committee, visited the mission in Alaska on different occasions at their own expense, thus showing the deep interest they have in the missionary and school work on Douglas Island. The distance from Kansas to the island is three thousand miles.

Hannah E. Sleeper has written me that the mission is about half a mile from the bay, and elevated nearly two hundred feet. Pine timber, blueberries and some other wild fruit grow in abundance. There is very little soil in sight, and no vegetables—not even lettuce—can be grown on the mission premises, and rarely on the island. It is wet and cool in summer—never muddy. In summer, "it is a delightful climate. If I had my choice I would always spend the summer in Southeastern Alaska. The atmosphere is very bracing and salubrious."

"Robert Harris, a native Chilkoot Indian, has labored efficiently as a minister of the Gospel among his people, and his gift has been recognized by Douglas Monthly Meeting of Friends. The meeting and Sabbath School have gradually increased in interest and in numbers. Within the last five years several of the children have been sent to the States to receive a higher education than can be offered them. All of the children appreciate this opportunity and are making commendable progress. . . . With no home, no Bible, no Christ, in their language, they need the fostering care of the followers of Him who said, 'Go ye and make disciples of all the nations.'" (See "Friends' Mission, Douglas Island, Alaska," by Hannah E. Sleeper.)

This mission is under the care of Oregon Yearly Meeting of Friends.

Kaak Island is about one hundred miles south of Douglas Island, Alaska. It is inhabited by about five hundred of the Kaak tribe of Indians, who subsist principally on wild game and fish. They cultivate potatoes and other vegetables, which grow abundantly on the island. They procure large quantities of fine furs. The island is reported to have a good agricultural climate and soil, with abundance of good timber. The natives are an intelligent class of people, and are very eager to receive the Gospel. Silas Moon and wife, and Fannie Liter, went to the island as missionaries in 1893. Soon they were visited by the chief, who said, on behalf of his people, " We so glad you come. Now our children be like white man's children. Now we have the light." Prior to Silas Moon going there the Government had erected a schoolhouse for Charles Edwards (the murder of whom is mentioned in the account of Douglas Island Mission).

To the schoolhouse has been built an addition of one room, and in 1896 a two-story log house was erected eighteen feet square. A day school has been taught, which averaged forty-five in the winter of 1895 and 1896. They have Sabbath School, church service and a Christian Endeavor Society, all of which are well attended. There is cause to believe that some of the natives have been converted. The missionaries report " a decided change in the lives of many of them."

In the summer of 1896 Fannie Liter returned home, and Anna Hunnicutt and Lizzie Morris were sent there by the Young People's Society of Christian Endeavor of California Yearly Meeting. " Lizzie Morris has a primary class in the Sabbath School numbering thirty-four, which is very satisfactory." Their interpreter is a native young man, who attended school at Douglas Island, and afterwards at the Indian Training School, near Salem, Oregon, where he learned the shoemaking trade.

The missionaries, and one man who has a store, are the only white people residing on the island. The merchant is not a Christian, and the missionaries and committee are very anxious to have a Christian merchant there, also that a sawmill may be built. Mary E. K. Edwards writes: " The Lord has most marvelously owned and blessed the work. Funds have come from unexpected sources. Our missionaries have had wonderful access to the hearts of the people. Now, if we only had the money to start the store and erect a sawmill, and place Christian people in charge, the work might be made self-supporting, and untold good might be done. We are trusting God, and believing, in His own time and way, it will come about if we do our part."

The report for 1898 shows that the mission work progressed under the efficient care of Silas and Anna Moon and Lizzie Morris. The latter had a school with enrollment of seventy-four pupils, some of whom " pray very fervently " on some occasions, and are ridiculed by the camp Indians for being Christians, but they " stand up for the missionaries." The school is in session only a small part of the year, as the Indians scatter out to hunt and fish, to procure means for subsistence.

From seventy to one hundred Indians attend church service and Bible School when they are near the mission, and several of them were trying to take a stand as Christians. Church service is sometimes held at their camps.

The address of the missionaries is Kaak Village, via Point Barrie, Rupreanoff Island, Alaska.

THE MISSIONARY WORK OF CALIFORNIA YEARLY MEETING OF FRIENDS WITH THE ESQUIMAU INDIANS.

During the summer of 1896 Anna Hunnicut, of California, while engaged as a missionary in Southern Alaska, felt a burden to undertake missionary work further north, where no missionary station was established. Dr. Jackson, the efficient Christian Superintendent of Indian Government Schools in Alaska, during his travels far north, met with Esquimau Indians, who were very anxious to have a missionary, and he knowing the desire of Anna Hunnicut recommended them to the Friends of Douglas Island, where Anna Hunnicut was laboring. Soon two or three of them started in their boat to travel some fifteen hundred miles in pursuit of a missionary. On their arrival at Douglas, Anna Hunnicut was absent, but Charles Replogle, the missionary there, was interested in the case, and went to Pasadena, California, to present the subject to Friends of California Yearly Meeting.

Here was a personal call from the Indians, and Anna Hunnicut believed that she was called of the Lord to go to them, and to go as soon as practicable, which would be in May, 1897, as no other opportunity would occur for a year. There were no persons in sight to go with her, and no funds on hand to meet expenses, and only two months to prepare. Robert Samms and Carrie Rowe were engaged to be married, and thought it would be right for them to accompany Anna Hunnicut to her field of labor. Voluntary contributions of about one thousand dollars was handed to the missionary committee. Preparations were made; Robert Samms and Carrie Rowe were married, and they started on their bridal tour of several thousand miles with Anna Hunnicut to the far, far north land. They located at Kotzebue Sound, north and east of Behring Straits, where three large rivers enter the sound, and not far from the Arctic Circle. It is a great summer resort of natives from these river valleys and from the coast of Alaska to Siberia. Thousands congregate there to trade furs for goods, and have summer festivities. It is thus a centre from which influences flow out to all that Northern region. In the winter season the Indians go up the rivers to hunt, and to other parts, leaving but few near the mission station.

The natives are a band of the Esquimau tribe of Indians, but are taller and more energetic than some of the other bands. They are mostly gentle and peaceable, and very superstitious and ignorant. They knew nothing of growth from seed until they saw the missionaries plant some. They seem capable of learning rapidly, and are very loyal to the missionaries. The report of the first year's work is very encouraging. The younger Indians want to adopt civilized life, and there is cause to believe that several of them have accepted Christ as their Saviour.

The work is one of great privation and difficulty. The most of the year they are absolutely cut off from the rest of the world by ice. The short summer is quite hot. During a portion of that time the sun is in sight nearly twenty-four hours during the day. During the summer vessels reach them with provisions and mail. The accommodations of the missionaries are very rude, and they had sometimes to go ten or twelve miles for fuel during the first winter.

It seemed providential that they went as soon as they did, as it gave them a year's time to learn the language and gain the confidence of the natives before the rush of gold seekers to that region, in the summer of 1898. There is urgent need of mission stations up the rivers at the winter quarters of the natives. Along these rivers are extensive forests, and during the brief summers there are multitudes of flowers, and a few acid berries. The

INDIAN GIRL, AS PROFESSIONAL NURSE
Trained at the Indian Industrial School, Carlisle, Pa.

abundant arctic moss furnishes ample food for reindeer. Salmon and other fish are plentiful in the summer, as well as water fowl. The temperature at the mission ranged from forty-four below zero to ninety above. In the interior it is colder in the winter. The prevalent diseases of the natives are consumption, rheumatism, and a loathsome contagious malady introduced by whalers and traders.

CARLISLE INDUSTRIAL SCHOOL.

Although this school is in no sense under the care of Friends, yet Friends, with many others who have the welfare of the Indians at heart, have an especial interest, if not a commendable pride, in what that school has already achieved, and what it is likely to accomplish if it should be kept under proper management. Friends, with other philanthropists in and about the city of Philadelphia and elsewhere, have on various occasions aided Captain Pratt in his great enterprise, and therefore a brief account of the school may not be out of place in connection with the foregoing. It was the first school of the kind in the United States. Since the school was started Captain Pratt has been promoted to Major.

Captain R. H. Pratt, after having control of seventy-four incorrigible Indians at Fort Marion, Florida, for three years, who were taken from Southwestern Indian Territory (now Oklahoma), and seeing how readily some of the younger ones applied themselves to school learning, conceived the idea of taking Indian children entirely away from the Indian reservations and keeping them in school for a term of years, with the thought, as he expressed: "The quickest way of getting civilization into the Indian is to take the Indian into civilization."

After conferring with government authorities, Captain Pratt obtained permission to use the Government buildings at Carlisle, formerly used for a United States fort, for an Indian School. It is located in Cumberland County, Pa., about one hundred and twenty miles northwest of Philadelphia. The school was started in 1879, with one hundred and thirty-nine students, which number was increased to eight hundred and sixty-seven in 1898, from seventy-four different tribes. His plan has been, in addition to school lore, for all the boys to be taught farming and horticulture, and in addition most of them are taught various kinds of trades. The girls are all taught to do housework, and a number of them are trained in other industries, as dressmaking, type setting, trained nurses, etc. Half the students are in school four hours in the forenoon, while the other half are at manual labor. In the afternoon they change places. The school owns two hundred and sixty acres, and sometimes other land is leased. The boys must have work.

An important feature of this school is the "outing system"—i. e., the pupils, boys and girls, by the hundreds, work out during vacation of school on farms, or where they can procure work, and retain the wages they earn. Of the large number who are hired to farmers, or

PUPIL TEACHERS AT THE INDIAN INDUSTRIAL SCHOOL, CARLISLE, PA.

One of the most helpful features of the School is the manual training given students who show ability, and deserve to qualify as teachers. This department becomes more and more important each year, as the students thus trained increase in number, and go out to fill positions in other Schools.

who help in families, it is seldom that any are returned
to the school for not being competent, or for other cause.
Here they are separated from their Indian associates, and
thus they learn how to labor with white people in the
practicable duties of life. They are cordially received
into the churches and Sabbath Schools. At the close of
vacation they return to school with cash in their pockets.
Then there is another important business lesson to be
taught them. What shall they do with their money?
A portion of it is usually spent for clothing beyond what
is provided by the school. It is their own money, and
they have the right to use it at their discretion. But
they are encouraged to save it, so as to have some to take
home with them. To aid in this they can deposit their
funds on interest. They have sometimes had more than
$15,000.00 on deposit.

During 1898 "the earnings of the boys aggregated
$13,541.30, of which they saved $5,208.61; and the
girls' earnings aggregated $8,184.20, of which they
saved $3,098.50, making a total earnings of $21,725.50,
and the savings, $8,307.11. The earnings belong to the
earners individually. Through a savings system established at the origin of the school, each pupil has a bank
and account book, and by supervision of its use the
pupils are taught the value of money. The pupils go
out at their own request, and almost invariably have a
pride in doing well, so that, through their good records,
the demand for pupils each year is multiplied, and we

have constantly to deny places at good homes." (Major Pratt's Annual Report, 1898.)

Some years ago the boys contributed $1,851.00 towards building quarters for the large boys. The building is 292 by 36 feet, three stories high. It has accommodations for three hundred boys, with library, reading, assembly, bath and clothing rooms. The balance of the funds, $14,500.00, for erecting and equipping the building, was donated by friends of the school. At a later date the pupils gave nearly $5,000.00 towards the erection of a gymnasium, more than $4,000.00 being added by friends of the school and $4,000.00 by the Government. In the early period of the school Congress did not have sufficient faith in Indian education to appropriate funds to erect those buildings. It was easier for it to appropriate millions to wage unjust war against the Indians. But that day, we hope, has passed.

The term of schooling at Carlisle is five years, at the expiration of which time the scholars are usually returned to their homes. If, however, they wish to pursue their studies further, they can, if approved by the superintendent, remain another term of five years. Many have taken the benefit of this, and have then gone to college or other higher institutions and have honorably graduated as lawyers, or ministers of the gospel, or have entered other professions. The first class of graduates from Carlisle was seven young women and seven young men, ten years after the opening of the school, since which some

DR. CARLOS MONTEZUMA
CARLISLE INDIAN SCHOOL PHYSICIAN

Dr. Montezuma is a living representative of what education will do for an Indian
when removed from his tribe at an early age. He was captured when small
by a band of Indians at war with his own tribe, sold to a travelling
photographer, brought East, went to public school in Chicago,
graduated from the Illinois State University, and
then from the Chicago Medical College.

have graduated each year. In 1896 there were twenty-five in the class from fourteen different tribes.

In order to graduate they have to be proficient in Language (English Grammar and Rhetoric); United States History; Civil Government; Arithmetic; Elements of Algebra; Geography, Political and Physical; Elements of Botany; Elements of Physics; Physiology; Hygiene and Drawing.

Major Pratt is a church member, and there is a religious influence pervading the school. Religious service is held in the institution each Sabbath afternoon, usually conducted by a minister of one of the congregations in the city of Carlisle. The students all attend this service; also a prayer meeting in the evening, and they can attend the church services in town in the morning. A large percentage of the students have been converted, some of them before going to Carlisle. Near two hundred are members of the Young Men's Christian Association, and a larger number of the young ladies are members of " The King's Daughters' Circles." Some of the students belong to the Christian Endeavor Societies in town. It seems very evident that Carlisle School is largely blessed of the Lord, to whom be the praise. Since this school has proved such a grand success, the Government has erected buildings in various parts of the United States, where schools are conducted on a similar basis.

In the first half of this century the United States expended small sums in carrying out treaty stipulations for the education of Indians. During that time the Government furnished different churches with a small amount of funds to carry on their denominational schools. For instance, in 1820 there were twenty-one schools carried on by different religious societies, which were aided by the Government to the extent of eleven thousand eight hundred and thirty-eight dollars, which was about one-sixth of the amount expended by the societies themselves for these schools. (" Report of Commissioner of Indian Affairs," 1897.)

During the same half century the Government expended four hundred million dollars to kill the Indians, or an average of eight million dollars a year! In 1870 a radical change was made in their treatment. Congress appropriated " one hundred thousand dollars for the support of industrial and other schools among the Indian tribes not otherwise provided for." For the fiscal year 1898 there was appropriated to conduct the ordinary operations of the Indian Department seven million three hundred and forty-two thousand eight hundred and eight dollars. Of this amount three million one hundred and twenty-three thousand eight hundred and seventy-one dollars was to fulfil treaty obligations, which included six hundred thousand dollars for the support of reservation schools, and two million six hundred and thirty-one thousand seven hundred and seventy-one dollars for the support of schools other than of treaty

THE SEVENTH CLASS OF GRADUATES, 1895, INDIAN INDUSTRIAL SCHOOL, CARLISLE, PA.

Thirteen Indian tribes are represented in this graduating class. They are: Assinaboine, Seneca, Chippewa, Wyandotte, Piegan, Oneida, Nez Perce, Crow, Sioux, Sac and Fox, Omaha, Cherokee.

stipulations, so that three million two hundred and thirty-one thousand and seven hundred and seventy-one dollars was appropriated for the cause of Indian education—a large sum, but less than half the amount that was formerly used to fight them, while for that year there were no funds expended to fight them.

Between three and four million dollars have been invested in Indian school plants, in some of which there have been introduced the most scientific and best mode of bathing. As a number of buildings have been set on fire by the use of coal oil lamps, electrical and other modes of lighting have been introduced in some of the large Indian school buildings.

SENATOR DAWES' BILL.

" An act to provide for the allotment of land in severalty to Indians on the various reservations, and to extend the protection of the laws of the United States and the Territories over the Indians and for other purposes." Approved February 8th, 1887, with amendment approved February 28th, 1891.

The allotment law provides, that at the discretion of the President of the United States he may have Indian reservations surveyed, " and to allot to each Indian located thereon one-eighth of a section of land "; that is, eighty acres, provided there is sufficient land in the Indian reservation for that purpose, and if not they are to have pro rata less. And provided further, when the lands " are only valuable for grazing purposes, such lands shall be allotted in double quantities." Indians are to make their own selections, with the assistance of their agent. If, in four years after the President has ordered an allotment, any Indian fails to select one, the agent shall select an allotment for him.

Said allotments are held in trust by the United States for twenty-five years, " And that at the expiration of said period the United States will convey the same by patent to said Indian, or his heirs as aforesaid, in fee, discharged of said trust and free of all charge or incumbrance whatsoever ; provided, that the President of the United States may in any case, in his discretion, extend the period."

After allotments are made the Secretary of the Interior may negotiate with the Indian tribe for the purchase of the balance of their reservation, and then it may be sold to bona-fide settlers. The purchase money " shall be held in the Treasury of the United States for the sole use of the tribe or tribes of Indians to whom such reservations belonged; and the same, with interest thereon at three per cent. per annum, shall be at all times subject to appropriation by Congress for the education and civilization of such tribe or tribes of Indians or members thereof."

By United States law, Indians become citizens when they are taxed. Therefore, when they take allotments, and their chattel property is taxed, or poll tax assessed on them, they become citizens.

DATE DUE

JA 3 '72			
MR 28 '72			
NO 1 '76			
GAYLORD			PRINTED IN U.S.A.